Guide to Good Speech

JAMES H. McBURNEY

Dean, The School of Speech
Northwestern University

ERNEST J. WRAGE

Chairman, Department of Public Address
and Group Communication
The School of Speech, Northwestern University

GUIDE TO GOOD SPEECH, third edition
McBurney and Wrage

Second printing. . . . . . August, 1965

PRENTICE-HALL INTERNATIONAL, INC., *London*
PRENTICE-HALL OF AUSTRALIA, PTY., LTD., *Sydney*
PRENTICE-HALL OF CANADA, LTD., *Toronto*
PRENTICE-HALL OF INDIA (PRIVATE) LTD., *New Delhi*
PRENTICE-HALL OF JAPAN, INC., *Tokyo*

Library of Congress Catalog Card Number: 65-16576

Preface

This edition of *Guide to Good Speech*, like its predecessors, is designed to present a concise statement of the principles of good speech as a basis for speech improvement. The result, we hope, is exactly what the title claims—a book that will guide young men and women to good speech in all their personal and public relations.

We believe that good speech is best achieved through a working *knowledge* of basic principles, by directed *practice* in the application of these principles, and by competent *criticism* of this practice. The book has been redesigned to deal directly with these matters in the first three chapters, thus setting standards and suggesting methods at the beginning. What follows is a refinement of these considerations in some depth that may be gone into as the study progresses.

The other changes in this edition have been made to give greater emphasis to principles of first importance, to achieve sharper and more felicitous statements of doctrine, and to provide additional illustrative matter. Noteworthy among these are a new chapter on critical listening, a thoroughgoing revision of the chapter on reporting, and a doubling of the number of sample speeches at the end of the book. All of the revisions are reflections of our continuing experience with the basic course in speech and our efforts to make *Guide to Good Speech* a more useful aid to teaching and learning.

We are indebted to colleagues and students who have used earlier editions and offered suggestions for improvement. We are especially indebted to Naomi H. Wrage for her contributions and to Maurine Lewis of Prentice-Hall, Inc., for her assistance and counsel.

JAMES H. MCBURNEY
ERNEST J. WRAGE

About the Illustrations

Opposite the first page of each chapter is a voiceprint, a rather artistic creation of the machine, tracing the pattern of a male voice as it pronounces the number of each chapter. A voiceprint of the title, *Guide to Good Speech*, is reproduced on the cover.

Made from a speech spectogram developed by Bell Telephone Laboratories, the prints are used in research concerning speech and acoustics.

Voiceprints provide fundamental knowledge that is essential to the understanding of unique features of naturalness of the voice. Basic similarities and differences become apparent among voices of different speakers saying the same words.

Going from machines to men, we illustrate the anatomy of speech with Lorelle Raboni's excellent drawings, and some points in the text are graphically presented in charts.

Other illustrations throughout the book give us glimpses of the famous of the twentieth century speaking in a variety of situations: in government, the arts, labor, religion, the military, and business—from Wilson to Warner Brothers.

Contents

ix

Guide to Good Speech

one

What Is
Good Speech?

"I venture to say," speculated Edwin A. Locke, Jr., "that all the thefts and embezzlements that corporations suffer each year do not cost the economy as much as verbal incompetence."[1] There is, of course, no known method of measuring precisely this alleged drag on our economy, but this comment by an American industrialist dramatizes a deplorable condition that has become commonplace. From industry, from the professions, from training and research centers, from homes and schools, the lament grows louder: Most people are sadly inadequate in situations that make more than minimal demands on their capacity to communicate.

Although we express ourselves and relate ourselves to others in many ways, speech is, and always has been, our most universal mode of communication. But in today's world, we can no longer take our speech for granted, as we do the air we breathe. In our swift-paced, crowded, and complex world, talk that is meaningless, misdirected, and inaccurate only adds to misunderstanding and clamor. It does not further rational purpose, whether that purpose be self-actualization, relating ourselves to others, or social and political participation.

In response to a questionnaire that sought to assess the goals of a liberal education, almost four thousand graduate engineers rated

[1] Quoted by Marion Odmark, "Sloppy Speaker Costs Money," *Chicago American*, March 6, 1962, Sect. 2, p. 9.

highest the goal "to express one's thoughts effectively." They gave top priority to college courses in speech and English composition. The most highly regarded second and third goals were "to acquire and use the skills and habits involved in critical and constructive thinking" and "to learn to get along with people." [2] These three goals, taken together, offer an acceptable account of what a soundly conceived course in speech is all about.

WHAT IS SPEECH?

Speech is the communication of ideas and feelings by means of visible and audible symbols originating in speakers and listeners. It is a dynamic process based on stimulus and response, of unfolding interactions between speaker and audience. A skillful speaker consciously strives for a specific response from his audience through symbolic representation of information, ideas, and feelings, and he is continuously guided by the developing reactions from his listeners. As we shall see, effective speaking is far more complex, subtle, and demanding than simply delivering messages in the manner of transporting freight from one point to another.

Speech follows a pattern of its own that is best described as circular rather than linear. It originates as an idea in the mind of a person. His brain, acting much like a radar system, scans his available store of symbols and then speedily converts the idea into its verbal equivalents. The speaker's nervous system activates appropriate muscle groups to express these symbols overtly. Sounds and gestures are then transmitted by air and light waves which impinge upon the sensory systems of the audience. Their nervous systems relay these symbols to their brains for decoding and interpretation, resulting in a determination of the meaning and the implications of what they heard. Having evaluated the message, members of the audience tend to react in some way, with signs of approval or disapproval, encouragement or discouragement, indifference or excitement. Sometimes these reactions are nothing more than a nod of the head, or a sour smile, or a grimace; sometimes the audience responds verbally. Whether covert or overt, response is inevitable in some degree and guides the speaker. If he is equal to his task—

[2] "Engineers' Need of Liberal Arts," *The New York Times,* May 4, 1958, p. 9B.

if he is as intelligent, wise, sensitive, and resilient as we want him to be—he will accept the flow of incoming cues and adapt to them in a manner that enhances his prospects for winning the desired response. If he senses hostility, he may slip in some humor to relieve the tension and disarm his auditors. If attention wanes, he may retrieve it with a lively illustration. If technicalities threaten to bury a point, he will strip it of encumbrances. As you perceive, then, speech is a dynamic process from beginning to end.

WHAT IS GOOD SPEECH?

This question is usually answered in one of four ways. Speech may be judged (1) by its results—the nature of the response, (2) by the truth—the soundness of the speaker's message, (3) by the trust-worthiness of the speaker's motives and intentions, or (4) by principles of the art of good speech. What is the best answer?

Let's begin with the theory that speech is good if it gets results and poor if it fails to get results. We ask: Did the student persuade his professor to give him an "Incomplete," rather than flunk him? Did the salesman sell his product? Was the campaigner elected? Did the lawyer win the case? Did the father persuade his daughter to finish school before marriage? Since we always speak to win response, it might seem logical to judge a speech by success or failure in getting the desired response. This plausible theory, however, suffers from one fatal defect: It ignores the fact that in every speaking situation there are many factors that influence the outcome. Some of these factors may be so stacked against the speaker that they will prevail despite his own brilliant performance. The professor may be moved by the student's appeal for a revised grade in a course, but he cannot ignore university standards. The salesman cannot sell to a customer who has neither money nor credit.

Outside factors may also work *for* the speaker. Listeners committed to a fixed belief, their minds tightly locked to hold that belief, will not only accept a speaker who tells them what they want to hear; they may even endow him with eloquence he does not demonstrate and "hear" arguments he did not advance.

Thus, a good speaker, through no fault of his own, may fail to get results, and a poor speaker may win approval in spite of his weaknesses. The results theory is an example of the old fallacy of attributing effect to a single cause where many causes are operating. From this mistake come false evaluations of speech and misleading advice to students.

Other critics have tried to judge speech by its *truth* or by *the character and motives of the speaker.* There is no question whatsoever that any speaker who sticks with the truth is on sound moral grounds. And there is no question that speakers of good character and high motives are preferable to scoundrels. Unfortunately, however, these theories get us into new difficulties.

We have all seen the best causes—the truth—suffer at the hands of poor speakers. And we have seen speakers with the finest character and most worthy motives fail to perceive the truth or defend it poorly if they do see it. Good causes and worthy motives help the speaker, but they can seldom do the job alone.

There are further difficulties. Truth is often relative to time, place, and circumstances, and motives are always personal and elusive. We cannot always be sure we know the truth, nor can we be certain of the speaker's motives. Judging speech by these standards is precarious at best.

How, then, *can* we judge speech? The only adequate answer is to judge speech as an *art* based on established principles. We hold speech to be good when it conforms to these principles and poor when it does not. But what are these principles? How are they derived? And how reliable are they?

Since stimulus and response are the essence of all good speech, we must search out the principles of good speech by identifying the stimuli that have proved successful in getting desired responses. And if we are to avoid the mistake of judging by results, we must isolate the influence of outside factors from the stimuli that are provided by the speech itself. In short, we must rely on controlled experimental studies and on careful investigations of speakers and the circumstances under which their speeches are given.

As Aristotle put it over 2,000 years ago, ". . . when the practised and the spontaneous speakers gain their end, it is possible to investigate the causes of their success, and such an inquiry, we shall all admit, performs the function of an art."[3] For centuries, men have been recording their observations on speaking and speakers. And these observations are still being checked and refined in an effort

---

[3] *The Rhetoric of Aristotle,* I. 1. Translation by Lane Cooper.

to provide directives and bases for evaluating speech. These are the principles that give us the most reliable answer to our question, "What is good speech?"

PRINCIPLES OF GOOD SPEECH

There are ten basic principles of good speech that you can apply both in learning how to speak more effectively and in evaluating speech—your own and that of others.

1. Good speech is socially responsible

A socially responsible speaker is aware of his potential influence on attitudes, values, traditions, and institutions, and he reveals his awareness by his respect for facts, logic, and informed judgments.

Woodrow Wilson, 1913.
(*The Bettmann Archive*)

In short, speech is responsible to the degree that a speaker comprehends the social context of his remarks, strives to make intelligence prevail, and is accountable for the consequences of his discourse.

2. Good speech reveals a speaker with good personal qualifications

Listeners always size up a speaker, and their judgment of his personal qualifications influences their attitude toward what he says. The speaker who exhibits competence, intelligence, and good will wins attention and respect.

3. Good speech is guided by a specific purpose

The specific purpose is simply the response that the speaker is seeking, the objective toward which he directs all his efforts. Without purpose, speech is random and aimless. And if the speaker without a purpose gets any response at all from his audience, it is not likely to be one that he values.

4. Good speech deals with worthwhile subjects

We talk about countless things—experiences, events, problems, hopes, aspirations, joys, sorrows, and fears. Some of these subjects are so urgent that they cannot be denied. They *must* be talked about. Others are tempting simply because they seem to be worth exploring. The *subjects* people talk about affect the level and quality of speech. Good subjects tap the best resources of both speaker and listener.

5. Good speech has worthwhile content

Effective speech reflects the best supporting facts, arguments, illustrations, and other material that a speaker is capable of bringing to his subject. Form is important in speech, but form without substance is mockery.

6. Good speech is analytical

Speech always takes place in a context—a setting. This setting is created by the subject, the audience, the occasion, and the speaker himself. *Analytical speech is speech that takes these factors into account.*

A good speaker is sensitive to every element in the setting. He sizes up the situation. If the speaker has made a poor analysis of his *subject,* he may deceive both himself and his audience. If he makes a poor analysis of his *audience,* his speech will miss its mark completely. If he makes a poor analysis of the *occasion,* he may stumble into improprieties of the worst kind. And if he makes a poor analysis of *himself* in relation to all the other factors, he may display attitudes that will block communication.

Analysis is involved at every step along the way, from the moment of choice of subject until delivery of the last word.

7. Good speech is based on sound method

The speaker's method is his plan of attack, dictated largely by his purpose and by his analysis of the situation. Four primary purposes of speech are served by four basic methods: inquiry, reporting, advocacy, and evocation. We shall explain these purposes and methods in later chapters. Suffice it to say here that a good speaker knows *when* and *how* to use the appropriate method. It is a fair test of any speech to ask: Has the speaker used the method best designed to accomplish his purpose?

8. Good speech claims the attention and interest of the listener

Communication stops when attention is lost. And attention will not persist very long unless the audience's interest is engaged. The best speech is rewarding to both speaker and listener, for then the speaker is motivated to give his best, and the audience is motivated to get the most out of what he says. This kind of motivated speech is realized only when the speaker analyzes and adapts to his audience and when the listeners analyze and adapt to the speaker.

9. Good speech makes effective use of voice and bodily action

Without voice and bodily action there can be no speech, for they carry the symbols out of which all speech is fashioned and the symbols to which listeners respond. The human voice and body are flexible instruments with enormous potentialities for sensitive communication far beyond the relatively simple demands of making oneself heard and seen. Good speakers exercise artistic control over these means of communication.

10. Good speech expresses itself in acceptable
     language, style, and diction

The ideas of a speech are invigorated, clarified, and enhanced by appropriate words, accurately selected and arranged, and correctly pronounced. Standards of good taste and usage are always changing, but the speaker ignores them at his peril. Diction, language, and style are not ends in themselves. Rather, they facilitate communication by giving it precision, vigor, and beauty.

A NOTE TO THE READER

These ten basic principles represent our analysis of the art of good speech. They are derived from our conception of the nature of speech and our interpretation of the evidence bearing on the sources of good speech. For the most part, these are time-tested principles sanctioned by the authority of tradition. But there is no reason in the world for you to accept them at face value. You will find them far more meaningful if you test them for yourself. The chapters that follow are designed to help you make this test, both in your speech class and in all the years of speaking that lie ahead of you.

Do not expect to find a one-to-one relation between principles and chapters, for many of the principles appear and reappear in several chapters. As you come to understand the principles, you will have no trouble identifying them when you meet them.

POINTS TO KEEP IN MIND

1. Speech is the communication of ideas and feelings by means of visible and audible symbols originating in speakers and listeners.

2. There are four ways of evaluating speech: by its results, by its truth, by the motives of the speaker, and by the principles of the art of good speech. The principles of the art offer valid and comprehensive standards for judging speech.

3. Ten basic principles of speech will guide you in improving your speech and in judging the speech of others.

EXERCISES

1. Choose a subject of genuine interest to you and prepare a short talk on it. Your purpose is to highlight *one* of the ten principles of good

speech. Choose the one that you think may give you the most trouble. Actually, of course, you will try to follow all ten principles, but give special attention to one of them. After your speech, tell the class which principle was uppermost in your mind. Ask the class members to discuss how well they think you may have succeeded in putting it into practice.

2. Think of a speaker whose speech exemplifies in strikingly effective ways any one of the basic principles of speech. Give a talk in which you explain the principle and then describe as vividly as you can how the speaker gains special strength through the application of this principle.

3. Make a short talk on a meaningful experience you have had. Your purpose here is to interest your listeners enough so that they will try it for themselves. Use the why-not-try-it approach, but without stating the question outright. Emphasize those aspects of your experience that will mean the most to your listeners. Here are some ideas.

Breaking a bad habit

Overcoming stagefright

How to interpret Matthew Arnold's poem "Dover Beach"

A church you have attended

A magazine you read regularly

A course you have taken

Participating in a community project manned by students

4. Read to the class a short passage that you feel has literary merit. Choose one you enjoy enough to want to share with others. Let the strength, beauty, and impact of the language and ideas come *through you*, as the writer's agent. When you have finished reading, give your own interpretation of the passage: What message does it carry? What points does it make? What are the sources of its strength and beauty?

5. Divide the class into groups of from eight to twelve people. Appoint a leader for each group and carry on a discussion for forty to fifty minutes on a question of campus policy. Here are some suggestions.

Should your college adopt the honor system for all examinations?

Should attendance be required at classes?

On what basis should scholarships be awarded?

Should students be permitted to have automobiles while at college?

two

Guidelines
for Speaking

An understanding of the basic principles of speech is the first step toward speech improvement. Practice in the application of these principles is the second step, and criticism of these applications is the third step. In your course in speech, these three activities—learning about speech, giving speeches, and listening to these speeches—will go on concurrently. The first three chapters in this book will help you get started: Chapter 1 has given you an introduction to the principles of good speech; in this chapter we give you preliminary advice on preparing and presenting speech; and in Chapter 3 we lay down guidelines for the criticism of speech.

Learning to speak better can be an exciting, stimulating adventure if you know what good speech is, if each practice speech represents your very best effort, and if you and your colleagues in this enterprise do your best to help each other.

EXTEMPORANEOUS SPEAKING

Most speaking occasions are relatively informal and flexible, seldom governed by rigid rules of procedure. Questions are asked and answered by several people who take their turns at speaking and listening.

The best preparation for meeting these typical, life situations is classroom experience in extemporaneous speaking—unmemorized speech that you prepare in advance. You investigate, analyze, select, and outline your material so that you know beforehand what you want to say and the order in which you will say it. You prepare thoroughly, but you avoid freezing the talk into a language mold. Since the language is not canned, you rely upon your resources to supply the appropriate words at the moment of delivery. The best extemporaneous speech is built upon a solid foundation of rigorous preparation. On this assured ground, you will find the freedom, flexibility, and spontaneity that you will need to adapt to the shifting reactions of your listeners.

True, there are times when you have little or no opportunity for advance preparation, and there are times also when it is wise to write out a speech in its entirety, then read it from a manuscript or to commit it to memory. We shall provide for those occasions too. But keep in mind that extemporaneous speaking is basic to all other approaches, and through it you acquire skills that have general utility.

PREPARATION OF EXTEMPORANEOUS SPEECH

Speech, like water, cannot rise higher than its source. Good speech is not achieved through casual musings and random thinking. It calls for hard, sequential thought, an intellectual weaving of ideas into a fabric so tight that it will withstand probing questions and objections. Norman Cousins aptly describes the process this way: "The route must be anticipated between the present location of an idea and where it is supposed to go. Memory must be raked for relevant material. Facts or notions must be sorted out, put in their proper places, then supplied with connective tissue. Then comes the problem of weighting and emphasis." [1]

In the preparation and presentation of speech, sequential thinking consists of a set of fairly discrete steps that follow a chronological order.

SUBJECT AND PURPOSE

First, decide on what you should talk about and the specific response you hope to achieve. You will find your best subjects at those junctures where your liveliest interests and concerns overlap

[1] Norman Cousins, "Not So Fast," *Saturday Review,* July 6, 1963, p. 14.

those of your listeners. Once you have made your decision, then state your specific purpose as concisely as possible in a single sentence.

Usually you will come to this purpose sentence by stages. The topic "Our changing educational scene," although too broad and indeterminate, suggests other possibilities of narrower scope, such as "The new admission policies now being applied by State University" or "Making higher education available to all who can benefit from it." But these somewhat narrower topics still lack the limitation, specificity, and direction that characterize the following purpose sentences: "Intense grade consciousness among students in my dormitory has killed extracurricular activities," or "I intend to show that excessive grade consciousness is killing intellectual life on campus." A worthwhile subject and a carefully devised purpose sentence provide a solid foundation on which to build your talk.

DEVELOPING YOUR TALK

Having formulated your purpose sentence, presumably you are already in possession of some information and ideas for developing your talk. Make the most of what you already know and have thought, for every good speech bears the authentic stamp of a speaker's individuality. Effective speeches are never mere collections of items taken from something that others have said or written. This does not mean, of course, that good speeches can be fabricated from thin air. When talking about matters of consequence, responsible people exercise utmost care to be sure that the information they have on hand is both accurate and sufficient; whenever necessary, they take pains to supplement it with additional facts, statistics, examples, and other materials that will help to give credence to their views. Experienced speakers draw upon their own resources, but they also verify and augment their knowledge of a subject through additional observations, interviews, and reading.

Your purpose sentence will not only guide your investigations, but it will help you to formulate key points in your talk. In one way or another, you have come to a conclusion now formulated as a purpose sentence; but if you hope to convince others, you must speak to the basic questions that are likely to arise in their minds. If your purpose sentence is well considered and sharply stated, it will offer strong indications of the points you must take up. Suppose your purpose sentence were this one: "I intend to show that excessive grade consciousness is killing intellectual life on campus." Analyze this statement thoughtfully, and you will quickly see that your listeners must be satisfied on various basic points before you can reasonably expect to gain their assent. You would need to show that (1) because of many pressures, the pursuit of grades seems to be foremost in the minds of students today; (2) although good grades are not incompatible with the intellectual life, excessive grade consciousness—grades for their own sake—stifles curiosity and joy of learning; (3) we ought to and can nourish a spirit of learning that relegates grade acquisition to a by-product.

A careful analysis of a well-conceived purpose sentence, you can see, virtually prescribes steps to take in developing your talk.

OUTLINING YOUR SPEECH

An outline organizes the results of your analysis and investigation. It charts the main points and subpoints along the course that your speech will follow. Main points support or explain your purpose sentence; subpoints support or explain either your main points or still other subpoints to which they are subordinate.

Visualizing the form of an outline helps to fix in mind these relationships among the points.

I. Main point that supports or explains purpose sentence.
   A. Subpoint that supports or explains main point I.
      1. Subpoint that supports or explains subpoint A.
      2. Subpoint that supports or explains subpoint A.
   B. Subpoint that supports or explains main point I.
II. Main point that supports or explains purpose sentence.

With this form before us, we can begin to develop an outline that supports our specific purpose.

Purpose sentence: I intend to show that excessive grade consciousness is killing intellectual life on campus.

I. Emphasis upon grades overshadows other motivations for learning.
   A. High schools seem less interested in inculcating the spirit of learning for its own satisfaction than in getting students admitted to prestige colleges and universities.
      1. Counselors are forever reminding students of requirements for admission to Ivy League schools.
      2. Teachers are driven to "lay on" the work in order to qualify students for these colleges and universities.

B. In college it is the same thing all over again.
   1. Outside pressure to qualify for admission into college is exceeded only by pressure from the inside to get the grades required to stay in college.
   2. Students with scholarships must make consistently high grades to hang onto their stipends.
   3. Students with ambitions for graduate or professional schools become greasy grinds instead of intellectual questers.
II. Widespread grade consciousness today actually fosters anti-intellectualism on our campuses.

What you have just seen is but a segment of the body of a speech. A fully developed outline is divided into three main sections: an *Introduction*, which stimulates audience interest, paves the way for good relationships between the speaker and his audience, and discloses the speaker's subject and possibly his particular line of attack; the *Body* or *Discussion*, which is the major part of the outline, unfolds the steps in the development of the speaker's theme; and the *Conclusion*, the capstone to the entire talk. For examples of full-length outlines, turn to pages 99–102.

REHEARSING THE SPEECH

Students often ask, "Should I practice extemporaneous speeches before delivering them to an audience?" The answer is "Yes!" This is the time to spot and iron out problems that become evident only after you try to articulate your thoughts. Rehearsing helps you to test your ideas, fix the outline in mind, and develop an ear for the sound and swing of your talk. But keep thinking out your speech as you talk it out. Should you hit upon especially felicitous words and phrases along the way, make a mental note of them, but don't come to depend upon them. The good ones will probably stick with you and turn up when you speak to an audience. There are exceptions to this rule, of course. For example, it is usually wise to think up a few good sentences as insurance against a fumbling start and an inconclusive conclusion.

Practice beforehand, but avoid turning these private sessions into sterile, mechanized exercises. Begin early and space your practicing. Make each session a means to personal development and an opportunity to enrich your talk.

"May I use notes?" you ask. Use them by all means to report

complicated information or extended quotations. Notes insure accuracy and remove the strain of memorizing. Usually there is no reason why you should not use prompting notes, such as a skeleton outline, if your speech is technical or long and if you use them sparingly and unobtrusively. Use practice sessions to acquire skill in handling notes effectively. You will have some assignments, however, in which notes are unnecessary and inadvisable. In any event, your instructor will let you know whether notes are an aid or a hindrance to your progress. When you need notes, these suggestions may help:

1. Make your notes simple.

2. Put them in proper sequence before you speak.

3. Write your notes legibly. (It is best to type them out in double-spaced lines.)

4. Place your notes on the desk or speaker's stand where you can consult them easily.

5. Resist the impulse to retreat into your notes. Use them only to jog your memory and keep you on track.

6. If you read quotations or other material, hold up your card, sheet, or book for easy reading. Look up and out at your audience from time to time.

DELIVERING YOUR SPEECH

All of your preparation is brought to bear either directly or indirectly in the delivery of speech—in your voice, words, and bodily action. Your goal in private practice, in the classroom, and in public is to talk *with* people, not *at* people.

THE CONVERSATIONAL NORM

Make a point of analyzing some invigorating conversation you overhear, and you will quickly perceive that *interaction* among participants is its most vivid characteristic. Listeners respond to the speaker through the alert posture of their bodies, changing facial expressions, bursts of laughter, sounds of protest or agreement, and still other overt signs of involvement. Speakers, through their words and comments, their voices and manner, respond to the developing reactions of the listeners. An analysis of this interaction suggests two key concepts that underlie it, basic components of all good speaking: *empathy* and *rapport.*

Empathy is a process by which you involve yourself imaginatively and sympathetically with the thoughts and feelings of another person. You adopt his interests, try to see things as he sees them, to feel as he feels, even though you may not subscribe to his views. Empathy is the opposite of self-preoccupation and egocentric behavior. When both the speaker and listener project themselves into the mind and emotion of the other, the interaction that follows is known as *rapport,* the hallmark of good speaker-audience relationship. Without rapport, the communicative act is always incomplete and therefore imperfect; sometimes it is completely blocked.

Since lively conversations exemplify the attributes of communicative delivery, the conversational norm furnishes the best guide to the delivery of all speech. Qualities of voice and action that characterize lively conversation—directness, animation, variety, and spontaneity—are appropriate to all speech, formal as well as informal. Many people suffer from a mistaken notion that public speech calls for an oratorical manner that is mysteriously different from the natural mode of their more private speech. The truth is that if you can talk easily, directly, and responsively in conversation, happily, you may proceed with assurance in adopting the conversational norm of informal speech for your public speeches—with only two precautions.

Remember, not all conversation qualifies as good conversation. We are seriously misguided if we accept as our models the mumblers and bumblers we hear on all sides. To take our standards for public speaking from the dull, rambling, inept conversations we all overhear (or engage in) every day of our lives is to heap undeserved torture on listeners. Remember, too, that public speech differs from conversation in several obvious ways. The speaker does all or most of the talking; audience response is largely covert rather than overt; more people are present; and the speaker usually stands in front of an audience, often on a platform. Accordingly, the public speaker must alter his delivery through heightened output to accommodate himself to these special conditions. Even so, he can and he should retain the *sense of communication* that is rooted in elements characteristic of good, conversational speech.

HOW TO TALK WITH PEOPLE

Here are several suggestions that will help strengthen your delivery in both conversation and public speech.

Idea consciousness should supplant self-consciousness

The first requisite of good delivery is an evident interest in what you are saying and in the people with whom you are talking. Given this interest in your subject and your listeners, many of the most common problems in delivery will vanish. Even a highly polished delivery will seem false and empty unless you are motivated by a desire to share your ideas and feelings with your listeners. As soon as you make delivery an end in itself, your speech becomes an artificial, devitalized act.

Think of what you are saying while you are saying it

Mental and emotional drifting can be spotted in a second, for the speaker's manner and voice will give him away. You have listened to people talk from memory or from a manuscript who obviously did not have their minds on what they were saying—and no one else did, either.

An extemporaneous speaker, of course, has no choice but to keep his wits about him. He must think as he talks and talk as he thinks. We expect talk to go forward with fluency, but not at the expense of the speaker's thoughtful reactions to his own remarks. Do not be distressed if you have to pause now and then to pick out the right word. Listeners regard occasional hesitations, on-the-spot revisions, or short digressions as signs of an active mind at work. Rattling glibness betrays a rattling mind. No speaker is really communicating unless he is in touch with what he is saying as he says it.

Respond to your audience

Think about what you are saying while you are saying it, but *think about it in relation to your audience*. Every audience sends out signals. Tune in on them to see if they carry messages of understanding, puzzlement, interest, boredom, weariness, or disapproval. Ask yourself: "Am I making myself heard? Would another example

Franklin Delano Roosevelt cups his hand to his mouth as he talks across the table with Lord Halifax, British Ambassador. (*Press Association, Inc.*)

help? Am I spinning this out unnecessarily? Did this sound too flippant?"

Most audiences will go more than halfway in giving you a fair hearing. But if you see that the audience is backing off or slipping away, take positive steps then and there to reestablish contact. Perhaps you need to change pace, or increase or decrease the force of your delivery. Don't hesitate to break in and underscore items with remarks like these: "The point I'm trying to make is this. . . ." "I want this to be perfectly clear. . . ." Throw out some questions: "Have you ever had this experience?" "Have you ever thought of it in this light?" Pointed remarks and questions help to retrieve wandering attention.

A good audience is a stimulus; a difficult audience is a challenge. But speech without any audience at all is a fiasco. Hold on to your listeners by talking things over *with* them instead of just talking *at* them.

Use your voice to carry meaning and feeling

The greatest value of the conversational norm is that it guides you in the use of your voice. Listen to the ordinary conversations around you. You will hear pleasant and unpleasant voices, clear and slovenly enunciation, good and poor diction—dialectal differences, mispronunciations, and grammatical errors. But through it all will come remarkable purposefulness and vitality. There will be exceptions, to be sure. But people do have a way of making their voices work for them. A student asks a question, and an instructor replies; a foreman directs the workman on a job; a girl explains to an anxious housemother why she is late; the cast talks over the play after rehearsal. These people are not thinking about their voices, but they have important business on their minds. Accordingly, their voices are remarkably flexible and expressive.

One of the most common problems among beginning speakers is learning to use their voices with this same flexibility when they are speaking to larger groups. Why do sight-seeing guides lapse into singsong speech? Why do radio and TV announcers, extravagantly extolling lawn fertilizers in one breath and skin balm in the next, speak in souped-up tones? Why do oldtime political orators intone? Why do so many beginning public speakers talk in flat, dull monotones? Speech has become routinized for the sight-seeing guide; announcers who cannot speak from the heart must artificially pump up enthusiasm; the political orator has established bad vocal habits that he thinks are good; and the beginning speaker is inhibited and nervous. In all these cases, *the speaker has lost contact with his ideas and feelings.* His voice has been cut off from its supply of vital energy and has been rendered lifeless. This is the principal cause of breakdowns in voice communication.

Speak with physical animation and directness

Speaking is action in which mind and body cooperate. Bodily action supplements and reinforces words; it energizes thought; it reveals you as a person who is self-confident rather than self-conscious. A listless person fails to sustain interest for very long; an anxious, distracted person communicates his distress; an overwrought person wears us out by trying too hard. A nice balance between relaxation and tension contributes to poise and directness.

People like personal attention. When you look your audience straight in the eye, you are taking notice of them. You are saying, "I invite you to share this information or observation." This simple gesture contributes to good human relationships. It also helps you to adapt sensitively to the reactions of others.

If you are talking to a large group, you cannot focus your attention on everyone at once. Simply shift your attention unobtrusively from one segment of the audience to another, so that no one is excluded. You can do this easily and naturally without swinging your head back and forth like a busy airport beacon. Usually there is no need to single out individuals unless you happen to be especially interested in their reactions. Even then, be careful not to fix them with your eye until they squirm in their seats.

Avoid annoying mannerisms

You have seen speakers shift uneasily in their chairs or pace restlessly up and down the platform. You have seen some who rock back and forth on their heels, jingle coins in their pockets, or aimlessly take their glasses off and put them on again. You have been distracted by speakers who induce little artificial coughs, who clear their throats every few seconds, and who clutter their speech with stray sounds such as *ah, uh,* and *er.* These mannerisms call attention to themselves and distract listeners from what the speaker is trying to say. If fellow members of your speech class make you aware of such mannerisms, welcome their criticisms and take steps to eliminate the offending habits.

Observe the courtesies of the occasion

When you are introduced to a stranger, you acknowledge the introduction in a warm, courteous manner. Similarly, when you are introduced to an audience, you acknowledge the chairman's introduction and greet the audience with a friendly salutation and remarks appropriate to the occasion.

Good rapport with listeners calls for respect for their feelings. If someone asks a question, don't brush him off or punish him for his audacity. Assume that he is asking his question in good faith. Pugnacity, sarcasm, and defensiveness repel listeners, even when they know you are being goaded by a boor. A friendly, urbane manner helps to win them over.

OTHER METHODS OF PRESENTATION

Some occasions call for special competence in impromptu speaking, speaking from a manuscript, and speaking from memory.

IMPROMPTU SPEAKING

Much of our conversation is nothing more than a series of short, impromptu talks—speech that we have had no opportunity to prepare beforehand. Suppose you are attending a get-together of twenty or thirty people. You are all set to sit back and listen to someone else. Suddenly, the chairman turns to you and asks you to say something to the group. As you get to your feet, you must swiftly decide on the substance, purpose, and plan of your remarks. In short, you have to compose and deliver your talk at the same time.

There is no magic formula to help you become a skillful impromptu speaker. Actually, the best preparation for impromptu speaking, whatever the circumstances, is preliminary experience in extemporaneous speaking. The facility you acquire in finding subjects for extemporaneous speech, in analyzing and organizing materials, and in adapting your language to the occasion will immeasurably increase your readiness to deal with impromptu speeches.

SPEAKING FROM MANUSCRIPT

With a manuscript clutched firmly in your hands, you are free from the fear of making slips of the tongue, from relying on catch-as-catch-can language, from the danger of running overtime or being cut off before you have finished. Sometimes these advantages are compelling. Yet few people read a manuscript with enough skill to communicate successfully. They plant themselves behind a lectern, bury their faces, and then lapse into a singsong recital of words while their minds wander off into unknown realms.

If your material or the situation demands that you use a manuscript, then make a sincere and serious effort to get your ideas across the barriers. Here are some suggestions that will help you avoid glaring mistakes when speaking from a manuscript.

Write your speech for the ear and not for the eye. Make sure it represents your best oral style. Keep your sentences short and simple. Weed out the long, complex ones. Favor colloquial words. Use the active voice rather than the passive. Write the talk in your most direct, personal, and graphic style, just as if you were talking person-to-person without a manuscript. Try it out on a friend and ask if it sounds like you.

After you have finished writing your speech, don't toss the manuscript aside and forget about it. Return to it from time to time. Review, rethink, and revise your ideas and language. Make your speech a living, growing thing. You will develop a richer feeling for it. This is the best way to keep your writing from turning cold and to keep your delivery from becoming mechanical.

Maintain contact with your audience while speaking. If you prepare well, you will be free to talk directly with your audience. You will find it easy to catch at a glance the sweep of a sentence, even a paragraph, and to concentrate on getting it across. And if you have your speech well in mind, you can work in on-the-spot comments that will keep it geared to the developing reactions of your listeners.

SPEAKING FROM MEMORY

Memorizing a talk frees you from the manuscript and preserves the advantages of a carefully written speech. Special events, such as a formal ceremonial occasion, sometimes call for speeches that exhibit finesse in composition. If reading a manuscript seems out of place, you may decide to commit your speech to memory.

One hazard of a memorized talk is that it often leads to mechanical delivery. Some people become so engrossed in recalling words and in behaving elegantly that they lose touch with the sense and sentiment that prompted the speech in the first place. Listeners quickly detect a "canned" speech and are likely to dismiss it as a schoolboy performance. A second hazard is that you may forget your speech. The fear of forgetting may itself make your mind go blank.

But you can reduce these hazards. You will discover that skill in extemporaneous speaking will help you when you speak from memory. In extemporaneous speech, you acquire the habit of first focusing your mind on a basic outline of points. Extemporaneous speaking also promotes habits of flexibility and directness that will help you to improvise when necessary and to preserve the conversational norm.

If you memorize a speech, avoid memorizing in rote fashion, line by line. Instead, begin by studying the pattern of ideas you worked up in your preliminary outline. Fix in your mind a picture of the talk as a whole, then take up the separate units as part of a logical structure. You will memorize with greatest efficiency if you spread your study sessions over a period of time.

POINTS TO KEEP IN MIND

1. Competence in extemporaneous speech—well-prepared but un-memorized speech—equips you to meet the widest range of speaking occasions in today's world.

2. The preparation of extemporaneous speech begins with a worthwhile subject and purpose, proceeds through thorough investigation of appropriate sources and careful analysis of steps, and culminates in a well-devised outline.

3. Rehearsing your speech is sound procedure for uncovering problems before you speak in public and for making necessary revisions.

4. Mutual empathy of speaker and audience leads to rapport, which is the condition for genuine communication.

5. The conversational norm, with adaptations, is appropriate to the delivery of all speech.

6. Effectiveness in delivery can be strengthened by disciplined effort

and by focusing on sensitive aspects of delivery that greatly affect communicativeness.

7. Some occasions require impromptu speaking, speaking from manuscript, or speaking from memory. Each type makes its own demands, but skill in extemporaneous speaking contributes to success in all.

EXERCISES

1. A series of open-forum assignments on controversial subjects stimulates good delivery. Each talk should be extemporaneous. Reserve half of the period for questions and answers. Appoint a chairman to preside. In the open-forum period, insist that each person stand when he speaks and that no one speak for more than one minute. Allow time for a critique of all the aspects of delivery in this chapter.

2. Make a short extemporaneous talk. After the other speakers scheduled for the day have spoken, you will be recalled to expand on the points of your talk or to offer additional ones. Invite the rest of the class to comment on your poise and communicativeness in your two appearances. Were there any differences? Analyze the differences.

3. Divide the class into three or four groups and have members of each group investigate independently a topic of general interest to the group. Appoint a leader for each group. On a scheduled day, have the leader open the discussion of the general topic in an easy, informal way. As the discussion proceeds, the leader will invite each member to rise and speak briefly to some point on which he is prepared to speak extemporaneously.

4. Each member of the class contributes two nontechnical subjects that are suitable for short impromptu talks. Then each person draws two subjects other than his own. After thinking them over, he rises and speaks briefly on the one he chooses.

5. Choose a subject, investigate it, and write out your talk, word for word. Test your writing on someone who knows you well, to see if it is in keeping with your best oral style. Be as communicative as you can when you read the speech to the class.

6. Prepare a short talk that will be largely extemporaneous. Write out and memorize only short passages of it. After you have delivered it to the class, find out if your listeners were able to detect the portions you memorized. If they were, try to find out how they managed to spot them.

7. Choose a passage of prose or poetry. Prepare a short introduction and a conclusion that enforce the point of your passage. Read communicatively, as if you were talking with people.

three

Guidelines
to Criticism

This chapter is designed to help you apply principles of good speech in criticism. You ask questions such as these: Did the speaker do a good job? Did he use all the available resources to best advantage to achieve his purpose? What were his strengths and weaknesses as a speaker? Why and how did he succeed or fail? What can he do to improve his speech?

The old saying "practice makes perfect" is only a half-truth at best. Practice makes "permanent." What you practice in and out of your speech class will become habitual. If these habits are to be good ones, then you must start with an understanding of good speech and submit your practice to appraisal by competent critics as the basis for improvement.

In your speech class, as elsewhere, you will respond vigorously to arresting ideas, for their own sake, and you will thereby contribute to a lively forum that furnishes the best kind of an audience any speaker could want. But at the same time, you are cast into the role of critic in the fullest sense. You will need to be aware of the *totality of the speaking process* if you are to help the speaker improve while achieving for yourself a finer grasp of principles and methods that underlie the art of speaking well.

WHAT CRITICISM MEANS

If you recoil from the word *criticism*, it may be that you equate it with fault-finding, as you do when you say, "You're too critical—

too negative. Don't stick pins in me." Perhaps you have come to prefer substitute words such as *comments, suggestions,* or *reactions.* The fact is, however, that the word *criticism* has a well-established and scholarly meaning for which there is no adequate substitute. For those who use the word in a professional sense, it does not imply negation; it is associated with *appraisal.* In all branches of the humanities, the word *criticism* is as meaningful and useful as is the word *diagnosis* for the physician.

Criticism may be defined as an intellectual process by which we seek to understand and to assess a work of art by applying to it the principles appropriate to that art form. Until we know what principles distinguish any art form, we are without criteria for judging it. Given these criteria, the critical process involves analyzing speech objectively to pinpoint strengths and weaknesses in the talk you hear—your own and that of others. Looked at in this way, criticism is an essential procedure for improving the quality of discourse.

YOUR ROLE AS A SPEECH CRITIC

Until now, chances are you have been preoccupied with the speaking responsibilities you face in the weeks ahead. This is understandable, since the preparation and delivery of talks at spaced intervals always looms large in a speech course. But consider now your role as critic. Whenever you are a listener, you are, perforce, a critic—whether or not you make your reactions known publicly. It is essential that you make the most of every opportunity to listen perceptively—in the dormitory, at home, and especially in the classroom—if you are to become a proficient speaker.

Look upon your speech course as laboratory learning. Here you will gain practical experience in the art of criticism, just as you do in the art of speaking. As time goes on, you are likely to discover that there is less and less shooting from the hip and more and more thoughtful comment. With experience, idiosyncratic reaction arising from the mood of the moment or from personal feeling about the speaker tends to be replaced by greater objectivity and rigor.

As you have undoubtedly surmised, the criteria for criticism are the principles of good speech you encountered in Chapter 1. These principles may be worded differently in other books, but there is consensus among experts on their substance. Later chapters will acquaint you with methods by which these principles are put into effect. Thus, as your speech course unfolds, you will see that there is reciprocity between your understanding of speech doctrine and your development as critic, between your growth as a speaker and your ability to make use of the insights you acquire from the daily exercise of giving and receiving criticism.

We recognize that criticism does not produce scientific certitude, but through regular practice each of us can become more perceptive in his observations and more reliable in his judgments.

SPEECH AS THE OBJECT OF CRITICISM

Although our immediate interest is in the criticism of classroom speeches, our approach to criticism must take into account all speaking—speech under any circumstances that we can imagine—long talks and conversational tidbits, prearranged talk and speech that accidentally falls on our ears. Merely to note the range and variety of our daily speaking-listening experience justifies the conclusion that of all forms of human expression, speech is undoubtedly the most evanescent. You can return to a painting or statue to check your initial responses. By rereading a novel or poem, or anything that is in written form, you catch meanings that escaped you the first time through. Not so with speech. Usually you listen without benefit of text. You seldom have artifacts to consult after the event. Normally, you take in the wholeness of the speaking event, now or never, with all of your senses acting like antennae picking up signals.

A speech critic performs multiple acts, simultaneously or in rapid succession. He looks, listens, and searches for half-hidden meanings, probes for implications, and tries to analyze all the subtle interactions among speaker, audience, and occasion. He does more than follow the speaker's words. His criticism is complex. He considers voice, gestures, style, subject, or whatever single features we might name, but he judges the value and effectiveness of speech from the *wholeness* of the event.

The complexity and dynamics of speech place a heavy load on the critic's power of attention. He must listen to understand the speech and must continuously isolate, analyze, and evaluate essential elements that affect the value of the enterprise. Some factors may escape his attention because of the strong competitive or compensatory influence of other rhetorical elements. Thus a great voice may create the illusion of great ideas. Conversely, great ideas may escape notice because they move sluggishly on a thin trickle of voice. Sometimes a glamorous personality half-hypnotizes listeners into believing that the speaker is saying something important. Later, the few people who read the text in cold print or listen to a transcription learn to their chagrin that they had mistaken malarky for a message. A speech that sounded fine in class may come close to sounding like gibberish when you hear it on tape. Because of the fleeting nature of speech and its susceptibility to rhetorical distortions, the art of criticism is demanding. It is mastered only by effort, discipline, and considerable experience.

To make close criticism, you will find a text, recording, or—if at all possible—a film with sound track to be invaluable. In live recordings, you can examine in detail various features of speech—ideas, structure, style, and aspects of delivery; but even so, to repeat a fundamental truth, the fullness of a speech exists only at the moment of its delivery in the presence of an audience. When you listen to it live, you are closer to the wholeness of the speaking event than you can ever be again.

Let us turn now to practical suggestions that you can put to use in criticizing classroom speeches.

PARTICIPATING IN CLASSROOM CRITICISM

Ours is an age of machines that seem capable of doing *almost* anything that people can do. Still, it is unlikely that a mechanism will be invented into which we can feed raw data about speaker, audience, occasion, and speech, and then quietly sit back until the gadget coughs up an acceptable punchcard critique. How may we as human beings, then—not machines—best put our human resources to use?

Total concentration

Deliberately put aside whatever threatens to distract your mind. Intense concentration is needed to step up your visual and auditory acuity. You will need to attend to what the speaker is saying, how

Marianne Moore talks with a group of student poets. *(Wide World Photos)*

he works at his job of communication, and how the audience responds. Attentiveness is not criticism, to be sure, but unless you have a full comprehension of what was said and what went on, your ultimate appraisal is bound to be incomplete and distorted. If you need a further reason for concentrated observation, remind yourself that in a speech class, where everyone works to improve his skill in speaking, we create a system of reciprocity: You give me your best attention, I'll give you mine, and we'll both get something out of it. As a speaker, you will quickly spot pretended listening that shows up in artificial expressions people sometimes plaster on their faces; and you will learn that few things are more disheartening than visible evidence of boredom on the part of your audience.

Should a critic make notes as he listens? Yes, if they help him to recall points later on. If note taking is necessary, do it as unobtrusively as possible. As a critic, your attention can be diverted from the speech by writing elaborate notes to yourself, and the speaker may be thrown off as he tries to communicate with an audience that is busily scribbling.

The critic's dual role

As must be evident from all we have said, the critic is not a mere sponge. Empathic involvement with the speaker helps you to see the speaker's job as he interprets it, and feeling-in with the audience enables you to make a finer assessment of their reactions. Unless you succeed in getting outside yourself, you are likely to limit your criticism to highly subjective reactions instead of making a judicious appraisal of the speaker's achievements. But if empathy is required of a critic, so is detachment. You must be able to stand aside in order to assess the nature and value of the rhetorical process. Each of us continues to make subtle psychological and intellectual adjustments in shifting from one role to another. Understanding the mixed demands for empathy and detachment helps to make a critic out of a listener.

Critical objectivity

As you listen to your classmates, you will hear a variety of views on many subjects coming from people of diverse backgrounds and personalities. You may be attracted by some views and personalities, repelled by others. As you listen, you are tempted to extol a speaker whose views support your own, especially if these views are under attack; or to denounce a speech that runs counter to your thinking. We are all prone to biases, but we must control them. A fair-minded critic is on guard lest he vote his private prejudices. He neither endorses a poor case in behalf of a cause of which he approves, nor does he withhold approval of a strong case for a cause he dislikes. One mark of maturity in a critic is his ability to judge speech by its artistic merits rather than his private predilections.

Applying standards

Before the speeches of the day begin, quickly review the principles of good speech summarized in Chapter 1. A complete critique evaluates a speaker through the application of all of these principles. Usually, each assignment prescribes a focal point in your learning of doctrine, which, in turn, prescribes the frame of reference for criticism. The focal point will shift from assignment to assignment. Thus, one class exercise may highlight the subject and purpose; the next may feature organization and outlining; a third may concentrate upon content and the development of ideas. As you progress, the orbit of your rhetorical knowledge widens, and topics for criticism become cumulative too.

Although your criticism will take on breadth as you go along, it is usually wise to make one thing central. More is accomplished by probing deeply than by ranging widely and superficially over a multitude of matters. Since the object of class criticism is to help a speaker to improve, you will succeed only by analyzing a problem thoroughly. Suppose you tell a speaker only that his delivery is ragged. This may add to his discomfort but probably will not help him at all. You will aid him by specifying the random activity, clumsy syntax, and physical indirectness that made his delivery seem ragged. Better still, try to get behind surface symptoms to the causes of his problem. Does his "raggedness" appear to be rooted in poor speech habits? Was the speaker responding to stress that can be circumvented by a change in his attitudes or in outside circumstance? Had the speaker spent enough time preparing? And what about his mode of preparation? Often a diagnostic inquiry will disclose the true nature of a problem and thereby enable the speaker to deal with it in a fundamental way.

Expressing criticism

The way in which you express your comments makes a world of difference in the way they are received. Rapport between critic and speaker is just as important as it is between speaker and audience. A speech class is doomed if members get in the habit of blackslapping each other or if they look for opportunities to trade low blows. Criticism is productive when intelligence, integrity, and good will prevail. When thoughtful observations are accompanied by evidence of respect for a speaker's feeling, they are almost always welcomed. Frankness is essential, but so is tact. A dogmatic, opinionated statement is resented and often provokes reprisals that destroy class morale.

To their credit, students sense these things without exhortation. Intuitively they tend to open their critiques by stressing a speaker's strong points before indicating matters that need to be improved. This is sound procedure. Without putting it into words, most students realize that criticism must be expressed in a stimulating manner and made persuasive to the speaker before he will act on it.

Timing criticism

Suppose there are five speakers scheduled for a class hour, with the remainder of the period to be devoted to discussion and criticism of the speeches. Should you talk about each speaker immediately after he has finished? Or should you hear all five of them before you criticize any? Is there any rule to guide us?

Perhaps it is best to decide after trying both procedures. Which do you prefer? After a speech, one is usually eager for reactions. On the other hand, a speaker's mind and emotions are so involved while he is talking that it takes time for him to disengage himself from preoccupation with his speech. With his own words ringing in his ears, he has difficulty attending closely to words spoken by others.

Consider, too, the feelings of students who are waiting to speak. When class discussion follows immediately upon the heels of each speech, the waiting period seems to stretch inordinately for speakers eager to get going and inhumanely for those whose apprehensions mount with the ticking of the clock. Still other considerations must be taken into account. Students who are waiting to speak are seldom good critics until they have disengaged their minds from their own talks. Hearing out all the speakers before criticizing any of them helps to maintain a good class schedule, and it enables critics to make comparative observations based on all of the speeches of the day. There is much to be said for dividing a class period into two parts: all the speeches first, then the criticism. But since there is no invariable rule to follow, perhaps it is best to experiment and choose the system that works for the class as a whole.

METHODS OF REPORTING CRITICISM

Oral comment in class

This widely established practice is justified by its values for speaker and critic. The open exchange of ideas can be immensely stimulating both to speaker and listener. Speakers soon learn that not every comment can be taken as valid, but they learn, too, that sensible judgments rise to the surface and prevail over notional reactions.

Usually it is good to have several members of a class involved in criticizing each speech, but variations are possible and sometimes advisable. For example, a member of the class may be singled out in advance and invited to serve as the principal critic of a speaker.

Written comment

Instructors commonly write comments on the backs of students' speech outlines or in the margins; but students, too, may be asked to prepare written evaluations. The written critique may mention delicate, personal matters that you might hesitate to bring up in class, or criticism that would eat up class time better devoted to matters of general importance. Usually prepared after the class period, written comments enable the critic to react retrospectively, with benefit of detachment. In summary, occasional written critiques afford a useful supplement to oral comment.

Demonstrations

One of the best ways to criticize and correct individual speech problems, especially problems in the delivery of speech, is to recall a speaker and then work with him in the presence of the class. Showing one person how to improve his own projection of voice, vocal variety, physical and vocal indirectness, stance and bodily action can have utility for the entire class. Through on-the-spot improvements in one speaker, other students gain insight into the *value* of vocal projection, for example, and into the *means* of achieving it.

Check sheets

On these shorthand devices, based on a list of rhetorical elements, the student indicates his reactions to a speaker and his speech. The critic reports his judgments by means of a checkmark in the blank space, by circling the appropriate index number, by underlining a word or phrase, or by still some other invention. Opinions differ sharply on the value of such criticism sheets. They can be administered easily and afford a quick, quantitative judgment of the speakers' success in exemplifying a large array of rhetorical factors. On the other hand, check sheets are arbitrary and do not lend themselves to the kind of qualitative criticism required by a particular speech. Moreover, since the basis of the critic's judgment is as important as the judgments themselves, critic sheets are useful as adjuncts to oral or written criticism, at best, and ought not to supplant detailed, analytical commentary.

POINTS TO KEEP IN MIND

1. Make the development of your critical capacities one of the primary purposes of your speech course.

2. As a critic, you will learn to apply the principles of good speech as standards for appraising speech—your own and that of others.

3. There is high reciprocity between your growth as a speaker and your growth as a critic.

4. Because every speech event is fleeting and exceedingly complex, you can expect to render a reliable judgment only by discipline and training.

5. Participating in classroom criticism will help you to acquire attitudes and practical procedures that will work for you outside the classroom.

EXERCISES

1. Make this an exercise in comparative criticism. Select a major speaking event that you may listen to on television. If possible, make a tape recording. Write your criticism of the speech based on your TV viewing. Now play back the tape recording. What differences did you pick up between the TV version and the taped version of the speech? How sig-

nificant are these differences in your judgment of the speech? Look for the newspaper accounts of the speech and take note of the criticism you find. What seems to be the basis or criterion of criticism that you found in the press? Finally, what insights into the art of criticism did you acquire from this exercise?

2. Attend a speaking event on campus. Write a précis of the talk to prove to yourself and others that you understood what was said. Then go on to write an appraisal of the talk, using the ten principles of good speech as your standards. Have a classroom discussion of the event, using student critiques as the bases for a criticism of criticism.

3. Find the text of a speech that once excited a great deal of attention but one that you have never read. Examples might be Wendell Phillips, "The Murder of Lovejoy" (1837); William Jennings Bryan's convention speech of 1896; Franklin Roosevelt's first inaugural address, 1933. First read the text without benefit of additional material. Then look up newspaper items on the speech and its times, general histories, and biographies of the speaker. With benefit of these materials and the exercise of historical imagination, reconstruct the speaking event by putting it into the context of its times. Comment on the meaning of the speech with and without the historical context.

4. Read two or three essays on the criticism of individual speakers that you find in W. N. Brigance, ed., *A History and Criticism of American Public Address*, 1943. Select one for an oral report. In your speech, make clear how the critic went about his job, what his findings were, and your judgment of his criticism.

four

The Personal ✓
Equation in Speech

Speech is an intensely personal act. One person speaks; others react. You will master all the basic principles of speech much more easily if you first master yourself.

We deal with two closely related problems in this chapter: how to make a good personal adjustment in speech and how to establish good personal relations with your audience. These are two sides of the same coin. Understanding the personal equation in speech contributes to poise and maturity in human relations.

YOU CAN'T ESCAPE

You as a person inevitably influence everything you say. You must call on your personal resources when you speak, and your listeners inevitably form impressions of you. You can't escape. Nor should you wish to. Your speech gives you some of your best opportunities for personal identification and fulfillment.

You have already discovered that it is easier to talk with some people than with others. You know, too, that tension mounts when the occasion is important to you, or more public than you are accustomed to, or more complex and demanding. These tensions may be energizing factors that spur you on to greater effort, or they may impose serious handicaps. In either case, your speech will be better if you are in full control of yourself.

Good personal adjustment in speech is achieved first through the discovery of personal qualities that will serve you best and, second, by learning how to call on your best personal resources to relieve tension.

Many corporations employ public relations experts to enlist the good will of audiences; but as a speaker, you have to do this job for yourself. Your audience sees you as you are. And remember that you represent the cause you are pleading, as well as yourself. Rightly or wrongly, attitudes toward *you* rub off on your subject. Here again, there are two things that you can do: first, discover the personal qualities audiences react to most favorably; second, learn how to enlist these qualities in establishing good personal relations with your listeners.

PERSONAL QUALITIES THAT CONTRIBUTE TO GOOD SPEECH

The personal equation in speech varies from speaker to speaker, from audience to audience—and fortunately so, for differences in personality give freshness and variety to human relations. It is hardly necessary to point out that success in speech is achieved by persons of very different temperament, personality, and capacity; and that peoples of different cultures, backgrounds, and motivations react differently to speakers. But do *not* jump to the conclusion that this variety and complexity in human relations means that any kind of behavior is acceptable. Far from it! Beneath individual differences, there are certain personal qualities that will help any speaker do a better job. Students of speech have been aware of these qualities for centuries, and there is a remarkable consensus in their findings, despite differences in time, place, and circumstances.

The most rewarding personal resources in speech are a compound of intellectual, emotional, moral, and social qualities. Taken together, they may describe a person of considerably more stature than many of us are likely to achieve. But this is not a fair test. If it is true that any speaker will be *more effective* to the degree he possesses these qualities, then we have established a goal worthy of our best efforts.

Intellectual qualities	Emotional qualities	Moral qualities	Social qualities	
$\begin{Bmatrix} \text{Insight} \\ \text{Judgment} \\ \text{Imagination} \end{Bmatrix}$	$+ \begin{Bmatrix} \text{Stability} \\ \text{Control} \\ \text{Strength} \end{Bmatrix}$	$+ \begin{Bmatrix} \text{Integrity} \\ \text{Sincerity} \\ \text{Courage} \end{Bmatrix}$	$+ \begin{Bmatrix} \text{Warmth} \\ \text{Sympathy} \\ \text{Sense of} \\ \text{humor} \end{Bmatrix}$	$= \begin{matrix} \text{Good personal ad-} \\ \text{justment and good} \\ \text{personal relations} \\ \text{in speech} \end{matrix}$

Most of the qualities in this equation are familiar enough in your day-to-day life. But how do they affect your speech? And how can you use them to best advantage? Let us identify them briefly and then see how they can be made to work for you.

Intellectual qualities

A speaker with clear insight, good judgment, and imaginative power is well equipped intellectually. He understands his subject and how it is related to his listeners, the occasion, and himself—he has clear insight. He thinks straight and evaluates men and ideas carefully—he has good judgment. And he is creative in coming up with new ideas or clever applications of old ones—he has imaginative power and vision.

Emotional qualities

Even well-prepared speakers with their best intellectual powers at work may fail to do themselves justice if they lack emotional stability, control, and strength. We all have experienced frustration in speaking because we were nervous, ill-tempered, or apathetic. Emotionally stable people are objective in their reactions to potentially disturbing situations. Their emotions are disciplined. Yet, they have the strength and the emotional drive to fight for important causes in which they believe.

Moral qualities

The moral component in your personal behavior can make or break you as a speaker. Let your listeners doubt your integrity, sincerity, or moral courage, and you will soon be without an audience. Integrity is a matter of choice—it is within the power of all of us. Sincerity means genuineness—freedom from affectation, smugness, and little conceits. It also means forthrightness and good intentions. Moral courage is the will to hold fast to your deepest convictions, even when they are unpopular. It does not call for churlishness or stubbornness, but it does call for self-respect and firmness when firmness is required.

Social qualities

The social qualities—warmth, sympathy, and a sense of humor— are closely related to your feelings and attitudes toward other people. Warmth and friendliness are relaxing, outgoing qualities that make speaking easier for you and your listeners, who are likely to respond with the same attitudes. Acceptance and understanding of human differences breaks down barriers, wins respect and a fair hearing. Sympathy is the power of entering into the feelings of another—appreciation and understanding of the attitudes and points of view of other people, whether or not you agree with them. This is the way to effect close rapport between speakers and listeners. It will almost always make communication easier, too, if the speaker has a good sense of humor and the capacity to bridge misunderstandings without rancor.

HOW TO IMPROVE YOUR PERSONAL ADJUSTMENT IN SPEECH

We have no magic for you here. Self-improvement springs from experience, and it often is a pretty slow process. But we have seen students improve their speech immensely by acquiring better understanding of their personal resources and by learning to use them with greater sensitivity and assurance.

1. Self-appraisal

This is the first step. What kind of a person are you? What are your personal assets and liabilities as a speaker? What are your intellectual, emotional, moral, and social qualifications? How well do *you* measure up to the personal standards we have set?

We are not referring to the reflection you see when you look in a mirror. This is less important than you think. What we have in mind is what you discover when you honestly and objectively assess your strengths and weaknesses as an individual, particularly in your relations with other people. Make this appraisal a continuing process throughout your course in speech.

2. Compare yourself with others

Observe the personal behavior of others when they speak. Why do you respond favorably to one speaker and not to another? What are the special strengths and weaknesses of these speakers in personal adjustment and human relations? How do these strengths and weaknesses compare with your own? Which of the speakers you have heard show the personal qualities you would most like to possess?

Cicero, in his *De Oratore*, tells the story of a young Roman, Sulpicius, who made great strides as a speaker by deliberately modeling himself after Crassus, one of the distinguished orators of his time. Cicero cautions the student to select the best model and "to strive with all possible care to achieve the most excellent qualities of the model he has approved," without imitating mannerisms in "pose or gait" or other eccentric habits.[1]

You can often pick up valuable pointers by studying the personal qualities and adjustments of other speakers. No one wants you to make yourself a carbon copy of another speaker, however successful he may be. But to emulate the best qualities of good speakers is a way of profiting by their experience.

3. Adopt positive attitudes

Chronic self-derogation is self-defeating. Be realistic in self-appraisal, but always work with a positive image of yourself at your best.

One of the surest ways to build up tension is to dwell on all the disasters that may befall you in the speech you are planning: "I might drop my notes. . . . Maybe she'll hang up on me. . . . I'd rather drop the course than give that speech. . . . He wouldn't possibly consider me for the job. . . . I just know I'll forget my lines. . . ."

You cannot turn confidence on and off like a water faucet, but you can direct your mind to thoughts that build confidence.

4. Plan a role for yourself

In preparing for a speech or conference, planning the disposition of your personal resources is as important as planning your case. Ask yourself these questions: What will be in good taste? What conduct will be appropriate? What approach will do justice to our

[1] Cicero's *De Oratore*, II. XXII.

cause? What behavior and what attitudes will help convey my ideas?

If you make firm decisions on these matters beforehand, you will avoid mental and emotional drifting when you begin to speak. But what is more important, you will narrow the areas in which tensions are most likely to develop.

5. Relax physically

One good way to relieve emotional tension is to relax physically. This relatively simple expedient is one of the better ways of restoring the poise and ease essential to good personal adjustment. We shall have more to say about this in Chapter 15.

6. Profit by experience

In spite of your best efforts, you may sometimes come away from a conversation, conference, or speech with the sick feeling that you have handled yourself very poorly indeed. The best therapy for this feeling is to make an objective analysis of what went wrong, devise a plan for improvement, and resolve to do better next time.

Every speech you give really consists of three speeches—the one you give in anticipation, the one you give to your audience, and the one you give to yourself on the way home. This third one is often the best of the lot, for then the pressure is off and you can profit by your mistakes while they are fresh in your mind. If you make these "third speeches" standard practice, you are likely to do better with the one that counts.

HOW TO IMPROVE PERSONAL RELATIONS
WITH YOUR AUDIENCE

As you gain experience, you will find that the personal adjustments that make life easier for you as a speaker are also well received by your hearers. If they see you as a well-adjusted person—intellectually, emotionally, morally, and socially qualified—you have gone a long way toward winning their confidence. How can you capitalize on these qualifications in gaining personal acceptance?

We have six suggestions. The first two are basic and fundamental. The others are special applications for many situations.

1. Project an effective ethos

The way your listeners regard you as a person has been discussed for many centuries as the *ethos* of the speaker. More than 300 years before Christ, Aristotle held that ethos may very well be "the most potent of all the means to persuasion." If listeners see the speaker as a competent person who knows what he is talking about, as an honest, decent man of good character, and as one who is concerned about their well-being, they will be favorably disposed toward him and toward his recommendations. Here is the way Aristotle put it:

As for the speakers themselves, the sources of our trust in them are three, for apart from the arguments (in a speech) there are three things that gain our belief, namely, intelligence, character, and good will. Speakers are untrustworthy in what they say or advise from one or more of the following causes. Either through want of intelligence they form wrong opinions; or, while they form correct opinions, their rascality leads them to say what they do not think; or, while intelligent and honest enough, they are not well-disposed (toward the hearer, audience), and so perchance will fail to advise the best course, though they see it. That is a complete list of the possibilities. It necessarily follows that the speaker who is thought to have all these qualities (intelligence, character, and good will) has the confidence of his hearers.[2]

In brief, then, the qualities an audience respects in a speaker are intelligence, character, and good will. Consciously or unconsciously, your audience will size you up in these terms and make judgments concerning you, whether you like it or not. These judgments are inevitable and inescapable. And they will have a powerful influence on the outcome of your speech. A wise speaker will know that these appraisals are being made, and he will try to present himself in ways that command respect.

It may be true that ideas should be accepted or rejected on their own merits without regard to the person who presents them, but this rarely occurs. Especially is this the case whenever the listener must necessarily rely on the competence and integrity of the speaker. In our complex specialized society, we cannot possibly attain the kind of expert knowledge required to make independent decisions in many of the areas that touch our lives. We call on tradesmen we trust, and we rely on their judgment. We cast our votes on the basis of personal or party endorsements of many issues that we do not fully understand. Although our educational system attempts to equip us to make critical judgments of our own, there is an ever

---

[2] The Rhetoric of Aristotle, II. 1. Translation by Lane Cooper.

widening gap between our personal competence and the many decisions that we are called upon to make. We often have to act on faith, and we try to reside this faith in people we think we can trust.

It is further true that many of us will prefer, if the cost is not too great, to go along with people we like and respect, even though we are fully capable of independent judgments.

2. Reveal your best self

Your ethos as a speaker is determined primarily by the choices you make and the reaction of your listeners to these choices. Every time you speak, you make certain choices—in *what* you say and *how* you say it. Most of the visible and audible symbols you offer your listeners are within your power to control, and every choice you make says something about you. Here is the way one writer describes it.

When an individual makes a voluntary selection of words to use in any human situation, he describes himself. To be sure, a person may recite, "Two plus two equal four" without giving himself away. But if he talks of anything more intimate than that—anything about which he has a free choice of what to say and how to say it—we do not have to listen long before we can guess what we can reasonably expect of him as a human personality.

That words reveal personalities is not accidental. Language serves the purpose of giving public form to otherwise private thoughts. Words, in short, get people out into the open. They may think they are talking about something quite other than themselves—about a stranger who cuts across their lawn; or about an editorial in the morning paper; or about an educational experiment, a minister's sermon, a housing project, a strike, a radio program. But it is *they* who are doing the talking, who choose the words and the tone of voice, and who, with those words and that tone of voice, recite their own philosophy, their own attitude toward human beings and human arrangements.[3]

The list of controllable factors is endless, but here are a few of them: the subjects you choose to discuss, the emotions you display, the interpretations you make, the stories you tell, the evidence you present, your attitudes toward yourself and others, your movements and gestures, your vocal inflections, your choice of words, pronun-

[3] Bonaro W. Overstreet, *Freedom's People* (New York: Harper & Row, Publishers, 1945), pp. 60–61.

ciation, diction, and so on. Out of this welter of clues, the listener traces out his opinion of you as a person.

You *do* reveal yourself—your personal qualities—through the many choices implicit in what you say and do as a speaker. Unless your listeners know you well, they have no other way of judging you. Sometimes they are right, sometimes they are wrong; but their respect and confidence is almost invariably important, in any situation, and being able to gain it is worth considerable time and effort. To the degree that the ability is developed, it then becomes a saver of time and effort.

You will soon discover, if you have not already, that most people are pretty shrewd in their judgment of speakers. A clever actor may be able to simulate qualities he does not possess, but he usually gives himself away in the hearing of critical listeners. It is exceedingly difficult to fake knowledge you do not possess or to disguise rascality and intolerance. The best way to *appear* effective is to be effective; the best way *to appear* honest and decent is to be honest and decent. And the best way *to make your listeners think you are concerned* about their welfare is to feel that concern.

It is a sad fact, however, that because many able men are poor speakers, they fail to win confidence. The capacity to conduct yourself in ways that reveal your best self is an important part of the art of good speech and should be a basic concern in every course that has skill in speech as its primary objective.

3. Adapt to your audience and to the occasion

An understanding of your listeners and sensitive awareness of the circumstances under which your speech is being received will often dictate the choice you should make in developing your subject and presenting your speech. Adaptations can always be made within the limits of accuracy, honesty, and good taste. Accommodations of this kind establish rapport with your listeners and mutual respect.

4. Adapt to your reputation

People have a tendency to form an opinion of a speaker before they ever hear him. They draw on press reports, public relations releases, personal associations, conversations with people who know him, introductory remarks by the chairman, and many other clues. This initial impression may work for, or against, you as a speaker.

The subject of James Brown's speech is "Let the People's Voice Prevail." His argument is a solid one, yet his listeners greet it with raucous laughter. Such is the price of Brown's reputation as the Machiavelli of Siwash. But reputations work the other way too. Helen Green is known as a thoroughly democratic person. So when she defends the right of a social organization to be as exclusive as it pleases, she receives a fair hearing, even though most of her listeners disagree with her position. John Jones has flown fifty missions in a Sabre-Jet and has been decorated for bravery. Even though he has a quaver in his voice, none of his listeners will question his courage.

You may discover that your reputation has followed you into your speech class. You will either have to live up to it or else live it down.

5. Make a good first impression

First impressions have a way of growing into lasting impressions. You meet a person for the first time and you make a quick appraisal of him. Once this judgment is made, you are likely to stick with it unless later evidence forces you to revise it. A speaker who makes a poor opening has to work hard to overcome this disadvantage. And one who makes a strong impression at the start can draw on this strength throughout the conference or speech.

6. Give information about yourself

A speaker usually provides a certain amount of information about himself during his speech—either inadvertently or for a specific purpose. That specific purpose is often to establish himself as someone who knows what he is talking about: "I have always been a friend of the farmers; I should like to take this opportunity to make my voting record on farm aid a matter of public record. . . . I have three sons in service and I know how vital this matter is to you. . . . I spent two years of my professional life in the Orient and I have seen these things for myself. . . . I wrote the labor platform and I have kept my promises to the working men and women of America. . . . You can't tell me anything about dormitory food; I've been eating it for four years."

We all issue such guarantees—both in conversation and in public speech. The very fact that we do is proof of how important this matter of personal status is both to speakers and listeners. We know that in one way or another we must establish ourselves as worthy of our listeners' attention if we hope to get a fair hearing. But remember that careful listeners will check your credentials, and a false guarantee is sure to be detected.

POINTS TO KEEP IN MIND

1. The personal equation in speech is made up of intellectual, emotional, moral, and social qualities that contribute to good personal adjustment and good personal relations.

2. You can improve your own personal adjustment in speech by (a) self-appraisal, (b) comparing yourself with other speakers, (c) adopting positive attitudes, (d) planning a role for yourself, (e) relaxing physically, and (f) profiting by experience.

3. You can improve personal relations with your audience by (a) projecting an effective ethos, (b) making choices that reveal your best self, (c) adapting to your audience and to the occasion, (d) adapting to your reputation, (e) making a good first impression, and (f) giving information about yourself.

EXERCISES

1. Write an analysis and appraisal of your own personal qualifications in making a satisfactory adjustment in speech. What are your strengths and weaknesses? What special problems do you face? What steps can you take to meet these problems?

2. Write an analysis and appraisal of some speaker you admire—a speaker whose personal qualifications enable him to make effective adjustments in speech. Make a list of his special strengths—the personal qualities you admire and the ways he manages his personal resources. Conclude your paper with a list of specific suggestions for your own speaking.

3. Use the analysis in Exercise 2 as the basis for a class speech. Characterize the speaker you are discussing and explain what you believe to be the personal resources that contribute to his strength. Be specific. Give examples drawn from the speech or speeches you have heard him deliver.

4. Bring to class a published speech that exemplifies the methods a speaker uses to establish his competence on his chosen subject. You may have to read the speech more than once to discover all the methods he uses. Read the speech to the class; then tell what methods you think the speaker has used to establish his competence.

5. Prepare a short talk in which your primary aim is to establish your competence to speak on a particular subject. Try to win your listeners' confidence without parading your qualifications. If you are describing an event, and if you were present when it occurred, say so. If you are talking about another person, tell your audience how well you know him. The important thing is to establish your right to talk about your subject, but to do so unobtrusively.

five

Speaking with a Purpose

Efficient performance starts with a clear objective and a definite plan of attack. Speech has its basic purposes, and there are superior methods of achieving each one. A clear-cut decision on your objective will lead you to choose an appropriate subject, guide your investigation, and help you to develop a soundly structured speech around your subject.

PRIMARY PURPOSES

The universal purpose of all speech is to get a *response*. When we communicate with others, we translate ideas and feelings of our own into symbols that others can see and hear, in the hope that they will react to them in meaningful ways. In short, we seek a response of some kind from someone.

At first sight, the conceivable purposes of speech seem too numerous to classify. After all, anybody can talk about anything for any reason under the sun. But if we look more closely, we find that there are four primary purposes that encompass all the important objectives of speech. These basic purposes will guide you in identifying and accomplishing your specific purpose, whatever it may be.

INQUIRY

Much of our speaking is a search for information or insights. We may simply ask someone a question in the hope that he can give us a helpful answer. Or we may try out our ideas on another person to see what he thinks of them. Or we may join with a group of people to discuss a common problem, in the hope that we can solve it or at least understand it better.

The common denominator in all speech of this sort is *inquiry*— or call it exploration, problem solving, investigation, or discovery. The occasion may be private conversation or public deliberation, but the purpose is always this searching for knowledge and understanding. In a sense, when we speak to inquire, we are doing what the scientist does in his search for facts and hypotheses. The laboratory and the conference table may have little else in common, but both can yield new insights of great social significance.

REPORTING

Most of you will be called on to make reports—in class, to business associates, to your clubs, and innumerable informal reports to friends and other people whom you meet in your daily activities. Here you are presenting information to your listeners. In your capacity as a reporter, you are not searching for information—you already have it, or think you have. Your purpose now is to inform or to instruct others who hope to learn from your report. What they do with this report may be of real concern to you, but your job as a reporter is well done if you have conveyed your information clearly, accurately, and in ways that sustain the interest and attention of your audience.

Reporting to inform or to instruct, like inquiry, is one of the four primary purposes of human discourse. In fact, most speakers will find themselves cast in the role of reporter more frequently than in any other. Like inquiry, reporting involves special skills and methods that every speaker must master.

ADVOCACY

The speaker who seeks to convince or persuade is an advocate. The advocate is not content just to provide his audience with information. He wants his listeners to adopt a specific attitude toward a proposition or to take action on it. He marshals arguments and appeals in support of a predetermined position—a position to which he is committed because he believes in it or simply because he has chosen to support it.

Advocacy is the third important purpose of speech. We practice it every day in selling, advertising, promoting, campaigning—in representing and defending causes that are important to us. Much of the practical decision making in our society is accomplished by advocates who defend competing ideas and yield to majority votes.

EVOCATION

The fourth primary purpose of speech is to inspire or to entertain. Here the speaker's intent is to evoke an emotional response—to intensify or allay feelings. You inspire people to greater efforts, comfort a friend in distress, tell a story to get a laugh, call for faith, reminisce, give encouragement, share your fears, stir up anger and resentment, express affection.

Such emotional experiences may be deeply moving, exciting, and exhilarating to the listener. Or they may be quieting and consoling. They may be pleasurable and entertaining, or stern and demanding.

All good speaking involves human emotions, of course, but in evocation the speaker's *central* purpose is to engage these emotions in a special way. It is an end in itself, to be enjoyed or valued in any way the speaker and his listeners see fit.

SECONDARY PURPOSES

One of these four primary purposes should dominate every speech, but secondary purposes may enter in along the way. In fact, even the primary purposes that we have mentioned may serve as secondary purposes when they operate in supporting roles. A funny story or an emotional appeal may be used to make a point or clinch an argument. Similarly, a speaker whose primary purpose is inquiry will almost always do some reporting, and may occasionally slip into the role of advocate. Advocates often use the reporter's approach in developing their case, and they have been known to use the techniques of inquiry for persuasive purposes. In short, any primary purpose, and the methods associated with it, may be used as a secondary purpose.

If secondary purposes are admitted, however, they must be kept subordinate to the primary objective. If a speaker's primary purpose is inquiry and he succeeds only in advocating his own point of view, his inquiry has failed; if his primary purpose is reporting and he succeeds only in entertaining, he has failed as a reporter.

THE SPECIFIC PURPOSE

Your specific purpose is your immediate goal in speaking to a particular audience. You should be able to state your specific purpose in a way that will point up your central idea and make clear precisely what you hope to accomplish. This statement should also indicate your primary objective. If inquiry is your primary purpose, you might put your statement of specific purpose this way: "How may we establish more efficient study habits?" or "We intend to investigate capital punishment as a deterrent to crime." If reporting is your primary purpose, your statement of specific purpose might be: "My object is to recount the highlights of the national Delta Sigma Rho Congress," or "I wish to explain the essential differences between boogie and cool jazz." If advocacy is your primary purpose, you might express your specific purpose this way: "My purpose is to urge the abolition of spring football practice," or "We must organize to oppose universal military conscription." If evocation is your primary objective, your specific goal might be expressed this way: "I wish to entertain my audience with an account of the rise and fall of Jenkins' Corners," or "I wish to stimulate appreciation for the poetic qualities in the sermons of John Donne."

Always phrase your specific purpose beforehand for your own guidance in preparing and presenting your speech. If you are to investigate a subject efficiently and organize your speech effectively, you need a clear and concise statement of purpose.

When, where, and under what circumstances you should disclose your specific purpose to your audience is quite another matter. Most often, perhaps, it is wise to state your purpose at the outset, so that your listeners will know precisely what you are trying to do from the very beginning. Sometimes, however, it may be wise to withhold your purpose until later in the speech. And there are times when you may decide never to state it at all. If your objective is controversial and likely to arouse a hostile reaction, pave the way for your proposition before submitting it directly. If you are after an emotional response of any kind, it would probably be naïve to spell out your purpose for your audience. Your purpose and your development of it can be implicit rather than explicit in any speech.

STATING YOUR SPECIFIC PURPOSE

Your statement of specific purpose should be

1. A complete sentence

Usually, a question is the most satisfactory form for speeches of inquiry. A declarative sentence is suitable for reporting, advocacy, and evocative speaking.

Inquiry: "Are telephone operators becoming obsolete?"

Reporting: "There are four basic procedures to be mastered to qualify for a position as telephone operator."

Advocacy: "Telephone operators should receive a ten-cent-an-hour pay hike."

Evocation: "Your telephone operator may be your life line."

2. One central idea

Your statement must present one idea, and only one. Many speakers find it difficult to compress their purpose into a unified sentence. They confuse supporting arguments or other lines of development with their specific purpose. Notice the confusion in this statement: "I want to acquaint my audience with Franklin D. Roosevelt's message to Congress in 1941 asking for a declaration of war against the Japanese Empire, because the step he was proposing was an important one in modern history, and it literally affected the entire world." Only the first part of this statement, ending with the word *Empire,* expresses intention or purpose. The rest of the sentence is a justification for talking about Roosevelt's message. These reasons should appear later, in the speaker's development of his talk.

3. Clear and concise

Be as terse and explicit as you can. Avoid ambiguity and vagueness. The statement "The best way to check inflation is to increase income taxes" is far more precise than "Something ought to be done about high prices."

ULTERIOR PURPOSES

A speaker may have a purpose in the back of his mind that he never reveals to his audience. This *ulterior* purpose is some indirect end toward which the speaker is moving, but which is unrelated to the form and substance of his talk. A candidate for a job might present a report on novel methods in advertising, but with the ulterior purpose of impressing his prospective employers. Speaking contests are good examples. Each speaker hopes to win the contest —that is his ulterior purpose. But each speaker tries to achieve this success by speaking to some specific purpose that is completely unrelated to winning or losing. Similarly, in your speech class, your ulterior purpose may be to win a good grade. But your speeches will be planned to inquire, report, advocate, and evoke in order to secure a specific response that is unrelated to the grade you get.

A FINAL OBSERVATION

We have stressed the value of having firm goals or purposes in speaking. To this we add a suggestion: *make your purposes worthy ones*. It's one thing to have a clear target, and it's another thing to have a target worth shooting at. The worthiness of your purpose brings several of the basic principles of speech sharply into focus: subjects that are worth talking about, speech that is socially responsible, and purposes that reveal you as a worthy person. Good speech is marked by worthy purposes as well as by clear-cut purposes.

POINTS TO KEEP IN MIND

All speech seeks some kind of response. You will have a better chance of winning the response you want if you define your objectives carefully.

1. Decide on your primary purpose. The one you choose will indicate the kind of response you seek and the best methods for winning it. Make one of these your primary purpose: to inquire, to report, to advocate, to evoke.

2. Decide on your specific purpose. This will be your central idea and will be in keeping with your primary purpose.

3. State your specific purpose in a clear, concise, complete sentence that contains only your central idea.

EXERCISES

1. Prepare a short talk based on (a) one of the four primary purposes set forth in this chapter and (b) a full and precise statement of your specific purpose. Speak to these purposes, but withhold any statement of them when you deliver your talk. After your speech, have your listeners write statements of what they understood to be your primary purpose and specific purpose.

Are your listeners in agreement? Now read to them the statements of your intentions. Did any of the listeners fail to recognize your intentions? What reasons do they offer for possible failure to understand your primary and specific purposes? How do you explain the discrepancies, if any? What conclusions may you draw from this experience?

2. Assume that you are to prepare a five-minute talk on each of the following statements of purpose. Is each an acceptable statement? If not, revise it to make it an acceptable statement of specific purpose. Then identify each specific purpose with some primary purpose that it might serve.

  a) The best way to keep down weight is to push yourself away from the table.
  b) College students are taller today than they were a generation ago.
  c) The owners of a big business are the American public.
  d) Something needs to be done about high prices and extravagance and lack of self-discipline.
  e) Radio and television have made "whistle-stop" presidential campaigns an anachronism.
  f) How should we study for the final examination in this course?
  g) Making assets out of our liabilities.
  h) Evansdale needs a public library and a swimming pool.
  i) The British Monarchy.
  j) There are many satisfactions in owning your own home, and you can finance it as cheaply as you can rent a house.
  k) Our vanishing forests and Indians.

3. Pick out a big, inclusive subject such as theater, fashion, door-to-door selling, Texas, trains, chemistry, automobiles. Divide this large subject into four subtopics, each suitable for a short class talk. Formulate a primary purpose and a specific purpose for each. Now prepare a speech on one of the topics. Have the class evaluate your talk in light of your avowed purposes.

4. Analyze the printed text of a speech that you find in a newspaper, in *Vital Speeches of the Day,* or in an anthology. Prepare and present a report that answers these questions:

  Who gave the speech? When? Under what circumstances?
  What is the speaker's primary purpose?
  What is the speaker's specific purpose? If it is not stated explicitly, what do you believe it to be?
  Is there any evidence that the speaker had an ulterior purpose? If so, do you regard it as commendable or justifiable?

5. Have four members of the class choose a single topic that is of interest to all of them. One will use this topic as the basis for a speech of inquiry. A second will use this topic for a report; a third for a speech of advocacy; and a fourth for an evocative speech.

six

Choosing ✓
Subjects

Subjects are the pivots of discourse. They control the orbit through which discussion swings. The value of our discourse turns on possibilities opened by the subjects we choose to talk about.

In everyday living, subjects spring naturally from immediate problems and events, from work and play. When you take your car to a mechanic, for example, your business with him dictates the area of discourse. There are other times, however, when you must initiate subjects and evoke interest in them. This is what you will need to do in your speech class. Here, in choosing and shaping subjects, you will acquire special abilities and a resourcefulness that will carry over into other life experiences.

FINDING SUBJECTS: A PERSPECTIVE

The catalog description of a course offered by a certain university ends with this requirement: "The only prerequisite is a persistent curiosity." Add to persistent curiosity the thoughtful probing of yourself and your reactions to your environment, and you have a working principle for finding subjects. Environment means total environment. Think of it in concentric circles, beginning with intimate, firsthand experiences and moving out to events, people, and ideas of widespread interest.

The key factor in your search for subjects is *reaction*. A subject for speech is not simply an event you have read or heard about. Neither is it a book, a memory, an acquaintance, or a concept. The subject lies (1) in your reaction to the book, event, person, or idea; and (2) in the possibilities it opens for inviting the interests of other people. Finding subjects is not like picking up rocks or seashells. It is a creative process in which reflection, imagination, and experience set your mind in motion.

REACTING TO THE WORLD AROUND US

The supersonic speed of our age makes Lewis Carroll, writing in the nineteenth century, a prophet of our times.

> Where Life becomes a Spasm
> And History a Whiz:
> If that is not Sensation,
> I don't know what it is.

Whatever charges may be leveled against our century—"the terrible twentieth century," as Winston Churchill once called it—nobody but a dullard would call it dull.

Ours is an age of revolution—revolution in transportation, in human relations, in communications, in education, in weaponry. Man is in revolt against repressive political systems, the inhumanity of machines, art forms, deprivation, disease. Religious and ethical systems are being re-examined, questioned, and sometimes repudiated. All of us have some part in the pageantry of our times. We exist, we act, and we talk in the context of a restless environment. This is our world, to be fashioned meaningfully through the power of human discourse.

But not all worthy subjects are world-shaking. Good subjects often reside in commonplace and even prosaic topics. The word *transportation* may suggest space flights to the moon, or it may suggest the hazard of scooters on a throughway, parking problems, or the incidence of bicycle thefts on campus. Ordinary conversational tidbits about haircuts, hairdos, and hair dyes become arresting when you catch their psychological and cultural implications. Spending a few minutes of reflective observation in a supermarket can send your mind in many directions—the effect of motivational research on packaging, the value of artistic displays, soft music and selling, our dependence on truckers, petty thefts, and courtesy in the check-out lines.

Often we are blind to good subjects right before our eyes—the effect of pesticides on food, the condition of our hospitals and schools, the roads we travel, and the billboards that block our view. A commuting student once complained he had nothing to talk about because he missed out on all of the campus activities. Encouraged to inspect his immediate environment more closely, he asked himself, "What do I look at each day without really seeing?" Among the things he listed were three used-car lots, each covering a city block. He took new interest in these car lots, asking questions such as these: Why do people dispose of cars that still have years of service left in them? Who buys these cars? What special sales pitch is used to sell them? Is there any other country in the world where you would find acres of used cars in a large city? What does the used-car business say about our economy? Does it mean that we are an enterprising or an extravagant people? Out of these questions grew the subject for an extremely interesting class talk: cars as a status symbol in our society.

REACTING TO THE IDEAS OF OTHERS

Be alert to possible subjects for speech as you scan the newspapers, listen to lectures, dinner conversations, or talks in your speech class. Jot down the ideas that turn up. A conversation on hypocrisy in religion may suggest a talk on hypocrisy in education, the law, or the home. A student who explained the theory of majority rule prompted a classmate to explain the doctrine of consensus practiced by the Society of Friends. A critic of the social ethics of advertisers aroused a member of the class to champion the advertising industry as essential to a free economy. A creative listener uses what he hears as a springboard to related topics.

PROBING PERSONAL EXPERIENCES
AND EXPECTATIONS

Nothing you say has meaning for others until it first has meaning for you. What is it like to travel the Trail Ridge Road in the Colorado Rockies at an elevation of over twelve thousand feet? Better ask the person who has made the trip. Does Boris Pasternak's *Doctor Zhivago* have the stature of a Tolstoy novel? Who can attempt to answer the question unless he has read both Pasternak and Tolstoy? How effective is the Woman's Judiciary Board in handling disciplinary problems on campus? A member of the board can offer facts that outweigh the opinions of the casual observer.

Oddly, students with special abilities and enthusiasms often dismiss rewarding subjects because of a mistaken notion that only fellow-specialists are interested in them. Here is a ski enthusiast, a collector of antiques, a cartoonist, an accomplished gardener. Here is someone wrapped up in thermodynamics, automation, puppetry, theater-in-the-round. Often your best subjects are your special interests. These are the things you can speak about with authority and enthusiasm. Through them you open a world only dimly known to others.

Examine your life as an unfolding process. Each of you has gone through infancy, childhood, adolescence, and into adulthood. Looking back over the years provides new insights, and looking ahead thrusts forward new questions and goals. A retrospective view of high school may reveal the way to revise study habits. A forward look into a law career may lead one to attend police court, an experience that may be stimulating or dismaying. Both experiences contain the raw materials for speech. Stretching out before you are a career, travel, marriage, parenthood, and active citizenship. Clustered around these experiences are scores of questions—real questions that open subjects for talk.

USING THE FOUR PRIMARY PURPOSES OF SPEECH AS GUIDES TO SUBJECTS

Inquiry

All of us carry in our heads unresolved questions that may perplex others too. When there is so much pressure to get into college, why do some students cut classes once they are admitted? Why does mononucleosis seem endemic to college students? You go with some friends to see a play. Some find it obscene, others do not. You decide to make a speech of inquiry on the question, "How does one judge whether or not a dramatic work is obscene?" You attend an evening lecture and discover that the audience is largely made up of townspeople and faculty. Why do so few students turn out for these lectures? You ask, "Should the university calendar be cleared of all extracurricular activities one night each week, to be known as Cultural Activities Night?" You cringe when you read the morning's headline: "Convicted Murderer to be Executed Tonight."

You are aroused to revive the long-standing question, "Should capital punishment be abolished?"

Use your speech opportunities, in class and outside, to state valid questions, to think them through with others, and to make some approach to satisfactory answers.

Reporting

Here are just a few subjects that students have used successfully in making reports.

Reactions to crisis: bailing out of an airplane
The proposed honor system
My life on a dude ranch
Uses of classical mythology in our modern world
Forerunners in the presidential sweepstakes
How the Secret Service protects the President
The life history of a bank check
Susie: a case study of a cerebral palsy victim
A new development in automation
The physiology of nutrition
Basic principles underlying cone re-entry
How a television show is put together
The process by which a new nation gains membership in the United Nations
The function of a computer's memory core

Make a list of things you have done, have seen, heard, or read that might be worked up into informative speeches that you would enjoy making.

Advocacy

We engage in advocacy whenever we seek to influence the belief or action of others. We engage in it daily. "Next time, take the train. . . . The Greeks get all the breaks on this campus. . . . If you don't start smoking, you won't have the problem of stopping. . . . You can lose weight on a high protein diet."

Cause-minded people never run out of subjects for speeches of advocacy. They are quick to encourage, defend, or denounce political, social, economic, educational, literary, or religious change. Here is a random list of propositions that students have used.

There is too much pressure to go to college.

A student judiciary should replace the faculty-student committee on discipline.

We need uniform traffic signs and signals throughout the Western world.

Everyone should take a vocational aptitude test at the end of his sophomore year.

Daylight saving time is a hoax.

The library stacks ought to be opened to undergraduates.

Pesticides are homicide.

Fashions make fools of us.

One foreign language should be required for graduation.

A computer is a creature without compassion.

Your convictions open prospects for subjects. They also furnish strong motivation for speaking and get you off to a good start in your early speeches.

Evocation

Your class offers opportunities for entertaining speech and for inspiration. We advance the civilizing process by illuminating accounts of men and women whose lives have enriched our own. Our love of the beautiful, our devotion to country, and our religious and humanitarian impulses impel us to share our feelings. These have been the titles of moving speeches:

Albert Schweitzer's reverence for life
Jane Addams changed Chicago
St. Francis of Assisi
A Scoutmaster saved my life
My favorite parable
The versatility of Robert Frost
John Glenn is more than an astronaut
The tragedy of John F. Kennedy

Classes have been entertained by light-touch speeches with titles such as these:

The secret language of women
My dog thinks he's people
Dollar signs without sense
What is "funny"?
How I tell my friends from apes

Basically, subjects for evocative speeches arise from your personal sense of values and find expression in either the inspirational or the light-touch speech.

FINDING SUBJECTS: SOME COMMON MISEVALUATIONS

All this advice on how to find subjects will be wasted on a person who habitually misevaluates himself and his responsibilities in speaking. What are some of these misevaluations?

"I'm not an authority on anything."

Being an authority is a relative matter. It depends on the situation and the problem at hand. If you have had first-aid training, you may take charge at the scene of an accident, but you will give way when the doctor arrives. Similarly, without being a psychologist, your job as a camp counselor may have qualified you to report on how unruly children were changed into socially cooperative youngsters.

Know what you are talking about. The more you know, the better; but it is wise to indicate the limits of your knowledge on a topic. Authoritativeness is never absolute. We might as well sew up our mouths if we have to know everything there is to know before we speak.

"Nothing I can say will interest my audience."

This lament arises from the false assumption that good subjects spring only from unusual experiences. Students complain: "She was in summer stock; all I did was go to summer school. . . . Lots of people in my class have been everywhere; I've never been outside the state. . . . He worked in Glacier Park; I worked in a service station."

Anyone who has ever listened to a boring travelogue knows that it is not the exotic experience *per se* that insures interesting talk. This point was brought home to one student who habitually drew unfortunate comparisons between his opportunities and those of others in the class. Having helped his father keep alive a family grocery store, he was encouraged to draw upon his personal experiences. He spoke with unmistakable authority on the threat of big business to small enterprise. The favorable reactions to his speech convinced him that audiences respect ideas and attitudes gained from firsthand experience, even if the experience is not glamorous. He saw, too, that he had needlessly belittled himself.

"I haven't any burning enthusiasms."

The subject you choose doesn't have to make the blood pound at your temples. You are not expected to set off a crusade or campaign in a five-minute talk. True, some people have more excitement in them than others. But all of us have interests that lead to worthwhile topics for class talks. Furthermore, as free men and women, we are under some obligation to strengthen our involvement in social and political affairs, and to think and talk about these matters.

**"Nobody has suggested anything
  that appeals to me."**

This clinging-vine attitude is rooted in the false notion that our own education is always somebody else's responsibility. You may pick up some good leads from something somebody else said or wrote. But in the final analysis, your own mind needs to reach out, take hold, and make the selection. You will never be able to speak convincingly until you can claim the subject as your own.

**"I have plenty of time to think up a subject;
  I don't speak for a week."**

You may have met this grab-bag specialist. The night before he is scheduled to talk, he scans a newspaper for the first time in days, gives an ear to a radio commentator, glances at some predigested magazine articles, or prowls through the dormitory badgering anyone available with a "Hey, I've got to make a speech tomorrow. Know any good topics?"

A last-minute speech is a talk of desperation—a batch of jumbled, pointless remarks on a topic chosen at random. There are no shortcuts to good speech. You have to live with an idea long enough to get acquainted with it. Select your subject early, so that you will be on familiar terms with it before you introduce it to others.

STAKING OUT YOUR TOPIC

Some topics are too big and shapeless for short talks or discussions. Others box you in so tightly that you cannot move. The big topics need to be pared down to size, and the undersized ones need to be enlarged.

LIMITING YOUR SUBJECT ✔

To limit your subject, move from the general to the specific. At first, you will probably cast about among general fields of interest, such as international relations, politics, science, art, literature, travel, and so on. Having chosen a general subject, divide it into smaller, more specific ones. For example, international relations may be classified in units, such as the history of our foreign policy, treaties, alliances, international tribunals and peace organizations, or programs for international understanding. Let us say that international under- standing strikes you as particularly appealing. But this is still too broad a topic; so you isolate seven factors that promote or block understanding.

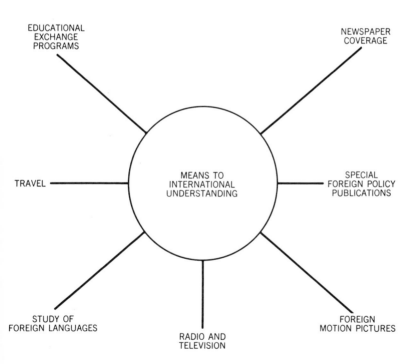

Any one of these seven subjects may be further subdivided. For instance:

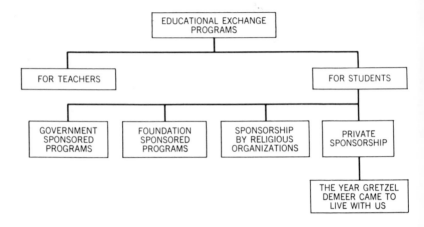

Of course, you won't always have to follow such an elaborate procedure. Once you pick up the trail of "Educational Exchange Programs," your mind might jump immediately to "The Year Gretzel DeMeer Came to Live with Us." The important thing is to grasp the principle behind the schematic device.

EXPANDING YOUR SUBJECT

Although you may be attracted by a subject on which you have strong feelings and opinions, you may decide to drop it because it seems too restricted and personal for others to be interested in. Before you discard it, however, see if you can detect certain implications that can be used to give it wider appeal.

Here is an example. A commuter is regularly late for his nine o'clock class because he can never find a parking place. His annoyance deepens every day, but he feels that a classroom is no place to air a personal gripe. Gradually, however, his annoyance gives way to inquiry and reflection. The building and grounds department tells him that the university has no more space for parking areas. The city officials tell him the same thing. The student realizes that his private problem is part of a critical problem in urban transportation. He also perceives that his personal grievance leads directly to urgent questions of general concern. Here, for example, are some of those questions:

Should the university grant parking privileges only to students who can prove a legitimate need for an automobile in residence?

Should the city undertake construction of subterranean and skyscraper parking areas?

Are automobile manufacturers doing all they can to redesign cars to meet mounting traffic and parking problems?

What are the prospects for redesigning and modernizing rail transportation to meet urban needs?

Subjects for conversation, discussions, and speeches often originate in a personal experience that, when explored thoughtfully, proves to have wide interest and application.

TESTING YOUR SUBJECT

Is my subject likely to yield solid values for me and my audience?

Some occasions call for small talk, but people who talk about only trivial things betray trivial minds. They cheat themselves and others. Discriminating listeners judge us by our interests. What you choose to talk about reveals how well you live up to your social responsibilities.

Am I able to deal with this subject competently?

Ask yourself, "Do I already know enough about this topic to discuss it responsibly?" If not, "Do I know how and where I can find the information I need?" If so, "Do I have the background to understand and interpret the material?"

Does my subject fit the interests and background of my audience?

An archaeologist returning from excavations in Egypt may hold fellow archaeologists spellbound with an account of complicated techniques for excavating and preserving remains. The same subject would probably fall flat in a speech to a woman's club. Here the archaeologist might be well advised to talk about tastes in home furnishings during various periods of Egyptian history.

Is my subject appropriate to the occasion?

A church group in a college town wanted to promote understanding and good interfaith relationships among students of different religions. Invited to a dinner meeting were Mohammedans, Hindus, Buddhists, Christians, and Jews. The main course of the Friday dinner was ham, the only prayer was to the Christian God, the only song was a Christian hymn, and the speaker topped it all off by extolling the Christian missionary spirit. So many blunders may seem incredible, but any blunder that offends the sensibilities of individuals and groups—their rituals, conventions, taboos—cuts off lines of communication.

Is my subject manageable?

Beginning speakers often make the mistake of choosing subjects of almost unlimited scope for a five-minute talk. They try to take a cross-continental trip instead of a short excursion. Instead of talking on "advertising" in all its phases, confine yourself to one specific aspect of the subject, such as ethics in advertising, artistic television commercials, scenery and signboards, hidden persuaders in our supermarkets.

POINTS TO KEEP IN MIND

1. When prospecting for subjects, make use of (a) your interactions with your social and physical environment, (b) ideas that arise from all levels of learning and discourse, (c) your personal experiences, and (d) the four primary purposes of speech as guides to topics.

2. Misevaluations of yourself and your resources may seriously impair your success at the very outset. Avoid down-grading yourself or otherwise ducking your responsibilities.

3. Limit or enlarge your subject beforehand, so that you can handle it successfully in the time at your disposal.

4. Apply the five tests of suitability to your subject before you finally adopt it for a speech.

EXERCISES

1. Start now to build a classified list of potential subjects for speeches. Be alert to possibilities—in the classroom, while reading a newspaper or magazine, while watching TV, in conversations, while studying, while listening to your classmates speak.

2. Think of three people you know well, and think of one subject you would like to hear each one talk about. Now apply the same test to yourself. Of all your experiences and interests, what might the class most enjoy hearing you talk about? If you still have doubts, ask your friends for their opinions. Prepare a short extemporaneous talk on the subject you choose.

3. Prepare a short talk on an occupation. Your speech should answer questions such as these: What is the nature of the work? What qualifications are required? How useful is it? What future is there in it? How interesting is it likely to be? What are some of its disadvantages? Here are some suggestions:

Playwright	Teacher	Radio and TV commentator
Landscape gardener	Farmer	Professional football
Personnel director	Clergyman	player
Electrical engineer	Salesman	Space pilot
Commercial artist	Psychiatrist	Nurse
Novelist	Fashion model	Architect

4. The lives of famous or infamous men and women—their ideas, pursuits, and deeds—serve as good subjects for speech. Choose someone who interests you greatly, then phrase a question or two you would like to ask him or her. From the writings by or about the person, figure out the answers he or she might give to your questions. Prepare a talk based on your questions and answers. Here are some examples of questions.

Albert Einstein: "Does a scientist have a social responsibility with respect to his specific research?"

Albert Schweitzer: "Why did you choose to pursue your philosophic, medical, and musical talents in an African jungle?"

Here are the names of other people to whom you may wish to put a question.

Frank Lloyd Wright	Greta Garbo	Norman Thomas
Ralph Waldo Emerson	John Glenn	Martin Luther King
Winston Churchill	Franklin D. Roosevelt	Conan Doyle
Dwight D. Eisenhower	Adolf Hitler	Mark Twain
Charles Darwin	Van Cliburn	Emily Dickinson
Eleanor Roosevelt	Babe Ruth	Charles Lindbergh
Leonard Bernstein	Ernest Hemingway	Robert Frost
Lee Harvey Oswald	Lyndon B. Johnson	Adlai Stevenson

5. Listen thoughtfully to all speeches given in class. Would you like to challenge the positions taken by some of the speakers? Did any of them suggest questions you would like to pursue? Did some speaker discuss an event or place (such as an educational experiment in high school) that calls attention to something you might like to take up in a future talk? Keep a running list of the subjects that occur to you.

seven

Exploring ✓
Your Subject

Two thousand years ago, the great Roman teacher Quintilian satirized the antics of lazy and erratic speakers who spent their days ducking painstaking preparation. His thrusts at charlatans of his age expose a root cause for vapid discourse in our own age.

. . . Owing to their contempt for method, when they are meditating on some future effusion, they spend whole days looking at the ceiling in the hope that some magnificent inspiration may occur to them, or rock their bodies to and fro, booming inarticulately as if they had a trumpet inside them and adapting their agitated movements, not to the delivery of words, but to their pursuit. Some again settle on certain definite openings long before they have thought what they are going to say, with a view to using them as pegs for subsequent snatches of eloquence, and then after practicing their delivery first in silent thought and then aloud for hours together, in utter desperation of providing any connecting links, abandon them and take refuge in one formula after another, each no less hackneyed and familiar than the last.[1]

The way to get on with the job is to stop rocking to and fro and to launch into an orderly, step-by-step program of analysis and investigation.

[1] *The Institutio Oratoria of Quintilian,* trans. by H. E. Butler (London: William Heinemann, 1920), I, 281-83.

PRELIMINARY SURVEY AND ANALYSIS

MAKE A PRELIMINARY INVENTORY

First, take stock of what you know or think you know about your subject before you scout out the "authorities." This kind of concentrated brain-cudgeling will jog your memory and stir up some original thinking. Talk that draws slavishly on the ideas and material of others sounds bookish and smells of somebody else's ink.

Make a list of your discoveries—key factual items, ideas, hunches, and questions that you can use as they stand or investigate further. What you turn up will probably look like a housewife's grocery list. If you were to turn this list over to someone else, it probably would not mean much to him. No matter, this is a sensible way to begin. It is a strictly personal record of self-investigation that may both please and dismay you. Some of your insights may excite you as genuine discoveries, but you will probably find some gaping holes that need to be filled in your background of information.

ANALYZE YOUR AUDIENCE IN ITS SETTING

When you work up a speech, visualize the audience as they will be when you meet them. For example, if you are getting ready for a ticklish conference, think of the people who will be there. Consider the range of their information, interests, and prejudices. Which points are urgent? Which points need to be mentioned without laboring them? Which points have to be introduced gingerly, or dropped altogether? Keep the time limits in mind.

Here is an actual case in which a little preliminary analysis of the audience and the occasion would have saved the day. A local civic group invited a public official, who was an expert on conservation, to explain proposals for reducing pollution and for checking the alarming depletion of local water resources. The speaker unwound with a detailed history of the government agency he represented, and then he sketched its nationwide organization. A half-hour of this, and the audience was summoning up courage for a sprint to the nearest exit. Public meetings are plagued by speakers who drag in material extraneous to the business at hand. Get into the habit of thinking about your audience's expectations as you explore your subject. Guard against allowing your private interests or even the seemingly logical dictates of your material to dominate your approach.

INTEGRATE YOUR INITIAL SURVEYS

You are now ready to make some tentative decisions. Go over your preliminary inventory again, this time with your audience in mind. Select the points that look most promising as big headings for your speech. Under each, list the observations and notations that are directly related to it. You may not be able to include all the items from your preliminary inventory, but you may come back to some of them later on. Your new list is an organized guide to further exploration of your subject. Let us look at a specific example of how you can put your preliminary survey and analysis to work.

THE THREE STEPS ILLUSTRATED

The experience of a student—we'll call him Arthur Lewis—provides us with an instructive example. You won't duplicate his procedure in every detail when you work up your own preliminary survey and analysis, of course, but you will have a clearer idea of how to go about it.

Lewis took this subject for a class speech: "The values of mastering a foreign language." A number of things had led him to his choice—his own progress in mastering French, his pleasure in overcoming an early phobia toward foreign languages, his trip abroad, and a story in *The New York Times* that reported an appalling deficiency in foreign languages among college students. As he proceeded, Lewis kept this purpose in the back of his mind: "I want to convince members of my speech class that they owe it to themselves to master at least one foreign language before they graduate."

Step one: Lewis' preliminary inventory

Lewis pondered his subject, analyzed it in various ways, and came up with this list of leads.

My summer abroad.
The study of foreign languages as an aid to English (debatable).
Being able to speak a foreign language helps to confer culture (belongs to the genteel tradition; probably not very convincing today).

With isolationism breaking down, the ability to read and write in a foreign tongue helps us to relate ourselves to our new world.

Today there are student exchange programs that enable us to live and study abroad.

Leadership in your chosen vocation makes language facility of practical value.

Business is becoming increasingly international. Many large department stores hold night classes in French, German, Italian, etc., for buyers and sales personnel.

Knowing a foreign language will help you professionally by giving you access to professional literature from abroad. Many professional meetings are held in foreign countries.

Government service is badly in need of specialists in almost all lines of work who can speak the language of the country.

You may want to enter graduate school someday, and you may have to show ability in one or more foreign languages.

Your pleasure in traveling abroad on vacations will be doubled if you can speak a language besides your own.

Opportunities for language study at our college.

Language phobia? How I overcame mine.

New techniques and aids in learning a foreign language.

Which language or languages should you study? Some of the variables that will affect your decision.

Government subsidies to colleges and students who undertake a concentrated program of language study.

Step two: Lewis' analysis of his
  audience in its setting

Through earlier speeches and class discussion, Lewis had already sized up the other eighteen members of his class. They were preponderantly freshmen and sophomores, people who still had plenty of time to make course decisions. About a third of the class were women, and he noted that their speeches ran to "cultural" subjects; most of the men seemed to favor more "practical" topics. He had a hunch that a few of his classmates would fall right in with his purpose; that some had already had a skirmish with a foreign-language course that left them reluctant to tackle another; that about half the class had thought little about the matter.

Not satisfied with guesses, Lewis put together a little questionnaire and asked each member to fill it out. The answers sharpened his analysis. He learned that (1) only three people talked or read a foreign language with any fluency, (2) a scattering of the class members had taken a high-school or college language course but had no strong desire to go on, (3) most of the class had no plans to elect a foreign-language course, and (4) several insisted that they lacked aptitude.

Step three: integrating his audience analysis with his preliminary inventory

Now that he had worked up an audience profile, Lewis was ready to make some tentative decisions on which items in his preliminary inventory would best serve his purpose. Now he had to pick and choose. He decided to concentrate on (1) the lifelong personal satisfactions that knowing a foreign language would bring, (2) the practical benefits, and (3) some novel and interesting ways to learn a new language.

Looking over his inventory, Lewis crossed out some of the items (though he decided that he might be able to mention a few of them in passing), and rephrased others. He settled on three big headings, under which he grouped other items from his inventory.

Fluency in a foreign language is a passport to travel and living abroad.
> Two personal experiences from my summer abroad.
> Interview some students who have lived abroad.
> Consult brochures on student exchange programs re language requirements and suggestions.

In today's world, your business and professional future may hinge on your ability to write and speak another tongue.
> New job opportunities are opening as business becomes increasingly international.
> Your chances for government service are greatly increased if you can speak the language of another country.

New devices and techniques make learning a language pleasant and speedy.
> How Professor Andrews teaches his language courses in French. (Check with him on the results of his three-year experiment.)
> The language "lab."
> Records and tapes that have helped me.
> My experience in learning French at the "language table" in Mc-Cullen Hall.
> Opportunities for language study at our college.

Lewis now felt satisfied that his preliminary explorations had opened the way to directed inquiry. He had no intention of freezing his analysis or settling for the information that he had on hand. He needed to know more, and he was quite willing to scrap or revise his analysis if further probing turned up something better.

EXTENDING THE INVESTIGATION

Your own preliminary analysis will put you on a trail that you can follow as far as you need to go. Along the way, you will encounter new ideas, points of view, facts, examples, illustrations, and all the other things that will enrich your perceptions, thinking, and speaking. You will not use everything, but in subtle ways "everything" will show through as you talk. Here, then, are some suggestions for pushing deeper into your subject.

INTERROGATION AND OBSERVATION

Talk over your ideas with someone whom you can
   count on to listen and give thoughtful reactions

As the writer Robert Penn Warren aptly remarks, "Very often it is in conversation during the germinal stage of a project that I stumble on my meanings, or they stumble on me. . . ." If possible, arrange interviews with people who have special knowledge of your subject.

Use paper-and-pencil devices for
   collecting information

When you want to survey specific attitudes and practices, try your hand at working out simple questionnaires and opinion polls. Since most of us lack the time and the special knowledge needed to prepare and use these devices scientifically, be realistic about the results. Be aware of their limitations and make those limitations clear to your listeners.

Take a field trip to see for yourself

This may mean that all you have to do is inspect a project so that you can talk about it with more familiarity; or it may mean some sleuthing. Agnes Watson kept hearing the charge that college students who drove cars were a menace to the citizens of Moresfield. She decided to investigate the charge. She went directly to the proper municipal offices and checked over the records of accidents during the past academic year. She interviewed a judge in traffic court. She talked to several traffic patrolmen. Her report was acclaimed as a masterful example of careful and productive field work. And incidentally, she learned that it was better to base her beliefs on research and critical thinking than on loose talk.

PUBLISHED SOURCES

For many subjects, the only place you can find the information you need is in the library. Logically, then, you will need a working knowledge of the basic tools and resources that you will find there.

Reference books

Learn to use *Guide to Reference Books* by Constance M. Winchell. Although this guide is primarily for librarians, you will find it invaluable and easy to use. We can list here only a few of the types of standard reference work listed in the Winchell *Guide.*

Encyclopedias are surveys of knowledge organized on a topical basis. Outstanding are the *Encyclopaedia Britannica, The Encyclopedia Americana,* the *New International Encyclopaedia,* and their supplements. You will also find encyclopedias that cover special fields, such as the *Encyclopaedia of the Social Sciences.*

Then you will find many collections of short biographies of prominent people based on time periods, geographical areas, and occupations. Outstanding collections of national and international figures are the *Dictionary of American Biography,* the *Dictionary of National Biography* (English), *Who's Who in America, World Biography,* and *Current Biography* (international). *Biography Index* is a guide to current biographical materials.

When you want factual data about the contemporary world, look in the Winchell *Guide* for the yearbook that is most likely to contain them. You will find that *The World Almanac* is a compendium of facts for each year. *The American Yearbook* is an annual record of events in politics, economics, business, social conditions, science, and humanities. *The Statesman's Yearbook* supplies information on governments of the world, on population, religion, education, crime, finance, industry, and so forth. The *Statistical Abstract of the United States* is a source book of facts covering social, political, industrial, and economic subjects. *Facts on File* is a weekly world-news digest. And there are many others.

Two well-known dictionaries are Webster's *New International*

Dictionary of the English Language and *Funk & Wagnall's New Standard Dictionary*. The *Oxford English Dictionary* and *A Dictionary of American English* are invaluable for information on the history and usage of words.

Bibliographies

A bibliography is a list of works on a particular subject. By looking in the *Bibliographic Index* you can locate lists of works on a great variety of subjects. *The Reference Shelf* series supplies bibliographies on timely, controversial questions that have been debated in schools and colleges.

Books

The card catalog is an alphabetically arranged index to all the resources of your library, primarily to books. The cards are usually filed in three ways—according to author, title of book, and subject of book. The speediest way to find an item is to look for it under the author's name or the title. But subject headings, in addition to supplying a third place to look for a particular item, often provide a list of additional works on your subject. If you cannot find your book in the card catalog, and if it was published in English during the twentieth century, look for information about it in *The United States Catalog* or its supplement, *Cumulative Book Index*. Look in the *Book Review Digest* to locate reviews of a book and to find short summaries of these reviews.

Periodicals

The Reader's Guide to Periodical Literature is indispensable in exploring subjects for speeches. It will pay you to study carefully its system of abbreviated entries. Use *Poole's Index to Periodical Literature* for articles published in the nineteenth century. Scholarly articles in the humanities and sciences are listed in *The International Index to Periodicals*.

Indexes to special fields

These indexes list all types of publications in a special field—books, articles, pamphlets, bulletins, and so forth. Examples are *Educational Index, Industrial Arts Index,* and *Public Affairs Information Service*. Look in Winchell for a guide to the special field you have in mind.

United States public documents

The *Monthly Catalog* is a current bibliography of government publications and tells you how to order them. *The Congressional Record* contains congressional debates, speeches, extended remarks of congressmen, and Presidents' messages.

Newspapers

The New York Times Index, published since 1913, is a chronological and alphabetical index to that paper's news items and other features. Actually, this index serves as a master key to current affairs reported in other newspapers as well.

RECORDING YOUR MATERIAL

Human memory is fickle. A good set of notes will save you from little and big errors, and will spare you a return trip to the library to recover information that you have looked up before. Writing a thing down carefully and thoughtfully increases accuracy. A good investigator checks on himself as well as on his sources of information.

There are four kinds of notes that you will want to make. Put a symbol on each card or slip of paper to show what type of note it is.

1. *Verbatim notes* contain somebody else's words and data exactly as he expressed them.

2. *Paraphrased notes* embody somebody else's ideas and data in your own words.

3. *Summary notes* are digests of a book, article, speech, interview, or conversation.

4. *Personal "idea" notes* are a record of your original thoughts and observations on a particular subject.

Each card or slip, in addition to the note itself, should carry a subject heading, designation of the type of note it is, the writer's name, a full and accurate statement of the source from which it is taken, and the page number. Sometimes information such as the library call number, the writer's identity and special qualifications, and any appraisal you care to make of the work proves valuable too. At the top of the next page is a sample note card containing the minimum essential information.

Abbreviation of the word ver-batim, *used by this writer to designate the type of note it is.*

HEADING {

Career opportunities for college graduates in the federal service   <u>Ver</u>

NOTE {

The Federal Service Entrance Examination (FSEE) is open to all college seniors and recent graduates regardless of their major field of study in college. Those who pass the FSEE are then considered for a wide variety of positions throughout the civil service. The FSEE is also used to recruit potential "managers," and those who wish to be considered for "junior-management internships" may qualify by passing addition-al tests. Although the FSEE is now the main entrance to the federal career service for college students, college training is also required for a great many professional positions, such as engineer, chemist, physicist, accountant, auditor, cartographer, dietician, geologist, intelligence specialist, mathematician, and meteorologist. Whatever a student's major in college, chances are he will find a career opening in the federal service, which will give him a chance to work on programs of national and international importance and will offer him training for positions of re-sponsibility and leadership.

AUTHORS AND SOURCE {

Marian D. Irish and James W. Prothro, <u>The Politics of American Democracy</u>, 3rd ed. Englewood Cliffs, New Jersey: Prentice-Hall, Inc., 1965, pp. 500-501.

Here are some useful rules for note taking.

1. Put notes for only one subject on each card, slip, or sheet.

2. Check and double-check your note against the original source. *Get it right* before you go on.

3. Never distort by lifting material out of context. Be faithful to the writer's or speaker's intended meaning.

4. Write legibly and follow a consistent style.

5. Before you file a note, be sure that you have indicated what type of note it is and have included all other necessary information about it and your source.

POINTS TO KEEP IN MIND

Follow a clear-cut plan when you are exploring a subject. Efficiency will save you time and yield better results.

1. Begin by making a preliminary survey of your subject, the audience, and the setting of your speech.

2. Go over your survey and select the key questions and main ideas that suggest lines of development for your speech.

3. Use these key questions and main ideas to guide you in an extended investigation and analysis of your subject.

4. Learn to be efficient, resourceful, and accurate when you go digging for material.

5. Be systematic and precise when you are taking notes.

EXERCISES

1. Prepare an extemporaneous talk. Turn in to your instructor the following items:

    a) Worksheets containing your preliminary survey of the subject.

    b) A list of all your sources of information.

    c) A few sample note cards.

2. Schedule a series of reports on specific reference material in your library. Have one speaker report on *The United States Catalog,* a second on the *Oxford English Dictionary,* a third on the *Encyclopaedia of Social Sciences,* and so on. Report on the purpose of the reference item, its history, its scope and limits, its location in the library. Explain how to use it efficiently.

3. Organize the class into teams of two or three investigators. Have each team interview a librarian who is in charge of one department of your school's library—the circulation department, the reference room, the reserve room, the documents department, the archives, the order department, the periodical department. Each team should seek information that is pertinent to an understanding of the materials and functions of the one department, and then hold a short discussion on its findings before the rest of the class.

4. Choose a topic on which you can make a firsthand investigation. Survey campus opinion, arrange interviews, make a personal check on conditions for yourself. Check and double-check your methods, data, and results. Make a report on your investigations.

5. Inform yourself on a speaker's habits and methods of preparation. Interview an outstanding clergyman, businessman, public official, or instructor. Or you may wish to read up on a speaker's work habits in biographies or in special studies such as those contained in *A History and Criticism of American Public Address,* edited, respectively, by W. N. Brigance and Marie Hochmuth.

eight

Outlining
Your Speech

Unorganized speech is the most difficult to deliver and to follow. Without a plan, the speaker wanders aimlessly, and his anxiety mounts as listeners show signs of impatience. But if he has an outline in his head or in his hands, these hazards are reduced. Even if he does make a few detours along the way, the outline will put him back on the track before he loses his audience forever.

ELEMENTS OF AN OUTLINE

Since we have already touched on the structural characteristics of an outline in Chapter 2, we need only review and amplify somewhat our understanding of these matters, thereby helping to perfect our practice.

When you explored your subject, you turned up facts and ideas, testimony and statistics, examples and stories—the raw materials of speech. The next step is to compress all these materials into separate statements or points and to assemble them into an outline. Think of an outline as an interlocking network of main points and subpoints with your statement of specific purpose as its control center.

Suppose your statement of specific purpose is this: I wish to show that the quarter system is better for our university than the semester system. One segment of your outline might develop in this way.

I. The quarter system meets the special needs of certain schools of our university.
   A. It has advantages for students in engineering and journalism.
      1. Many of these students spend one term each year picking up practical experience in industry.
      2. An academic year divided into four quarters enables them to graduate within four years.
   B. Most of the professional schools have many courses that lend themselves to concentrated treatment within a twelve-week term.
II. The student body likes the quarter system.

As you have observed, the mechanics of an outline consist of standard symbols and a system of identification.

I. Roman numerals designate main points.
   A. Capital letters identify the first division of subpoints.
      1. Arabic numbers enumerate the second level of subpoints.
         a. If you have a third level, use lowercase letters.
            (1) For a fourth division, use Arabic numbers enclosed in parentheses.

With these mechanics in mind, we can take a closer look at the principles that underlie all outlining.

PRINCIPLES OF OUTLINING

1. Phrase each point clearly and concisely

You want each point to etch itself on your mind—and on your audience's mind too. Long, involved sentences blunt points. This is cumbersome: "Our antiquated system for levying and collecting real estate and personal property taxes was devised in the last century when most people had their money tied up in land, homes, and personal belongings instead of intangible forms of investment." Sifting out the main point, you might begin with: "Real estate and personal property taxes are levied and collected through a system that belongs to the horse-and-buggy days." The time and basis of the system's origin, the reasons for its being outmoded can follow.

2. Limit each point to one distinct idea or fact

No point should overlap or duplicate another. Take this example:

I. Choose your camp site carefully.
   A. Keep the factor of water in mind.

1. Be sure you have a source of drinking water.
2. Pitch your tent in an area that is high and dry.
3. A swamp makes a poor camp site.

Note that point 2 overlaps point 3. Point 2 had already established the need for a dry camp site. Re-examine all points to insure that they are really distinct and self-contained. Test your points by looking behind the words for meaning. If two points say the same thing, drop one of them.

3. Assemble your points in proper relationships

Each point in an outline must either (a) *directly* support or explain the statement of specific purpose or (b) *directly* support or explain another point in the outline.

Items that have the same weight, value, or importance are called *coordinate* points. They have equal status in your outline. Thus, main points are coordinate because they directly support your statement of specific purpose. Your first series of subpoints, A, B, and C, are coordinate because they join in supporting a main point. If you give equal status to items that are unequal in importance, your outline will be defective. Notice what has happened here.

THE HIGH COST OF POLITICAL CAMPAIGNS

I. Running for high office is becoming prohibitively expensive.
II. Estimates run as high as $9 million spent by two candidates seeking nomination for President in a key state during the 1964 primaries.
III. We must take steps that will open the way for candidates of talent who lack great wealth.
IV. We can reduce costs by shortening our campaigns.
V. We must appropriate public funds to defray part of the campaign costs for high office.

All five points are assigned a coordinate status. Look closely, however, and you will see that only points I and III have equal status and are therefore coordinate. Point II supports point I and therefore should be made subordinate to it. And since points IV and V specify ways for implementing point III, they should be assigned a coordinate status and made subordinate to point III.

Unless a point is clearly self-supporting or self-explanatory, use *subordinate* points to give it the necessary support. For example:

I. The ability to speak and write a foreign language is an asset in the department store business.

A. The large stores need people who buy and sell for them in foreign markets.
  1. Carson, Pirie, Scott and Company offers courses in French and Italian to its representatives.

Here point A supports point I, and point 1 states a factual case to support point A. Include all reasons and data in the first draft of your outline and then be somewhat more selective in revised versions.

Make sure that each subpoint *directly* supports or explains the point to which it is *immediately* subordinate. The example below violates this rule.

I. There are compelling educational reasons for attending a good college for women.
  A. Students are freed from many social distractions present in co-educational schools.
  B. Its curriculum usually has a strong emphasis on cultural subjects.
  C. Eighty-five per cent of the students from women's colleges marry within five months of graduation.

Whatever the merits of subpoint C, it is not a "compelling educational" reason in the sense of point I, and it is therefore neither coordinate with A and B nor subordinate to point I. If point C is included in the outline at all, it must be made subordinate to some other main point, such as "A women's college does not isolate its graduates from normal human experiences."

PATTERNS OF ORGANIZATION

All speeches follow either a topical pattern or a logical pattern of organization. One pattern or the other may be followed strictly, or else the two may be combined for special purposes. As you will see later, either type of outline can be adapted to various orders of sequence. For example, the points in your topical outline might proceed from the familiar to the unfamiliar, or follow a chronological order. In a logical outline your arguments might unfold in an order of climax, or you may wish to advance them in sequence that you deem psychologically advantageous. In later chapters you will find sample outlines that combine the two basic patterns and that illustrate various sequential systems.

THE TOPICAL PATTERN

The topical pattern is based on a relationship of *parts to the whole*. The styles of houses on your street (the whole), may be classified as Georgian, Cape Cod, and ranch-style (the parts). If you had chosen some other factor—such as the size, age, history, or market value—to serve as the whole, you would have a quite different set of parts. Your statement of the specific purpose should make explicit the whole you expect to divide into parts.

Be sure your list of parts is accurate and consistent. If you were discussing popular models of automobiles (the whole), your outline would be hopelessly confused by this classification, which throws together name and body style: Chevrolet, convertibles, four-door sedans, Ford, hardtops, and Plymouth.

The topical pattern of outlining is ideally suited to descriptive, narrative, and expository speeches. For an example of a complete topical outline, see the specimen outlines at the end of the chapter.

THE LOGICAL PATTERN

The logical pattern of organization, quite different from the topical, is used in making a tight, logical case in behalf of some proposition. You ask your listeners to believe or act in a certain way on the strength of the reasons and evidence that you offer.

In a logical outline, the proposition serves as your control center. It may be a formal statement: "Resolved: That the library stacks should be opened to all undergraduates." Or it may be an informal remark: "Let's have dinner at six o'clock." The main points of your outline are the reasons that you are offering in support of your proposition. Your subpoints are statements of the premises that support the main point to which they are immediately subordinate.

The logical outline, then, is made up of one or more chains of reasoning that connect the central proposition with the facts, opinions, and the basic assumptions upon which it ultimately rests. Here is an example of a chain of reasoning:

I. Most traffic accidents occur in the early evening hours, because
   A. Traffic is heavier than at any other time, because
      1. Most people return home from work at the same hour.
      2. More and more they are relying on automobiles for transportation to and from work, because

        a. Rail transportation has been reduced by 20 per cent.
        b. Bus lines have not been extended to take up the slack.
        c. Many suburbs are inaccessible except by car.
   B. The driver's efficiency drops off at this time of day, because. . . .

The words *because, for,* or *since* are sometimes written into logical outlines to show linkage among points in a chain of reasoning. See the end of the chapter for an example of a complete logical outline.

DIVISIONS OF THE OUTLINE

An organized speech has a beginning, a body, and an ending. You can spot these divisions most clearly in public speech, but you will find them in informal talk, too. Don't think of them as formal and rigid. Rather, think of them as functions that the speaker must somehow perform. These divisions are closely knit, and their boundaries are sometimes indistinguishable. In an outline, these parts are usually labeled Introduction, Discussion or Body, and Conclusion.

THE INTRODUCTION

The introduction to your speech is an invitation to listening. It should create good relationships between you and your audience and pave the way for your subject. The length, ingenuity, and degree of formality of your introduction will vary with circumstances. Here are three general approaches that you can adapt to your needs.

KINDS OF INTRODUCTION

1. Quick disclosure of the subject at hand

Sometimes you need to come to the point quickly, with just enough comment to connect your speech with what has been said before and to show where you are going. This is typical of conversation: "I'll go along with you. We do need a better campus newspaper. But I think we can get it without pouring more money into it. What we need is a better staff." Having tersely stated the nub of the problem, the speaker continued with suggestions for recruiting a staff.

    Notice the way that Howard Hanson moved deftly and swiftly

to his central thesis when addressing students at a convocation of the Eastman School of Music.

> I would like to discuss with you some questions which have concerned me as a musician and educator for the past fifty years. Some of my own conclusions may surprise you—may even startle you. I believe that they are sound, but I am constantly reminded by the passage of time of Josh Billings' remark to the effect that so many folks know so many things that aren't true.
>
> Perhaps the surprising thing is that over the decades we hold to some beliefs which after the passage of time and experience do still seem to be true. My principal thesis is, in brief, that the arts in general—although I shall confine myself to my own field of music—are not fulfilling their mission in the life of our country and its people. This may be equally true of Europe, but I shall confine myself to the country which I know best.[1]

2. The motivated introduction

Sometimes you will have to use your introduction as a means of enlisting attention, especially if you suspect that your audience may be passive, disinterested, or downright hostile. A student advocating "Let the Handicapped Help You!" aroused interest at once with this opening.

> The world calls you and me normal people. We can see, hear, talk, walk, and learn. I know you're humane. You prove it every time I talk to you. If I stood before you today as a handicapped person, you'd be doubly courteous. That would do credit to your heart if not to your understanding of a handicapped person's psychology.
>
> Suppose you were an employer. Suppose a man or woman whom the world calls deaf and dumb applied to you for a job. And suppose this applicant was qualified to do the job. Would you hire him on the strength of his credentials? Or would you get skittish and give him the gentle brush-off?
>
> "Sure I'd give him the job," you say. Maybe you would. If so, you'd belong to a class of exceptionally enlightened employers. The blunt fact is that the handicapped person has a tough time landing a job, no matter how well qualified he is. I know, because my father belongs to that group of people the world calls deaf and dumb.

[1] *Vital Speeches of the Day,* November 15, 1963, p. 87. Reprinted by permission.

Let's see if I can convey to you some of the frustrations of the handicapped person in our so-called normal world. More importantly, I'd like to suggest that we deprive ourselves when we deprive the handicapped person of legitimate job oportunities.

Motivated introductions make use of personal experiences, stories, humor, challenging statements and questions, pat quotations, paradoxes, and other approaches. Whatever you decide to use, though, should be relevant, in good taste, and handled imaginatively. Notice how these elements spark the opening remarks by Adlai Stevenson in a speech at a convocation of the Center for the Study of Democratic Institutions.

When Bob Hutchins lured me here to speak at this meeting, he said, with customary modesty, that it would surpass in importance the Constitutional Convention. I thought he might be exaggerating a bit, but, looking around this room, I'm not so sure.

I understand all these famous and wise men, foreign and domestic, have been dissecting democracy morning, afternoon and evening for two days. I wonder if the time hasn't come to leave the poor thing alone to recuperate!

And my discomfort isn't relieved by the subject Dr. Hutchins has assigned to me: "The prospects for Democracy around the world!"

Have you no little questions, Dr. Hutchins? For I am neither prophet nor philosopher, but an ex-politician and a practicing diplomat, although many would doubtless dissent from both of these claims.

But if my qualifications for speaking to this exalted company are dubious, let me say that when it comes to faith in democracy, I refuse to take a back seat even for my distinguished predecessors on this platform. Because I believe in democracy and freedom, and I believe in their ultimate triumph with the fundamentalist fervor of a survivor of Valley Forge or a Presidential campaign—not to mention two! As Macaulay said of Lord Brougham, or vice versa, "I wish I was as sure of anything as he is of everything." Well the one thing I'm sure of is that constitutional democracy is that form of government, as Bob Hutchins says, which best fulfills the nature of man. Moreover, my faith, I remind you, has survived some rather disillusioning experiences.

And that's why I'm glad to be here among people of like convictions who are trying so hard to make freedom and democracy working realities. And that's why I toil in the tangled vineyards of the United Nations, where the leaders of the whole world are trying to practice parliamentary democracy on a global scale.

Bernard Shaw said that democracy was a device that insures we shall be governed no better than we deserve. The Center for the Study of Democratic Institutions, as I understand it, can be thought of, then, as a kind of national insurance plan—a way of making certain that we will deserve better and better.

For years Robert Hutchins talked about the need for a democratic version of the Platonic Academy, to deal with new questions of freedom and justice as they emerged on the changing horizon of our times. Finally, with the establishment of the Center, his dream came true.

Now, I gather from a few delicate hints that the time has come to think about an endowment policy for this insurance plan—and I am pleased to lend my endorsement to what the Center has already done and promises to do in the years ahead. For busy, battered bureaucrat though I be, I am a staunch believer in the leisure of the theory class.[2]

3. The explanatory introduction

If you are planning to explore a complex or technical subject in your speech, you will be wise to use an explanatory introduction in which you define terms, provide background, and offer a preview of the points you expect to take up. Here is an example of a businesslike explanatory introduction made by a man appearing before the planning commission of his city.

Gentlemen, my name is Roger Weldon. I am a businessman here, and I live at 1245 Kinsley Avenue. I am president of the Glendale Property Association, and I appear at the request of its members. This is a non-profit organization, whose members live and own property in the Glendale area, the southeast section of our city.

The Glendale Property Association is interested in all matters that affect the property values and the residential character of our neighborhood. Accordingly, we are concerned about the increasing traffic load on the streets of our area. Years ago the city dedicated a strip of land running through the heart of our neighborhood for the extension of Lake Road, now a dead-end road. Whether or not the road is ever extended, the possibility exists—and constitutes a threat to the property values and character of our area. I am here to request that the city authorities relinquish all rights to this strip of land now dedicated to the extension of Lake Road.

First, let us locate on a map the strip of land in question. Then I shall

[2] *Vital Speeches of the Day,* March 1, 1963, pp. 305–6. Reprinted by permission.

outline in detail why we think it should be vacated and what legal steps
need to be taken if you approve our petition.

OUTLINING THE INTRODUCTION

Outline your introduction just as you do the rest of your speech.
Here is a working outline for the introduction presented above:

I. I appear at the request of the Glendale Property Association.
   A. We are organized to protect homeowners in our area.
   B. We request that a strip of land dedicated to the extension of Lake
      Road be vacated.
II. I propose to discuss our petition under three headings.
   A. The description of the strip of land in question.
   B. The reasons why we ask the city to vacate the strip.
   C. The legal steps that need to be taken to vacate it.

THE DISCUSSION

This division of your outline is the body of your speech. It contains
all the main points and subpoints by which you explain or support
your topic or thesis.

1. How many main points and subpoints do I need?

This is a little like asking, "How many legs does a table need?" It
depends on the size and shape of the table, how strong the legs are,
and where they are placed. Some tables stand well on one leg, some
on two, and some need four or more. If you tell a person that he
should not drink the contents of a bottle because it contains poison,
that one reason is likely to be enough.

In a short talk, it usually is wise to limit yourself to between one
and five main points. One thing is certain: If you try to cover nine-
teen main points in a five-minute talk, you will be in a hopeless
position. Either limit your purpose and therefore the number of
your main points, or re-examine your analysis of the subject and
combine some of your main points into a few bigger points.

The same answer holds for the subpoints. Do not spin them out
beyond your own needs or those of your audience. If your outline
goes beyond two or three degrees of subordination, try recasting
it into a simpler form.

2. In what order should I arrange my
   main points and their subpoints?

The answer to this question lies in your subject or in the special needs of the audience and occasion.

The points in a topical outline may be arranged in one of several different ways. If you discuss labor organizations in the order of their appearance on the American scene, you would be following a *time sequence*. If you compared the mountain ranges of the United States, region by region from east to west, you would be using a *space sequence*. A speech explaining the physical needs of a school district might take up these needs in an *order of priority* —classrooms, laboratories, a lunchroom, and a gymnasium. Points in a speech analyzing the composition of *The New York Times'* Sunday edition might be arranged according to the *interests of the audience*. Speeches of instruction often move from the *familiar to the unfamiliar* or from the *simple to the complex*. Once you have chosen a method of ordering the items of your speech, stick with it consistently throughout any given series of coordinate points.

Customarily, logical outlines open with arguments that establish a *need for change* or a *cause for action*. There are times, however, when it is wise to depart from this formula in order to accommodate your speech to the psychology of your audience. If you know that your audience has a keen interest in one of your arguments, capitalize on that interest. Open with that argument. Then again, if you feel that all your arguments will sustain interest but that one is especially strong, you probably would use it as a clincher or climax. Should your audience be divided on a controversial issue, open with the point that is likely to win agreement, in the hope that your other points will be given a more favorable hearing.

3. Should I write transitions into my outline?

Transitional sentences link together points in your speech, offering a terse concluding reference to or summary of one point while foreshadowing the next. For example:

Having defined automation, let us consider its benefits to our economy.

We have declared that our first human "good" is survival, but that alone is not good enough. What other distinctly human values justify the human experience?

A speech may be overloaded with forced transitions, but the omission of these bridges is a more frequent fault. If your outline is tightly woven and if you have worked on transitions in your rehearsals, chances are that you will move easily and naturally from point to point without laboriously writing transitional sentences into your outline.

4. Should I use complete sentences
   or key phrases?

It is usually better to use complete sentences for main points and major subpoints, particularly in the discussion or body. Complete sentences force one to think through all the points clearly and to express them with precision. If you want to refer to an outline while you are speaking, then reduce your formal outline from complete sentences to key phrases.

THE CONCLUSION

A good conclusion ends smartly and strongly. Use the conclusion as a capstone for your speech, not as a dumping ground for leftover items. Think out your conclusion beforehand and make it part of your outline.

TYPES OF CONCLUSION

Three types of conclusion will cover most of your needs.

1. Summary

Often the best way to close is simply to restate clearly and forcefully the main ideas or points of your talk, as if you were to say, "Now before you go, let's be certain we understand each other." Note how Robert M. Hutchins succeeds in restating the central thesis of his speech, "Education and Social Improvement," and the perils to both education and society.

> We see, then, that the quest for social improvement is a perpetual one. What a better society is and how to get it has been one of the persistent problems of philosophy and one of the fundamental issues in the traditions of the Western World. Only those who recognize the important place that philosophy and the wisdom of the race must hold in education for citizenship can hope to educate men and women who can contribute to the improvement of society and who will want to do

so. The cults of skepticism, presentism, scientism, and anti-intellectualism can lead us only to despair, not merely of education, but of society.[3]

2. Epitome

A more dramatic and often, therefore, a more impressive type of conclusion encloses the essence of a speech in a capsule—a story, an illustration, or an example. In a lecture on culture and communication, Robert Oliver points out that international dialogue is possible only if we comprehend and adjust ourselves to the rhetorical demands of any given culture. The burden of his exposition and argument is neatly epitomized in this story:

I recall very well a scene some years ago, just as daylight was breaking on the island of Wake, in the mid-Pacific. The commercial passenger plane on which I was flying from Tokyo to San Francisco had put down to refuel, and we passengers were shepherded into the restaurant at the terminal building to have breakfast. All of us were sleepy, disheveled, and tired after a night-long flight. As a consequence, we did not feel particularly sociable. I took my seat at a small table along with two other American men, who appeared to be businessmen, and a middle-aged Japanese, who proved to be a college professor barely able to speak a few words of English.

None of us paid any attention to any of the others until I noticed that the Japanese was regarding his American companions with obvious distaste. Then I smiled at him and handed him the salt cellar for his eggs, holding it toward him in my right hand, with the fingers of the left hand lightly touching the base of my right hand palm—a typical Japanese gesture of respect. For a moment he looked unbelievingly at the unexpected behavior of this strange foreigner. Then his face broke into a broad smile of sheer relief and I could almost hear him say to himself, "Perhaps they are not barbarians after all." It was quite a lot to accomplish by a simple device such as knowing how to hold one's hands.

This, I think, is a good point at which to come to rest. The change in theory and method for which I am asking is neither complex nor considerable. But if we should make the shift and learn how to operate upon the concept of multiple rhetorics, the change in effect might be as great as was the change in medicine when Pasteur said to his colleagues, "It is not vapour or dirt, gentlemen, that carries the disease, but germs." [4]

[3] *Vital Speeches of the Day*, June 1, 1938, p. 501.
[4] *Vital Speeches of the Day*, September 16, 1963, p. 724.

3. Plea for acceptance or action

If you have made a good case for the proposition you urge, you have won the right to ask your audience to embrace your views and to act on them. You do your cause an injustice if you fail to enlist the vital interests and the sentiments of your audience.

The following example of a conclusion is highly specific in the action that is called for. Many speeches would be immeasurably strengthened by this degree of specificity.

Start building your library now. Buy good books and then make them your own. Your purchase slip gives you title to a book, but it doesn't confer real ownership. The marks of ownership are the questions and notations you scribble in the margins, the underlining of important ideas, the digests you write at the end of chapters, and the reactions you list on the blank pages. Never mark a book until you have established title to it. Once your title is clear, own the book. Owning a book calls for an active mind and a sharp pencil.

If you have been an effective advocate throughout your speech, you won't have to resort to stunts or high-pressure tactics to get action. Your audience will be ready to vote, sign up, buy, give, and even sacrifice.

In his memorable inaugural address of January 20, 1961, President John F. Kennedy had paved the way for his moving plea to men everywhere to join him in his mission.

In the long history of the world, only a few generations have been granted the role of defending freedom in its hour of maximum danger.

I do not shrink from this responsibility—I welcome it. I do not believe that any of us would exchange places with any other people or any other generation. The energy, the faith, the devotion which we bring to this endeavor will light our country and all who serve it—and the glow from that fire can truly light the world.

And so, my fellow Americans: Ask not what your country can do for you—ask what you can do for your country.

My fellow citizens of the world: Ask not what America will do for you, but what together we can do for the freedom of man.

Finally, whether you are citizens of America or citizens of the world, ask of us here the same high standards of strength and sacrifice which we ask of you. With a good conscience as our only sure reward, with history the final judge of our deeds, let us go forth to lead the land we love, asking His blessing and His help, but knowing that here on earth God's work must truly be our own.

OUTLINING THE CONCLUSION

Make your conclusion a part of your outline. The conclusion of a speech in behalf of the Red Cross, for example, might look like this:

I. Support the Red Cross throughout the year.
   A. Help keeps its blood-bank stocked.
   B. Contribute as much money as you can.
   C. Give time to hospitals and emergency relief.
II. The Red Cross may one day be your lifeline.

SPECIMEN OUTLINES

Up to this point we have been examining small sections of outlines as examples. Here are two full-length sample outlines for short speeches. One exemplifies the topical pattern, the other the logical pattern.

SAMPLE TOPICAL OUTLINE

Title: The Anonymous Doctor
Subject: The role of the pathologist
Specific purpose: My object is to inform my audience on the principal responsibilities of a pathologist in a modern hospital.

Introduction

I. The pathologist is a doctor's doctor.
   A. He works directly with internists and surgeons.
      1. His job is to analyze and interpret disease tissue.
      2. Every accredited American hospital has at least one pathologist.
   B. Since he does not treat patients, his work is little known by the public at large.
II. You owe it to yourself to learn more about his role.
   A. When you are a patient, this knowledge will add to your confidence in hospital procedures.
   B. Knowing about his work may suggest professional opportunities to you—a career as a doctor, technician, nurse, or hospital administrator.

Discussion

I. The pathologist is an indispensable partner to other doctors.
   A. His diagnostic reports may save both the patient and the surgeon.

      1. He warns the surgeon against operations that analysis shows to be unnecessary.

      2. Or he calls attention to an urgent need for an operation.

    B. Often the surgeon calls upon the pathologist to look over his shoulder while he operates.

      1. As a tissue specialist, he may make on-the-spot interpretations of unexpected discoveries.

      2. The surgeon may suspend an operation in progress while the pathologist makes a quick microscopic analysis of tissue.

    C. The pathologist prescribes for preoperative and postoperative care of the patient.

  II. The pathologist presides over hospital laboratory work.

    A. Each day brings its routine of laboratory analysis.

      1. Every organ removed in the operating room must be inspected.

      2. Every sample of blood extracted must go under the microscope.

    B. Much of the lab work is done by technicians, but the pathologist has final responsibility.

  III. The pathologist is a standard-maker.

    A. As a research man, he contributes to medical knowledge.

    B. He is a watchdog for the profession.

      1. He reports to the "tissue committee" all healthy tissue removed in an operation.

      2. He also serves as a member of the "tissue committee."

        a. This committee reviews and adjudicates doubtful procedures.

        b. It may call on a surgeon to explain his reasons for the procedure in question.

Conclusion

  I. The pathologist is the patient's anonymous doctor.

  II. He serves both you and the medical profession.

SAMPLE LOGICAL OUTLINE

         Title: Clear the Aisles
     Subject: A mock political convention
Specific purpose: I wish to persuade the Student Governing Board to sponsor a mock political convention during the spring term of the next presidential election year.

Introduction

  I. A mock political convention simulates a national political convention.

    A. It follows procedures common to the political conventions of the major parties.

    B. It drafts and enacts a political platform.

C. It brings to campus prominent political speakers from both major parties.

D. It nominates candidates for the office of President and Vice-President of the United States.

II. Since this proposal involves the whole school, the Student Governing Board is the logical group to get the ball rolling.

Discussion

I. This project would add to our political education, because

A. It would supplement our academic studies, for

1. It would strengthen our interest in the history of political campaigns and conventions.

2. We would apply information about political procedure that we learn in political science.

B. It would stimulate interest in contemporary political issues, because

1. We would have to read widely in current sources of information.

2. It would encourage informal discussion among students.

3. We would have a chance to hear and meet prominent political figures in person.

II. A mock political convention would contribute to the personal development of students, because

A. Many students would have opportunities for leadership in areas of their special interests, for

1. Money has to be raised and budgeted by students.

2. There would be publicity and public relations assignments for many people.

3. Technical arrangements would require students who have knowledge of electronics and lighting.

4. Staging the convention would bring students of theater and music into the act.

5. All who have political ambitions would gain experience in the art of politics.

B. Students generally would learn a great deal about group behavior, for

1. They would learn what it means to work together in order to get things done.

2. They would gain experience in cooperative decision making on controversial issues among partisans.

III. The convention would instill meaningful school spirit, because

A. Students would get to know each other better, for

1. Each house and dormitory would be organized to act as a state or territorial delegation.

2. Campaign activities are great mixers.

B. It would promote good student–faculty–administration relationships, for

1. Faculty members would be called in as advisers.

    2. Students and administrative officers would need to work closely on arrangements.

IV. A mock political convention is a feasible project, because
  A. Other colleges and universities have been successful at it.
  B. We have adequate building facilities.
  C. We can handle the financial side of it, for
    1. There is an accumulated surplus of $1,000 in our student activities budget.
    2. We can sell advertising space in convention programs.
    3. We can charge a door admission for all outsiders.

Conclusion

I. We should and can stage a mock political convention, because
  A. It confers valuable educational benefits.
  B. It will contribute to campus unity.
  C. It is a feasible project.

II. I ask that the Student Governing Board endorse this proposal and forward it to the administrative officers for their consideration.

POINTS TO KEEP IN MIND

1. A tightly developed outline is your best guarantee of a well-organized speech.

2. The items in your outline should conform to the rules governing phrasing, distinctness, and relationship among points.

3. Base all outlines on a topical pattern or logical pattern, or on a combination of the two.

4. Divide every outline into Introduction, Discussion, and Conclusion. Each division serves functions that are natural and necessary to speech.

EXERCISES

1. Each student writes the outline for a speech on the blackboard. Or better still, each outline is typed on a stencil, duplicated, and distributed to the class. Spend a class period or two analyzing one another's outlines and making suggestions for improvement.

2. Deliver a talk based on a carefully developed outline. Ask the class to jot down your main points and subpoints as they come through while you are speaking. If your prepared outline fails to agree with your listeners' records, either you need to improve your organization or to make it come through better *when you talk*.

3. Focus on introductions and conclusions. Plan and deliver an interesting introduction to a ten- or fifteen-minute speech; you need not go beyond the introduction. Revise and strengthen the conclusion of some

speech you have already given. Refresh your listeners' memory on the whole speech, then deliver your revised conclusion.

4. Analyze and outline a short, printed speech. Many speeches have ill-designed and rickety structures. But make an honest and diligent effort to find the main points, to see if they follow in sensible order, and to determine whether the whole outline holds up. Make a thoroughgoing critique of the organization.

nine

The Content of Speech

The substance of speech consists of facts, opinions, and interpretations of facts and opinions. These are the content of speech whether drawn from ordinary human experience or from specialized fields such as physics, medicine, economics, philosophy, or art. Facts, opinions, and interpretations gained from highly technical and esoteric fields often require translation for some segment—perhaps the majority—of the population. But given a mastery of both the content and the appropriate means of communication, the effective speaker will be able to make commonplace matters interesting, and the mysterious ones comprehensible. This chapter and the chapter that follows, "Developing Your Ideas," are two sides of the same coin.

FACTS

Facts are distinct items that we can verify. Facts are objective (they are based on reality), and, like sound money, they are negotiable. Facts are not created. They simply exist. They may be discovered by anyone who cares to look for them and who knows how and where to look. Facts are impersonal. We cannot talk them into or out of existence. Facts are not determined by majority agreement. Whole families have been wiped out because they mistook toadstools for mushrooms.

Most of us like to think we "face the facts." We hear people exclaim with a ring of pride, "I have the facts" or "Let's look at the record!" Since most of us want to talk facts, it is fair to ask: How do we decide what are the facts and what are not? How do we know who has the facts? Here are some ways of evaluating alleged facts.

Is the alleged fact consistent with human nature and experience?

It is hard to believe that a small child fatally injured a grown man by striking him with his fist or that a drug addict was completely cured by a five-day jail sentence. Whenever you offer a factual claim that seems to defy human nature or normal experience, be sure to double-check it before you use it; and if you do use it, be prepared to give an explanation that will make your claim believable. Remember, though, that what strikes us at first as being inconsistent with human nature and experience may only reflect the limitations of our own experience.

Is the alleged fact consistent with established facts?

This is a good test for checking up on speakers who tend to make loose or exaggerated claims. If the listeners are in possession of certain established facts, they will reject alleged facts that seem to be inconsistent with what they know to be true. If statistics published in local newspapers indicate a steady over-all rise in crime rate, the incumbent mayor's claim that he has greatly reduced local crime simply cannot be sustained. The mayor may mean that he has waged a vigorous battle against crime or that he has succeeded in reducing the incidence of particular misdemeanors or felonies— but the facts show that he cannot have reduced the crime rate. When such inconsistencies are pointed out, a speaker must qualify his claim, admit his mistake, or explain away the seeming inconsistency. Otherwise he will lose the respect of his listeners.

Are all the speaker's facts consistent?

Never be guilty of inconsistencies within your own remarks. A real estate promoter is trying to induce people who live in a crowded city to buy building lots in Suburbia. In one breath he claims that Suburbia possesses all the advantages of "spacious country living"; in the next breath he boasts that Suburbia is so attractive that its population has jumped from three thousand to ten thousand in three years. The wary listener, knowing the town limits of Suburbia, concludes that spacious country living and a skyrocketing population are incompatible. If inconsistencies turn up in your remarks, your listeners have the right to conclude that you may be right on one claim and wrong on the other or that you may be wrong on both; but you cannot be right on both.

Is the person who is reporting the alleged fact mentally and morally qualified?

Without being wantonly suspicious or cynical, be attentive for prejudice, exaggeration, rumor, inaccuracy, poor memory, and downright falsification that impede communication of facts. Guard against people who are given to loose talk or who have a motive for distorting facts. A common human failing is the tendency to report only those facts that support one's vital interests or that prove to be the least damaging to those interests.

Can the alleged fact be verified?

Whether you are a listener or a speaker, verify any alleged fact that seems questionable before you adopt it. One way is to make direct observations and inquiries. Do people in your locality believe that the voting age should be lowered to eighteen? Poll representative segments of the community to find out. Has there been a trend in the last five years toward increased juvenile delinquency? Check the records maintained by local law enforcement agencies and news media. Did the death of Ann Rutledge drive Abraham Lincoln to the verge of suicide? Consult the authorities. (Scholars such as J. G. Randall have concluded that the legendary impact of Ann's death upon Lincoln has been greatly exaggerated, if not fabricated.)

There are three ways, then, to verify an alleged fact: make direct observations, check records, and consult authorities.

OPINIONS

An opinion is some person's judgment of a matter that we are asked to accept because he is represented to us as an authority. If an opinion contains factual claims or an interpretation based on facts, we must test it just as we test facts and interpretations themselves.

But here we shall talk only about strictly personal judgments that are offered without factual support or interpretation—opinions that we are asked to accept solely because the person who makes them is presumed to be an authority.

Here are some tests that you may apply to personal opinions.

Is the opinion offered by an expert?

Obviously, we have more confidence in an expert's opinion than in a layman's. But remember that an expert in one field may know little or nothing about some other field and that a layman in one subject may be an expert in another. We may accept a layman's testimony on *matters of fact*, if it stands up to the tests of facts, but we must treat his *opinions* with extreme caution in fields where expertness is required.

For example, the opinion of a distinguished atomic physicist on the amount of energy likely to be released by an atomic explosion carries great weight. But his opinion on our moral right to bomb a city might be less useful than a clergyman's or philosopher's, or no more valuable than your own.

How does your audience feel about the expert you are citing?

If you offer the opinion of an expert in support of a point, your listeners must agree that he is really an expert. If he is unknown to them or if his qualifications are doubtful, be prepared to establish his competence. Show that his training, position, and experience qualify him to speak with authority.

Is the opinion being offered as a substitute for facts?

Most people prefer facts to opinions—when they are available and if they are comprehensible. Sometimes, however, the facts are complicated or technical enough to be effectively beyond the grasp of many people. A homeowner who must decide what type and quantity of wall insulation to install will very likely seek the recommendation of a trained engineer, rather than try to evaluate technical reports that have been published about the relative merits of rock wool, aluminum foil, and other insulators.

Always get the facts and interpret them for yourself whenever you can. But whenever it is difficult or impossible to get the facts or to understand them, make use of expert opinion. This is what you do when you accept a physician's diagnosis.

Is the opinion being used to confirm factual evidence?

For instance, you might state the facts on athletic facilities for women at your college, draw a conclusion about the need for additional space and equipment, then cite the opinions of members of the athletic staff and administrative officers to confirm your conclusion. Or you might begin with an expert's opinion, and then explain the factual basis for it. Either way, you strengthen your own conclusion by citing expert opinion, and your listeners have a chance to inspect the factual basis of the opinion.

Do the experts agree?

Expert opinions are stronger and more reliable if you can show that the experts agree. If they do not agree on the important points, your listeners are likely to reserve their own opinions.

INTERPRETATIONS OF FACT AND OPINION

Interpretations are the meanings we give to facts and opinions and the conclusions we draw from them. We make use of interpretations every day. We decide to take the dog for a walk and discover he has disappeared. When and where was he last seen? He was around an hour or so ago. Maybe another member of the family has taken him out. His leash is gone. That must be the answer. We pick up the evening paper and read about a threatened steel strike. An editorial suggests that the government is prepared to take over the plants. Is this a wise move? Can you blame the workers for asking for a wage increase with prices the way they are? On the other hand, can you expect management to absorb the wage increases without raising steel prices? You recall an article in a journal you glanced at a few day ago and pick it up to see what it has to say on inflation.

And so it goes. All these interpretations are based on inferences. We think or reason our way to conclusions from facts—or what we take to be facts—and opinions. Failure to interpret fact and opinion reasonably can be due to a variety of causes. We may wish for certain outcomes and simply rationalize our desires; we may be blinded by prejudice; we may be led astray by exceptional cases and coincidences; we may willfully distort under pressure; or we may lack the comprehension and perception that enables us to discriminate between straight and crooked thinking. In any case, speaker and listeners alike will benefit by an understanding of the several types of inference and by the ability to test their validity.

GENERALIZATION

A generalization is a conclusion that we reach on something common to a whole group of things after we have examined a good sample of the group. Speech abounds with generalizations. In fact, our daily life would be completely disorganized unless we generalized from our experiences and then acted according to our generalizations. When you eat in a restaurant, you act on dozens of tacit generalizations—that public buildings are safe, that restaurants do not put poison in their food, that public eating places are reasonably sanitary, and so forth. Here are just a few generalizations that were made in a single conversation: Country living is more healthful and wholesome than city living; the University Theatre produces the best plays in this area; football players are subsidized; labor leaders lack a social conscience; the food in England is terrible.

These examples show how often we use generalizations, and they suggest the danger of making hasty ones. Some of the examples appear to be false, and all of them are open to exceptions. How can you draw generalizations that are safe and useful? Here are some tests.

Have you examined enough samples?

Our confidence is quickly undermined when we hear a speaker draw sweeping, general conclusions from few or no facts. You are sitting in on a bull session with four or five other students. Each remarks that he is taller than his parents. So you all agree that the present generation of college students is taller than the last. Obviously, this generalization is not based on enough samples. All sound generalizations depend on an adequate survey of the field.

Are the samples examined typical
of the whole group?

Often we have to generalize without having time or opportunity to examine very many samples. So we must be careful to base our conclusion for the whole group on typical cases. Avoid basing generalizations on exceptional or bizarre examples. Suppose you declare that foreign motion pictures are superior to American ones. This conclusion is unwarranted and unfair if you see foreign films that have been carefully selected for export to the United States, but only go to Hollywood's B movies.

Have you accounted for the exceptions?

In our enthusiasm or in our desire to make a point, we sometimes overlook the exceptions to a generalization. Suppose we assert that summer vacations are now a standard practice among all Americans. No doubt you can think of many exceptions, and you would be quite right to insist that the generalization be scaled down to fit the facts. We might say that summer vacations are a standard practice among Americans *except for* farmers and other groups who have to work through the summer; or we might say that *many* or *most* Americans enjoy a summer vacation. Better still, if the statistics were available, we might supply the *exact percentage* of Americans who take summer vacations. Almost every generalization needs to be qualified in terms of quantity, time, place, or special circumstances.

ANALOGY

An analogy is an inference based on a comparison of two items. If you can show that the two items resemble each other in all significant respects, you may infer that they resemble each other in an attribute known to belong to one but not known to belong to the other. In contemporary international politics, the controversial opinion that new nations should form democratic governments is based on a tacit analogy between America and any other country that comes into existence by revolutionary means and seeks "freedom."

Apply the following tests to analogies before you accept them as valid.

Are the cases alike in all essential respects?

This is the key test. The success of a democracy in the newly independent United States in 1776 is no guarantee that it will succeed in any other country if it is smaller and has different traditions and standards of living and is emerging as a nation two centuries later.

Have significant differences in the
   cases been accounted for?

If you discover such differences, you must either show that they do not affect your conclusion, or else qualify your conclusion. Suppose that a colony existed today in which many of the so-called American values and attitudes, learned through textbooks and periodicals, were popular, and the people of that country rebelled against their colonial government for independence. However, the economy of the colony has been entirely agrarian and oriented toward domestic consumption. If you believe that this new country should become a democracy, you will have to show that the difference does not impair your conclusion.

CAUSAL RELATIONS

In establishing a causal relationship, we try to show the probable cause for some known event or condition, or we try to predict the effect of some event, condition, or proposal. We speak of the first of these two methods of interpretation as reasoning from a *known* effect to an *alleged* cause. The following questions will help you test *effect-to-cause reasoning.*

Did the alleged cause actually contribute
   to the known effect?

This is the first and most elementary test. Often the actual cause is obscure and lies below the surface. Did the men really strike because of poor working conditions? They knew that improvements had been made and that others had already been contracted for. Avoid hasty conclusions. Analyze the problem and scrutinize all possible causes, rejecting those that do not seem to have made significant contribution to the effect. One can be sure that this test is being applied—perhaps unconsciously—when one hears comments such as these: "No, it can't be the fan belt; I just had a new one put on." "Surely it's not a lack of water; why, I watered the plant every day."

Is the alleged cause the whole cause of the known effect?

Don't try to explain an effect by a cause that is only *partially* responsible for it. A man's poverty may be charged to his laziness when, in fact, poor health and lack of opportunity may have contributed to it. Whenever a known effect seems "too big" to be explained by the "little" cause assigned to it, treat the explanation with caution.

Is the alleged cause too general and vague to explain the known effect?

If the known effect is too "little" for the "big" cause assigned to it, look for a more specific cause. To say that Frankie's misbehavior at school is caused by a wave of juvenile delinquency sweeping the nation fails to tell us much about Frankie's problems. This alleged cause, even if it is remotely true, is too big and too far removed from Frankie's immediate difficulties to help us straighten him out.

Now let's reverse the process. We have a *known cause* and we want to predict its effect. This is what we usually do whenever we explain, defend, or attack a proposed course of action (offered as a known cause). For example, perhaps someone urged you to attend college because a college education would broaden your outlook, enable you to meet interesting people, or increase your earning power (alleged effects). A plea to lower our tariff schedules might be urged in the interest of "trade not aid," world economic stability, and world peace (alleged effects); the same plea might be challenged on the grounds that it would lower wage rates for American laborers, dislocate industry, and lead to inferior products.

The following questions will help you test *cause-to-effect reasoning*.

Is the known cause sufficient to produce the alleged effect?

Will insulating my house reduce my heating costs by two hundred dollars a year? Will eating Wheaties make me a champion? This is a good test to apply to many of the claims of enthusiastic promoters and salesmen. Never mistake a half-truth for a whole truth.

Will the known cause produce effects other than those alleged?

Even if insulating my house will save me money in the long run, its immediate effect may be to throw me into bankruptcy. Certain proposals for federal aid to education may mean better educational facilities as claimed, but they may also mean increased federal control of education. Try to discover *all* possible effects, good or bad, before you commit yourself.

Are the alleged effects too vague to be convincing?

"Turn the rascals out and return to good times" is a familiar political theme. Because the times are always a little upset in our imperfect world, this slogan appeals to disgruntled and undiscriminating voters. But before you accept as probable outcomes the general claims that are made for or against a proposition, reduce them to specific items. In politics, this would mean reviewing a candidate's position on definite issues.

CORRELATIVE RELATIONS

Correlative relations are simply implied relations between two or more items. You take the presence or absence of one as an *indication* of the presence or absence of the other. You take the familiar red-and-white barber pole as a sign of a barber shop. You interpret dark clouds to mean wind or rain. An open front door is taken to mean that someone is home. Rainy weather on election day is sometimes taken as a sign that the rural vote will be light.

As with other methods of interpretation, we must test the reliability of the correlative relations that we hear and use.

Is the known item a certain sign of the alleged item?

How close, how sure, how constant is the relationship attributed to the two items? We can answer these questions only after making close and repeated observations. If we're looking for a barber shop, we may head for the red-and-white pole with confidence. Less convincing are these inferences: "If he's so smart, why isn't he rich?"

"The food must be good here; the prices are high enough." Unless you have made enough observations to support a firm correlative relationship, qualify your conclusions, present them tentatively, and act on them with caution.

Is the relationship between the two items real or accidental?

Many superstitions and old wives' tales collapse under this test. Try it on these: Misfortune will stalk you if a black cat crosses your path. Potatoes should be planted when the moon is full. A horseshoe nailed above the door brings good luck.

Racial bigotry and prejudice thrive on accidental relationships. No race or creed is exempt from undesirable members, and thoughtful people are not easily duped by accidental associations. Yet it is tragically true that many people who are usually cautious seize upon the frailest kind of relationship for support when their prejudices are threatened.

Have special factors entered in to alter normal relations?

Black clouds probably mean rain *if* the wind is in the northeast. The party would have been well attended *if* the invitations had gone out on time. The deal was practically in the bag *until* his wife stepped in. Unforeseen conditions often upset what we would normally expect. An important part of the maturation process is the realization that few signs are absolutely reliable. We should try to anticipate as best we can the factors that might upset relationships between signs and that might destroy the conclusions we are tempted to draw or to accept uncritically.

POINTS TO KEEP IN MIND

Facts, opinions, and interpretations of facts and opinions are the raw materials of speech.

1. Before you accept an alleged fact, find out whether it agrees with nature and experience, whether it agrees with other facts, and whether it comes from a reliable source.

2. If you cannot find or understand the facts you need, turn to the opinions of authorities. Be sure your "authorities" are really experts on the subject.

3. Keep close watch on generalizations. Be sure that they are properly qualified and are based on a sufficient number of typical cases or items.

4. When you draw an analogy, see to it that the cases are essentially alike and that important differences are explained.

5. In reasoning from a known effect to an alleged cause, make sure that the "cause" actually did produce the effect.

6. In reasoning from a known cause to a probable effect, make sure that the effect is really likely and that it will not carry along with it undesirable effects.

7. Be cautious about accepting a conclusion based on correlative relationships. First find out whether the presence of one factor indicates the presence or absence of a second one. Be sure there is no third factor that will upset things.

EXERCISES

1. Prepare a short talk alleging at least three facts and specifying their sources. Convince the audience of the reliability of the sources and allow them to question you about the sources. This exercise encourages critical thinking by both speaker and listeners.

2. Maintain a list of statements alleging facts that raise some doubt in your mind. Conversations, public speeches, and printed material are good sources for such statements. The resultant list will be heterogeneous and may include statements by friends and other students. Apply the five tests for facts offered in this chapter. Present some of your analyses to your class and allow others to evaluate your reasoning. Confine the discussion to the factual acceptability of the statements.

3. Find a news story, editorial, magazine article, or advertisement to which you take exception because of (a) the alleged facts or omission of facts, (b) the opinions offered in behalf of the contention, or (c) the interpretations made of the alleged facts and opinions. Discuss the claim or contention, the support offered in its behalf, and your objections on the grounds suggested in this chapter.

4. Choose as your subject for a talk some problem about which you have limited knowledge and no settled opinion. It may be a problem in politics, medicine, architecture, literature, agriculture—any field. Locate some articles and speeches by people who seem to write and speak as authorities on the matter. Then find out all you can about the qualifications of these people. What tentative conclusions may you draw about the subject based on the several opinions and their sources? Discuss your findings and conclusions.

5. Prepare and present a talk in which you develop your subject *primarily* by means of *one* of the four methods of interpretation: generalization, analogy, causal relations, or correlative relations. Most of us use all these methods in our daily speech, but this time you are to

concentrate on one method. Make your inferences as tight and invulnerable as you can. After you have spoken, ask the class (a) to identify the method of interpretation you employed, and (b) to apply the appropriate tests of inference listed in this chapter.

6. Analyze the printed text of a recent speech. Identify statements of alleged fact, opinion, and interpretation of fact and opinion. Which predominate? After testing these statements, are you prepared to accept or reject the speaker's conclusions? Did you detect any significant fallacies? Present a written or oral report of your findings.

7. For this exercise, select the printed text of a speech by which the speaker won your confidence because of his respect for facts, his discriminating use of opinions, and his sound interpretations of facts and opinions. Offer it to the class as a model of straight thinking. Briefly review the speech as a whole for the class, point out its merits, and read portions of the speech to illustrate and enforce your conclusions about it.

ten

Developing ✓
Your Ideas

Although facts, expert opinions, and logical arguments may speak for themselves, they frequently need to be energized before they become meaningful to an audience. It is a *fact* that thousands of families "on the wrong side of the tracks" live in crowded, ill-ventilated, rat-infested housing, but this fact will have greater impact if you can tell a vivid, firsthand story of the plight of one of these families.

This chapter presents tested methods for amplifying and dramatizing your ideas. These methods are *not* substitutes for facts, expert opinions, or the reasoning process. Rather, they are supporting devices that help you to project your material with impact. Skillfully used, these methods will endow your speech with clarity, warmth, color, human interest, and emotional appeal.

METHODS OF AMPLIFICATION

DEVELOPMENT BY DEFINITION

Define important terms that may be unfamiliar to your listeners or that may be misunderstood. No one should take liberties with well-established meanings, but when a term has several possible meanings, make clear the one you are using.

A definition establishes boundary lines. It places a term in a general class or category and then shows how the term differs from other members of the class. If you can offer an example that further pinpoints your meaning, so much the better.

Suppose you wanted to define the word *manslaughter*. You might say, "Manslaughter means killing another human being without malice. If someone kills a person in self-defense or through reckless driving, he may be charged with manslaughter but not murder." Here you place manslaughter within a category of actions called killing. Immediately you draw distinctions, pointing out that manslaughter is limited to the killing of human beings, not other forms of life. And you add that it must be done without malice, which distinguishes it from murder. Finally, you offer two examples of killing under circumstances that warrant the charge of manslaughter.

Often we need to define our terms with great precision. Other times we wish only to highlight an already familiar term by throwing out a few points of reference that will help our listeners catch the special sense and importance we attach to it. Notice the somewhat satirical vein in which Robert M. Hutchins, former president of the University of Chicago, sets forth his conception of a university. Notice too how he first classifies his term, then separates it from other "communities."

A University is a community of scholars. It is not a kindergarten; it is not a club; it is not a reform school; it is not a political party; it is not an agency of propaganda. A University is a community of scholars.[1]

DEVELOPMENT BY EXAMPLE

An example is a *specific case in point* that supports or explains a general statement. Listeners appreciate examples that are relevant and that facilitate understanding of a point. There are *real* examples and *hypothetical* examples. A *real* example is an actual case that can be documented. A *hypothetical* example is one that you create for the occasion. The following excerpt from a statement by Adlai E. Stevenson to the United States Senate Subcommittee on Foreign Relations in 1963 is replete with real examples that support his general point.

I said a moment ago that the agenda of the Seventeenth General Assembly was a virtual compendium of the ongoing problems of the modern

[1] *Vital Speeches of the Day,* May 20, 1935, p. 547.

world. Listen to this list of trouble spots and sore spots: the Congo . . . the Gaza strip . . . Southern Rhodesia . . . South West Africa . . . Yemen . . . West New Guinea . . . and the Arab refugee camps.

Mark this string of contentious issues: Chinese representation . . . North Korea . . . Hungary . . . colonialism . . . Troika . . . and sovereignty over natural resources.

Consider, if you will, this list of universal concerns: disarmament . . . nuclear testing . . . outer space . . . world food . . . world trade . . . world science . . . and the training of manpower for economic and social development.[2]

In this instance, the listeners were familiar with the examples, and the speaker had only to name them to make his point.

Some examples, however, need to be developed in detail before they become convincing. Observe how Frederick Mayer uses a single example to give impact to his point.

I can think of one of my students as a freshman. She was a replica of Middle-Town, a product of what Sinclair Lewis described in *Babbitt*. She called Plato—Pluto. Her spelling was atrocious. Her first test was chaos roughly organized. Her taste in music was influenced by Elvis Presley. Three years later she is reading Kafka, Thomas Mann, and Gide. She has just written a superb essay on Albert Camus. . . . She is a different person today—alive, vibrant, idealistic. This shows what education can do.[3]

Sometimes an entire speech is developed through a single master-example. One student, arguing that it is possible for a small town to have a lively cultural life, based her entire speech on the example of a small town in Colorado. She recounted in detail how the residents stimulated community interest in literature, theater, and painting, and the resourceful means they used to bring an occasional artist and writer with national standing to their town.

In the following quotation from an address by Oscar E. Ewing, "What Health Insurance Would Mean to You," all the examples are hypothetical. Not one actual case is cited. All are introduced by *suppose* or *if*.

Good evening. I want to talk to you tonight, not about the nation's health, but about your own health. Suppose that tomorrow morning, you

[2] Adlai E. Stevenson, *Looking Outward,* ed. Robert L. Schiffer and Selma Schiffer (New York: Harper & Row, Publishers, 1963), p. 122.

[3] *Vital Speeches of the Day,* April 15, 1959, p. 414.

should become suddenly ill—seriously ill. Suppose you found that you needed an operation, with special medical care, and all kinds of x-rays and drugs. Suppose you had to stop working for some months while you went through your operation and your convalescence. Suppose the doctor's bill, the hospital bill, the bills for special laboratory services and medicines, added up to hundreds of dollars—maybe even thousands. Would you be able to afford it? . . .

If you have been lying in a hospital bed after an operation, worrying about where the money to pay the bills would come from, you know what I mean. If you have had to go to a loan company and borrow money to pay a hospital bill, you know what I mean. If you had ever received a note from your child's school, telling you that your little boy or your little girl needs adenoids or tonsils out, and wondered how you'd pay for it, you know what I mean. . . .[4]

Hypothetical examples are not always used this effectively, though, and most people prefer examples that are authentic. Listeners confronted by a plethora of contrived examples are likely to conclude that real examples do not exist or that the speaker cannot think of any. When used skillfully, hypothetical examples vividly dramatize reality and call up real examples in your listeners' minds.

DEVELOPMENT BY STATISTICS

An example is *one* case in point. Statistics are a shorthand method of summarizing a large number of examples.

Be accurate in handling statistics

Know the meaning of the unit you use. Statistics can be misleading unless you define your terms carefully. Suppose a university reports an enrollment of 5,000 students. Does that mean full-time students, or are part-time students included? If a student is registered in two different divisions, is he counted once or twice? In other words, the unit *student* must be defined before the statistics can be interpreted reliably.

Base your statistics on a fair sample. Offhand, it might seem that the records of a college health service should accurately reveal the incidence of common diseases among students. But if you investigate, you might find that commuting students seldom use the health service and that even resident students go to their family physicians when they are seriously sick. As a result, the health-

[4] *Vital Speeches of the Day,* May 15, 1952, p. 478.

service records alone do not give you an accurate picture. Statistics must be based on a sufficient number of representative cases if they are to be reliable.

Establish the stability of the unit in making statistical comparisons. Statistics compiled at one time and place may seem to be based on the same unit as those compiled at another time or place. A comparison of 1890 statistics on cancer with those compiled seventy years later might make it appear that the incidence of cancer is increasing. Actually it may mean merely that we now identify cancer more accurately. A fund raiser for a political campaign pointed out that the cost of Lincoln's campaign for the presidency in 1860 was $100,000. Today a half hour of TV time for political campaigning on a national network may cost this much. Granted, the cost of political campaigning has skyrocketed, but the comparison is misleading because the dollar has depreciated in value.

Be sure that your statistics measure what they say they measure. If you are reporting on the real income of wage-earners, statistics that give their income in dollars might be deceptive, since "real income" means dollars translated into things the worker buys. If women have fewer automobile accidents than men, can you conclude without question that women are better drivers? Or could it mean that women drive fewer miles than men and that they drive in places and at times when accidents are less likely to happen?

Use statistics sparingly and skillfully

A blanket of statistics may smother your listeners, particularly if the statistics are highly complex. Translate statistics into concrete items that your audience can grasp. In the statement below, C. Langdon White reduces to human terms complicated data on the land-population ratio.

Taking the world as a whole, there is only one acre of arable land available to each person and even in the United States only three acres per head. If the world population continues to increase at the present rate—that is, unchanged—in 600 years there will be only one square yard of land surface per capita. This "standing room" figure takes into account more than arable land; it includes all land—polar wastes, deserts, jungles, mountain tops, as well as available living space.[5]

[5] *Vital Speeches of the Day,* May 15, 1959, p. 462.

Use round figures when you can compare them strikingly to make your point. For example, in 1800 there were 900 million people on the earth; by 1962 the figure had grown to over 3 billion; and best estimates are that by 2050 the world's population will be between 9 and 13 billion. It may be more efficient and effective to convert figures into percentages. For example, saying that 20 per cent of the students are commuters may be more effective than giving the actual number.

Use statistics dramatically if you can do so without distorting them. The following "stix" story (so called because it is designed to make statistics stick!) is an example.

The first printing of the Revised Standard Version of the Holy Bible was 970,000 copies. These Bibles—each 1½ inches thick—stacked in one pile would tower 24 miles into the stratosphere—higher than 100 Empire State Buildings.[6]

Note the use of statistics in the following paragraph not simply to show the relative magnitude of salaries, but to emphasize distortions in contemporary values.

Elvis Presley, fresh out of army khaki, may not have returned from overseas as a conquering hero, but his claim to dubious fame as America's sex idol is still intact, it would seem; he recently received no less than $125,000 for one night's appearance on a network TV program. He did two wiggles and sang two songs, and for this received more than the yearly salary of the President of the United States and three times the yearly salary of the Chief Justice of the Supreme Court. An identical sum of money would pay the salaries of 25 school teachers, 42 ministers, or 63 farm hands in many of our states. It would provide a year's training for 30 or more nurses, would give 125 American young people a year in college, would stock ten mission hospitals with elemental tools and drugs, would feed 3,000 refugee children for a whole year. . . .[7]

DEVELOPMENT BY ILLUSTRATION

Although the word *illustration* is popularly used to cover many methods of developing ideas, we use it here to mean an extended comparison between two things drawn from quite different fields. An idea that is unfamiliar or doubtful is more likely to be accepted

[6] Bernard Kalb, in *The Saturday Review,* December 20, 1952, p. 8.
[7] *The Christian Century,* May 25, 1960, p. 630.

John F. Kennedy and Dwight D. Eisenhower leave the White House to ride together to the Capitol for the inauguration of Kennedy as President of the United States. *(Wide World Photos)*

when it is compared with something your listener knows or feels confident about.

In one of his fireside chats, Franklin D. Roosevelt sought to interpret the nature of the New Deal at a time when it really was new, and to counter charges that it was revolutionary. He used an illustration to assure the people that the New Deal was wholly consistent with the American political tradition.

While I am away from Washington this summer, a long-needed renovation of and addition to our White House office building is to be started. The architects have planned a few new rooms built into the present all too small one-story structure. We are going to include in this addition and in the renovation modern electric wiring and modern plumbing and modern means of keeping the offices cool in hot Washington summers. But the structural lines of the old Executive office building will remain. The artistic lines of the White House buildings were the creation of master builders when our Republic was young. The simplicity and the strength of the structure remain in the face of every modern test. But within this magnificent pattern, the necessities of modern government business require reorganization and rebuilding.

If I were to listen to the arguments of some prophets of calamity who are talking these days, I should hesitate to make these alterations. I should fear that while I am away for a few weeks the architects might build some strange new Gothic tower or a factory building or perhaps a replica of the Kremlin or of the Potsdam palace. But I have no such fears. The architects and builders are men of common sense and of artistic American tastes. They know that the principles of harmony and of necessity itself require that the building of the new structure shall blend with the essential lines of the old. It is this combination of the old and the new that marks orderly peaceful progress, not only in building buildings but in building government itself.[8]

The value of an illustration lies in its suggestive power. It should never be offered or taken as a literal or complete demonstration of a point. Fresh illustrations illuminate points and indicate originality; hackneyed illustrations suggest a dull mind. As Dr. George Buttrick said, "The little boy who held his finger in the dike to avoid the flood is now an old man and should be sent home for a much needed rest."[9]

[8] Fireside chat, "Reviewing the Achievements of the Seventy-Third Congress," June 28, 1934.
[9] *The New York Times,* September 29, 1937, p. L25.

DEVELOPMENT BY STORIES

We recount anecdotes and tell stories for pleasure, and we use them to cinch points. Some of these stories we draw from personal experiences, literature, or history; others we create to point up some true-to-life situation. A well-told story is one of the most effective means of kindling interest and dramatizing ideas. In a speech called "Awake the Dawn," Bishop Gerald Kennedy uses several well-placed stories to highlight ideas and strengthen points. Here is one example.

The late Bishop Francis J. McConnell was once president of DePauw University. He always liked to be on the land, and after retirement he lived on a farm in Ohio. When he was at DePauw he had a small acreage where he raised chickens. He said that everything went all right except in the middle of the night the rooster would start to crow and wake everybody up. He could not understand this behavior so he stayed up one night to find out the trouble. He said that along about two o'clock in the morning, the interurban train coming out from Indianapolis would swing around a curve, and the headlight would shine into the chicken house. The rooster, thinking it was the sun, would begin to crow. And the bishop said, "It is not only roosters that mistake headlights for dawns." Indeed it is not! If men can sometimes bring the darkness, so sometimes in their pride and in their limited knowledge they can promise dawns which never come, and bring disillusionment.[10]

The value of a story, of course, may be more apparent than real. Be on guard against stories that oversimplify and that substitute a pleasant, facile explanation for rigor and accuracy. Unless you speak merely to entertain, your story must bear sharply on the point. You may have heard listeners remark, "I became so interested in his story that I missed the point he was trying to make."

DEVELOPMENT BY QUOTATIONS

Quotations may be drawn from anything in the vast reservoir of human expression—from history, literature, biography, technical reports, newspapers, speeches, conversations. Apt statements by somebody else may lend weight to your own views or may simply be more impressive, beautiful, or amusing than anything you can

[10] A. Craig Baird, ed., *Representative American Speeches: 1956–1957* (New York: The H. W. Wilson Company, 1957), p. 185.

devise. A quotation loses its value, though, if it is laboriously dragged in or is too long. Make it clear that you are quoting and from whom you have taken your material.

J. Martin Klotsche uses many short quotations in his speech "On Being an Educated Person." Through these borrowed statements he sets forth with great economy a variety of views on education.

A former distinguished professor of the faculty of the University of Wisconsin once defined an educated person as one "who tries to understand the whole of knowledge as well as one man can." Mark Van Doren held that the purpose of education is to see that "each man becomes more than he is," while William Whewell thought of education as the means "to connect a man's mind with the general mind of the human race." [11]

DEVELOPMENT BY MAXIMS, PROVERBS, AND SLOGANS

A *maxim* is a general statement of principle, advice, or counsel on human conduct and affairs expressed in tight, epigrammatic form. To be effective, a maxim must suggest its idea with memorable deftness. Here are a few examples.

An Englishman is the unfittest person on earth to argue another Englishman into slavery. (*Edmund Burke*)

Men may be sorely touched and deeply grieved in their privileges as well as in their purses. (*Edmund Burke*)

Error of opinion may be tolerated where reason is left free to combat it. (*Thomas Jefferson*)

It is better to work on institutions by the sun than by the wind. (*Ralph W. Emerson*)

Only a people who can achieve the moral mastery of themselves can hope to win the moral leadership of others. (*Adlai Stevenson*)

Self-criticism is the secret weapon of democracy, and candor and confession are good for the political soul. (*Adlai Stevenson*)

It is my task to report the state of the Union; to improve it is the task of us all. (*John F. Kennedy*)

A *proverb* is a short, pithy saying that expresses a widely ac-

[11] *Vital Speeches of the Day*, August 1, 1957, p. 635.

cepted truth based on common sense and practical experience. Proverbs are really a type of maxim that embodies the folk-wisdom of a people. Benjamin Franklin's counsels, offered as the words of Poor Richard, are examples.

He that falls in love with himself will have no rivals.
'Tis hard for an empty bag to stand upright.
If you'd have it done, go; if not, send.

Many of the late President Kennedy's statements have the ring of proverb.

A stern heritage is a good teacher.
It takes two to make peace.

Skillful speakers use proverbs and maxims sparingly. Overabundant use of these techniques sounds stuffy, and if a speaker's advice is premature or unwelcome, he may alienate his audience by this imprudence.

A *slogan* is a short, catchy statement used as a rallying point by a person, group, or party. Some slogans have undeniable social value, such as "The life you save may be your own" or "Help fight cancer with a check-up and a check." But slogans that boost products and services are often half-truths designed to beguile the unwary. However valid, a slogan soon becomes trite and loses its appeal.

DEVELOPMENT BY REPETITION

A reader has the advantage of being able to go back to an earlier page, to refresh his memory and review important points in the light of what followed. A speaker may provide much the same advantage for his audience by repeating in new ways what he has already said. By repeating an idea, a speaker underlines it and clarifies it for his listeners.

Theodore Roosevelt was a master of the art of *meaningful* repetition. On April 14, 1906, he spoke on "The Man with the Muck-Rake," in which he recalled the man in Bunyan's *Pilgrim's Progress* "who could look no way but downward, with the muck-rake in his hand; who was offered a celestial crown for his muck-rake, but who would neither look up or regard the crown he was offered, but continued to rake to himself the filth of the floor." From this allegory, Roosevelt drew his theme: that dishonest men in public and private life should be exposed, but indiscriminate muck-raking dulls the public conscience and benefits the scoundrels. In various ways, Roosevelt restates this theme, repeating it over and over again, dinning it into public consciousness.

Avoid needless repetition, of course. And when you do repeat a point, find new ways of putting it.

DEVELOPMENT BY VISUAL AND AUDITORY AIDS

Visual and auditory aids include charts, maps, graphs, diagrams, outlines, pictures, cartoons, posters, lantern slides, moving pictures, models, tape recorders, and objects used in demonstrations. These aids are particularly useful in teaching and in other types of informative speaking. A great deal of our conversation take place in sight of the objects we are talking about. Television has an advantage over radio not only because the speakers can be seen as well as heard, but because they can use visual aids to supplement the spoken word.

Here are suggestions for the use of aids.

Let the aids supplement your words

Ask yourself, "Will visual and auditory aids help me achieve my purpose?" If so, use them. Fortunately, many ingenious devices are available. If you cannot find just what you want, homemade devices are well worth the time and effort spent in getting them together.

But don't drag in visual and auditory aids for their own sake. If your listeners conclude that you are simply parading a set of gimmicks, you will lose their respect as well as their interest. The best advice is this: Don't overload your speech with aids and never use them as mere "fill-in."

Make sure that your audience can see your visual aids without straining their eyes

An audience cannot be expected to take interest in an illustration that is too small or very minutely detailed or that is displayed in inadequate light. The thoughtful speaker will have clearly displayed aids, or, if that is not possible, will have small ones duplicated and distributed—at the proper time—to his audience.

Keep your aids simple and comprehensible

An "inventor" created a wonderful machine that would do the work of five men; but it took six men to operate it. If it takes more time and ingenuity for you to explain a chart than it would to explain the point you are trying to make, everyone will be happier if you skip the chart. The point of your exhibit must emerge quickly and easily, or else be lost.

Synchronize your aids with your remarks

To be effective, visual aids must become visible at exactly the moment they are needed. We have all seen lecturers who competed for attention with their own devices. They make the mistake of handing out charts, pictures, graphs, and the like before such aids are needed. As a result, the audience's attention is distracted from the speaker's words.

Have your aids in working order

Have you ever suffered along with a speaker who tried to use electrical gadgets that would not operate, lantern slides that were unnumbered or mixed up or upside down, maps that fell down, or demonstration kits that lacked an essential component? The strange thing is that some people seem not to learn very much from their own lack of preparation. Arrange things beforehand.

AXIOMS OF AMPLIFICATION

Why are definitions, examples, illustrations, visual aids, and all the other methods of amplification effective in speech? What are the sources of their strength and appeal? The axioms we offer here will throw light on these questions. In addition, they will serve as practical guides in selecting material and developing it. In general, any technique of developing an idea that makes use of the axioms that follow is likely to command interest.

Specific instances, items, and cases are usually clearer and more interesting than general statements

Specificity is particularly needed if your generalization falls outside the immediate experiences of your listeners or if it is a tired one that needs to be enlivened by the touch of reality. Without adequate attention to details and applications, speech tends to become vague, loose and indefinite.

Concrete things—actual substances and persons— hold interest better than do abstractions

Most generalizations are abstract, and specific instances may be. For example, the law of supply and demand is a specific instance of economic principles, and the law of excluded middle is a specific case of the so-called laws of reasoning. But neither is concrete. If you want a concrete example of the law of supply and demand, take your listener, figuratively speaking, to a used car lot and let him see how this law works; and if you want a concrete example of the law of excluded middle, draw a diagram of the sort you can find in any elementary textbook on logic.

Familiar references bring the unfamiliar within the experience of the listener

Rhetorical devices based on comparison and contrast are especially useful here, but all methods of amplification draw on this axiom. A specific case developed in concrete terms will usually be more effective if it deals with familiar places, persons, and things.

The novel—the rare, the unusual, and the different—also attracts attention

A novel way of putting a familiar idea, an unusual experience, or any method of amplification that contains an element of surprise relieves the monotony of ordinary talk and enlivens formal speech. But precaution is necessary: Bizarre materials that strain for novelty offend good taste and place the speaker under a cloud of suspicion.

Whatever strikes a person's vital interests will involve him most quickly and deeply

This story illustrates the point.

One evening in his club, a physician sat at the card table with three friends. Word was brought to him that a child had suddenly become desperately ill.

As he rose to go, one of his friends remonstrated saying: "Don't rush off; the child's mother is probably unduly alarmed over the situation. Stay and finish the game before you go; that will be time enough."

"That's what you think I ought to do?" queried the doctor.

"Yes," answered his friend, "fussy, nervous people have no right to call a physician after office hours, anyway."

"Very well," said the doctor, "I'll take your advice this time because it is your child who is ill." [12]

Allusion to our vital interests immediately removes a matter from the realm of the casual and impersonal. Let an instructor say "The normal distribution curve is illustrated by the grades I gave on the quiz you took yesterday," and his students are likely to take a quick and keen interest in the curve.

Proximity, recency, and immediacy lend impact

Illustrative materials that are remote from the listener's experiences are seldom so effective as those drawn from situations close at hand. If you can date your story "last night" or "today" and locate it "right here in this town" or "next door" or "in our sorority," you will see at once how quickly interest quickens.

Conflict—struggle, clash, and controversy—implies competitiveness, one of the strongest motivations in our culture

Who has not listened to comparisons between himself and others with mounting interest? The same kind of interest is evoked when a speaker compares one's town with a neighboring village or a local football team with its competitors. Interest in political conventions and TV debates is heightened by conflict. This device can be applied to any circumstances in which competing forces are at work.

Action arouses more interest than does quiescence

Motion pictures and visual aids with moving parts put this principle to use. Narrative discourse is a popular oral method because it is lively. Personification of abstract qualities and animation of inanimate objects are other frequent applications of the motion axiom.

---

[12] J. M. O'Neill and A. T. Weaver, *The Elements of Speech* (New York: David McKay Co., Inc., 1936), p. 257.

POINTS TO KEEP IN MIND

1. Normally, your speech will gain in clarity, interest, and impact as you acquire skill in making full use of various methods of amplification.

2. In future speeches, try to apply the following suggestions:

Define all unfamiliar or ambiguous terms of any importance.

Should your listeners need a "for instance," provide real or convincing hypothetical examples.

When you introduce statistics, be sure they are reliable and readily understandable.

An illustration will help your audience translate the unfamiliar into the familiar.

A human interest story dramatizes a point.

A quotation is useful if it lends authority to your ideas or if it expresses a point more effectively than you can state it.

Well-chosen maxims, proverbs, and slogans identify your ideas with the wisdom of the race.

Repeat main ideas in new ways to help clarify and instill them in your listeners' minds.

3. Bear in mind the psychological bases for developing your ideas embodied in the axioms of amplification.

EXERCISES

1. Choose a term that not everyone understands. Define the term and clarify your definition by using examples, illustrations, visual aids, or other support. Terms such as *cubism, thermodynamics, agronomy, socialism, semantics, neurosis,* and *group dynamics* are good subjects.

2. Prepare a "master-example" speech by devoting half or more of your time to development of a single example to make a point. Do not merely cite an example, but build an entire speech about it.

3. Choose a subject that calls for a statistical development. Limit yourself to an aspect of some general problem such as membership in campus religious organizations today as compared with ten years ago, tuition charges, popular interest in TV programs, automobile sales, depletion of natural resources. Be mindful of all instructions for the preparation and use of statistics. A visual aid may help you present them.

4. Develop a speech around one or more auditory or visual aids. A talk on voting machines might employ a miniature model; one on jazz might benefit from recorded excerpts. Follow the advice given in this chapter.

5. Make a place, event, institution, or process come alive through skillful description and explanation. Make your listeners see vividly the Bingham Copper Mine, a session of the UN, the inside of a prison, or the stages in getting a cartoon from the drafting board into a newspaper.

6. There are three steps in this exercise: (a) open your talk with an example, story, or illustration that discloses your purpose; (b) develop each main point with one method listed in this chapter; (c) conclude with a maxim, proverb, slogan, or quotation.

eleven

Language
and Style

Everyone has a speaking style, a characteristic way of patterning his words. But not all styles are born free and equal. Many people lack social, economic, and intellectual mobility because they are shackled by their own language habits. A command of language, oral and written, opens new worlds of thought, action, and human association. This chapter discusses common verbal impediments and suggests ways to improve language habits and develop an effective oral style.

MAKE YOURSELF UNDERSTOOD

Clarity is the first requirement of good style. Listeners must grasp what is being stated or asked before they can respond intelligently. Then they can take the next step—accept it, disagree with it, or disregard it, as they choose. Irwin Edman once said of Bertrand Russell, "He has the gift or the achievement of a style unfailingly lucid so that even when one disagrees with him, one knows exactly what it is with which one is disagreeing."

To establish clear lines of communication, (1) treat words as symbols, not "things"; (2) anchor your words to valid facts and thoughts; (3) practice good usage and strengthen your vocabulary; and (4) avoid saying things the hard way.

TREAT WORDS AS SYMBOLS

Words are merely sound waves that vibrate membranes of our ears, or light waves that excite sensitive parts in our eyes. Words are symbols that we endow with meaning. We should not confuse the symbol with the "thing" nor should we act toward the symbol as if meaning were inherent in it.

Words vary in the stability of the meaning we assign them. Technical words used by specialists tend to be more restricted in their meaning and therefore more stable than words used in ordinary parlance. With time, most words acquire a greater range and variety of meaning. As Charles C. Fries, a distinguished language scholar, points out, the *Oxford English Dictionary* records and illustrates from our literature 14,070 separate meanings for the 500 most commonly used words in the English language.[1]

Misunderstandings may arise when a speaker uses a word or when a listener responds to it as if it held exactly the same meaning for everyone. To say that a person is or is not a Christian invites as many interpretations as there are denominations and sects. "You call yourself a liberal, but you're antilabor." "You bet I'm a liberal, and I'm telling you that labor is the most reactionary group in the country." As the conversation warms up, we become heated champions of our labels rather than cool-headed investigators of the meaning they carry for other people.

Come to an early understanding with your listeners on ambiguous terms. Be particularly careful when you use words that are abstract, that are unfamiliar, or that arouse emotions, such as *the common man, socialism, big business, radical, reactionary, love,* and *existentialism.* Avoid trouble by saying at the outset, "Now when I talk about academic freedom, I mean limited and specific things. I have in mind these privileges, these responsibilities, for these people."

Since you can't always anticipate what words will spawn misunderstanding, be alert to signals of confusion, perplexity, or hostility from your listeners. Then pause to find out if they are reacting adversely to your language as such, or to what you are really talking about. You can often find out by asking, "Do I make myself clear?" Or, "I notice you seem to disagree. I wonder why?" Or, "Let me put it another way and see whether we understand each other."

---

[1] Quoted in Irving J. Lee, *How to Talk With People* (New York: Harper & Row, Publishers, Inc., 1952), p. 15.

Of course you may discover that your listeners are perfectly clear about what you mean but that they simply disagree with you. Then you must either accept these differences or work them out by recourse to facts and reasoning. But be sure that you differ on a *real* issue, not simply on what the words mean.

ANCHOR YOUR WORDS TO REALITY

Communication becomes an illusion whenever a speaker and his listeners cut loose from their moorings and drift off together in a cloudland of words.

Verbomania is a virulent disease to which many people have low resistance. Our world of talk is infested with empty words, platitudes, and clichés. They pass from individual to individual, from group to group, until, through social osmosis, they get into our nervous systems; we respond to them as a dog does to a whistle.

The epidemic of verbomania once inspired A. Parker Nevin to write "A Speech for Any Occasion," a minor classic of satire on speechmaking. Job E. Hedges said of it, "You can call it 'The Crisis,' 'Justice,' 'Solution,' 'Destiny,' or anything you want. It covers the whole range of human thought and is unanswerable." Here it is.

Mr. Chairman, Ladies and Gentlemen:

It is indeed a great and undeserved privilege to address such an audience as I see before me. At no previous time in the history of human civilization have greater problems confronted and challenged the ingenuity of man's intellect than now. Let us look around us. What do we see on the horizon? What forces are at work? Whither are we drifting? Under what mist of clouds does the future stand obscured? My friends, casting aside the raiment of all human speech, the crucial test for the solution of all these intricate problems to which I have just alluded is the sheer and forceful application of those immutable laws which down the corridor of Time have always guided the hand of man, groping, as it were, for some faint beacon light for his hopes and aspirations. Without these great vital principles, we are but puppets responding to whim and fancy, failing entirely to grasp the hidden meaning of it all. We must re-address ourselves to these questions which press for answer and solution. The issues cannot be avoided. There they stand. It is upon you —and you—and yet even upon me that the yoke of responsibility falls.

What, then, is our duty? Shall we continue to drift? No! With all the emphasis of my being I hurl back the message *No!* Drifting must stop. We must press onward and upward toward the ultimate good to which all must aspire. But I cannot conclude my remarks, dear friends, without briefly touching upon a subject which I know is steeped in your very consciousness. I refer to that spirit which gleams from the eyes of a new-born babe, that animates the toiling masses, that sways all the hosts of humanity past and present. Without this energizing principle all commerce, trade and industry are hushed and will perish from this earth as surely as the crimson sunset follows the golden sunshine. Mark you, I do not seek to unduly alarm or distress the mothers, fathers, sons and daughters gathered before me in this vast assemblage, but I would indeed be recreant to a high resolve which I made as a youth if I did not at this time and in this place, and with the full realizing sense of responsibility which I assume, publicly declare and affirm my dedication and my consecration to the eternal principles and receipts of simple, ordinary, commonplace *JUSTICE*.

For what, in the last analysis, is justice? Whence does it come from? Where does it go? Is it tangible? It is not. Is it ponderable? It is not. Justice is none of these, and yet, on the other hand, in a sense it is all of these things combined. While I cannot tell you what justice is, this much I can tell you: That without the encircling arms of justice, without her shield, without her guardianship, the ship of state will sail through unchartered seas, narrowly avoiding rocks and shoals, headed inevitably to the harbor of calamity.

Justice! Justice! Justice! To thee we pay homage. To thee we dedicate our laurels of hope. Before thee we kneel in adoration, mindful of thy great power, mute before thy inscrutable destiny! [2]

Nevin's speech was once read to a class of twenty adults, who were then asked to summarize the message and evaluate the talk. No two could agree completely on what it was all about, but most of the class seemed to think it was a fine speech. One person acknowledged that he hadn't the foggiest notion of what the speaker was driving at. None recognized the speech as satire, for all had been listening to "speeches for any and all occasions" most of their lives.

You may delude some of your listeners by tossing unanchored words about. You may also delude yourself. It is poor praise to be complimented for your ability to sling the King's English. It is high praise to be assured that you talked sense and to know that your listeners carried away a clear idea of what you wanted to get across.

Listeners have the choice of surrendering to the spell of language

[2] Robert H. Davis, "Bob Davis Recalls," *New York Sun*, March 22, 1927. Reprinted by permission.

or critically inspecting the speaker's ideas and words to see whether they are firmly anchored to reality. Critical listening is the best defense against verbomania, and how you react as a listener is likely to influence how you yourself behave as a speaker.

PRACTICE GOOD USAGE AND STRENGTHEN YOUR VOCABULARY

When you talk extemporaneously, you are privileged to take more liberties with language than when you write. By means of vocal inflection, change of pace, and emphasis, you are able to give force and clarity to a sentence that would not pass muster in writing. This liberty, however, does not give you license to disregard the accepted rules of good usage and syntax. Mangled sentences such as "I crossed in an airplane the distance of the continent that took my grandfather a week to ten days in eight hours" impose a considerable strain on listeners, who must reconstruct the sentence to extract the meaning.

All bad language habits can be corrected. Familiarity with the basic rules given in grammars, books on good usage, and dictionaries is a requirement that nobody can ignore without victimizing himself and his listeners. An effective speaker will supplement his study with practice sessions in which he experiments with various ways of expressing an idea until it emerges with clarity and economy.

To transmit our meanings accurately, we need an adequate vocabulary. We can recognize and identify many more words in our reading and listening than we use in our writing and speaking. To develop an effective working vocabulary, you will need (1) to add words to your recognition vocabulary from your reading and listening and (2) to recruit new words for speaking from your recognition vocabulary. Some people resort to word lists compiled by somebody else. It is more profitable to build your own list, drawing on the synonyms and highly expressive words that already constitute your recognition vocabulary.

Learn the meaning of new words and check your understanding of familiar ones. Pronounce them out loud and fix their spelling in your mind. Often the origin and derivation of a word will help to establish it in your vocabulary. Put each word into sentences and practice using it in private. Finally, assimilate each word by introducing it into your conversation and speeches. If you make a habit of following this procedure, you will begin to build a larger speaking vocabulary.

Many people, even college students, use barbarisms like *irregardless* and *irrevelant*—words that have no status in any lexicon. Betrayed by superficial resemblances between words, they reach out at random and grab whatever comes to mind. "My opponent flaunts public opinion," the politician charges. He means *flouts*. This building is inexhaustible," declares a travel guide; he means *indestructible*. "Our education takes up a great part of our formidable years," says a student, who means *formative*. "You excelled the speed limit," insists the traffic cop, meaning *exceeded*. A speaker who confuses *noisy* and *noisome* describes an attractive residential neighborhood as noisome because it falls within the traffic pattern of a metropolitan airport.

Our language is filled with words that have almost, but not quite, the same meaning: *amiable* and *amicable; comprehensive* and *comprehensible; impassive* and *impassible* (*impassable* means something different from either); *bellicose* and *belligerent; glance* and *glimpse; intrude* and *obtrude; minute* and *moment; rigid* and *rigorous.* Verbal acuity enables you to sense the distinctions between such words in various contexts. A good, standard dictionary is indispensable, and a useful adjunct is *A Dictionary of Contemporary Usage* by Bergen and Cornelia Evans. You will discover that the Evanses' *Dictionary* makes word study not only informative but fascinating as well.

AVOID SAYING THINGS THE HARD WAY

A plumber once wrote to a government agency, saying he found that hydrochloric acid quickly opened drain pipes. He wanted to know whether this was a good thing to use. A scientist at the agency replied that "the efficacy of hydrochloric acid is indisputable, but the corrosive residue is incompatible with metallic permanence." The plumber wrote back, thanking him for his assurance that hydrochloric acid was all right. Disturbed by this turn of affairs, the scientist showed the letter to his boss—another scientist—who then wrote to the plumber, "We cannot assume responsibility for the production of toxic and noxious residue with hydrochloric acid and suggest you use an alternative procedure." The plumber wrote back that he agreed—hydrochloric acid worked fine. Now greatly disturbed by these misunderstandings, the scientists took their problem to their chief. He broke through the jargon and wrote to the plumber: "Don't use hydrochloric acid. It eats holes in the pipes."

Be as economical as you can without impoverishing your thought. Choose a simple, direct way of expression or, at least, when there are several ways of saying the same thing, choose the simplest way. Simple speech is not to be confused with speech for the simpleton. Simple speech is unencumbered speech. As Dr. George Buttrick once remarked, "Great diction is not the linking of unusual words, but the unusual linking of usual words." [3]

USE VIVID AND ENERGETIC LANGUAGE

SPECIFIC LANGUAGE ETCHES IMPRESSIONS

Specific words and phrases focus attention and etch sharp mental images. Sentences made up of nonspecific language hint at vagueness and leave a blurred impression. Compare these examples.

Somebody told me that a good many people in this general area are down with an ailment of some sort.

Dr. Hewitt reports that there are thirty-two cases of bronchitis in Belleville.

CONCRETE WORDS RECREATE EXPERIENCE

Walt Whitman once said, "Language, be it remember'd, is not an abstract construction of the learned, or of dictionary-makers, but is something arising out of the work, needs, ties, joys, affections, tastes, of long generations of humanity, and has its bases broad and low, close to the ground."

Concrete words are linked in our minds with the things we hear, see, smell, touch, taste, and feel—so closely, in fact, that when we hear concrete words spoken our nervous system reproduces vicariously the sensory experience itself. When you hear somebody tell of a crackling fire, you can almost hear the crackle of a bonfire, campfire, or burning building.

[3] *The New York Times*, September 29, 1937, p. L25.

Compare these two descriptions:

In autumn the leaves display diversity in color.

In October the leaves go wild with color—purple and green, red and gold, all running into each other.

The first statement is clear and precise, to be sure; the second is just as clear and just as precise but, in addition, it is "close to the ground." Its language stirs associations and stimulates us to feel the tangy air and see the riot of color.

GOOD FIGURES OF SPEECH DRAMATIZE RELATIONSHIPS

Simile and metaphor point up the resemblance between two seemingly dissimilar things. They help us to understand something unfamiliar, abstract, or complex by comparing it with something familiar or simple. If the simile or metaphor is particularly deft, we are surprised by a resemblance we have never perceived before; if it is pertinent and fresh, it may also give us aesthetic pleasure or amusement.

The *simile* is a short statement in which the comparison is spelled out. Words such as *like, as,* and *as if* usually provide clues to a simile. For example: "She plays the piano as if she were wearing boxing gloves." "Talking is like playing on the harp; there is as much in laying the hands on the strings to stop their vibrations as in twanging them to bring out their music" (Oliver Wendell Holmes). Lincoln likened the thinness of Douglas' arguments on popular sovereignty to soup made from boiling the shadow of a starved chicken. "Once one knows which Communist line a Communist leader is using," declared Richard Rovere, "listening to him becomes almost as unendurable as hearing someone count to fifty thousand."

The simile calls attention to the fact that a comparison is being drawn. The *metaphor* merely *implies* a comparison. For example, a secretary of state, trying to show that the objectives of a certain country remain the same despite appearances to the contrary, once declared that "The switch is simply from hob-nail boots to carpet slippers." The implication is that only the tactics of the country have changed, not its objectives. Winston Churchill brought home

General Douglas MacArthur. *(Wide World Photos)*

a complex problem in international relations with a metaphor: "From Stettin in the Baltic to Trieste in the Adriatic, an iron curtain has descended across the continent." In his tribute to Mrs. Roosevelt, Adlai Stevenson said movingly, "She would rather light candles than curse the darkness and her glow warmed the world."

Our everyday talk abounds with similes, metaphors, and variations on these basic forms. Many of the figures we use are no longer novel and no longer catch our ear, but we go on using them out of habit and because they possess universal applicability. We say a person is a tower of strength, straight as a ramrod, a bundle of energy, has nerves of steel, is dirty as a pig. But these and hundreds of other familiar figures of speech are overworked and tired. If we rely only on the old expressions, discriminating listeners will conclude that our speech is trite and our minds dull. Fresh, vivid figures inject life and color into our speech.

Relaxed, competent speakers are vivid without straining to be original. Poorly devised and mixed-up figures are good vehicles for low comedy, but make a serious speaker appear ludicrous. For example, a young teacher groped for a figure to convey his impressions of teaching and said, "You carry all thirty of the students on your back, and just when you're ready to throw in the towel, you strike gold." Use metaphors intelligently.

PERSONAL FORMS ARE NATURAL TO SPEECH

We all like dialogue. We are familiar with its patterns, and we enjoy its intimacy and movement. Real and hypothetical illustrations used in informal and formal talk can often be couched in the form of dialogue. Notice how R. W. Jepson makes you a party to dialogue in a speech called "Potted Thinking: The Necessity of Going Deeper than the Headlines."

Have you ever come across the man who buttonholes you and poses you with a question and insists on your answering, "Yes" or "No"? He will say to you: "Now then, are you a Free Trader, or aren't you?" And you might reply: "Well, the removal of all restrictions and barriers on international trade would be an ideal thing to my mind. But as things are—" Then he will burst in and say: "Come along now, I asked you a plain question. Give me a plain answer." Once again you will probably stammer out a few "buts." Then he will tell you you are hedging. "Either you are, or you aren't," he will say. "Which is it? 'Yes' or 'No'?" You know the kind of person: the real whole-hogger.[4]

In public speaking, rhetorical questions help bring the listener in as an active partner in communication. Observe how Franklin D. Roosevelt created the sense of dialogue between himself and his listeners even though he didn't really expect them to answer back.

But the simplest way for you to judge recovery lies in the plain facts of your own individual situation. Are you better off than you were last year? Are your debts less burdensome? Is your bank account more secure? Are your working conditions better? Is your faith in your own individual future more grounded?

Use personal pronouns in formal talks much as you do in every-day speech. Remember, you are talking with people, not to manne-quins. The personal pronouns *I, you,* and *we* are natural, simple expressions of sincere speech. They help establish rapport. Imper-sonal substitutes for real persons are stilted and affected. It is less wooden and more direct to say "I think that . . ." than it is to say "In the estimation of this speaker, it is not an unjustifiable assump-tion to say. . . ." Of course, the personal pronoun may be con-spicuously overworked.

STURDY SENTENCES ADD STRENGTH TO SPEECH

Make your sentences stand on their legs and march. Flabby sen-tences start off with a limp and end in a crumpled heap. They begin, "And then there's another thing . . . And then there's some-thing else . . . and incidentally, there's still this that I might men-tion. . . ." They end, ". . . and things like that," ". . . and so forth," or ". . . several other miscellaneous matters."

Avoid overloading your sentences with so many phrases and clauses that they jostle each other.

Now my friends, we all believe in the purposes of public education, the great bulwark of our free country, our greatest heritage, but we also must be realistic and inquire closely into the financial feasibility of ex-panding our school plant at this moment when we contemplate an aug-

[4] *Vital Speeches of the Day,* December 15, 1937, pp. 135-36.

mentation of salaries for the instructional staff, whose members are charged with shaping our childrens' futures.

Because of the clumsy composition of the passage, it is difficult to form a sharp, clear conception of what the speaker is saying. Now note how easily the sense comes across when put into sturdy sentences that step along briskly.

We all want the best in plant, equipment, and staff for our public schools. We agree on this. But let's ask, "Can we afford to build a new gymnasium this year and at the same time improve salaries for teachers?"

Sturdy sentences feature nouns and verbs. Excessive use of clamorous words like *very, great, colossal, stupendous,* and *terrific* drowns out the essential ones.

Clinch your main ideas with climaxes. Before leaving an important point to go on to the next, drive home the sense and significance of what you have just said. For example, one speaker capped a key point on the threat of communism by saying, "The greatest danger communism presents to America is not by arms but by invitation." A series of strong, climactic sentences is particularly suited for the conclusion of speeches of advocacy and evocation.

USE LANGUAGE WITH PROPRIETY

SUIT YOUR LANGUAGE TO THE OCCASION

Ordinary speech is colloquial. We don't prepare our words when we are bargaining over the counter, asking someone to pass the butter, or exchanging the news of the day. But we all know there are times when our handy, everyday words are inadequate. Some occasions demand that we sort out our words and compose speech with distinction.

Compare the snatch of conversation below with a short passage suitable to a formal speech on the same subject. First the conversation.

A university is not out to please customers. It's more of a busybody than a business. Its job is to poke around, sniff out facts, air them—no matter whether people like 'em or not. It ought to puncture prejudices and platitudes. Let the bigots howl. A university is a people's hairshirt.

Now the formal speech.

A university that does not lead is a university only in name. A true university diligently pursues facts amid appearances. It is a critic of what is, and a standard-bearer for what ought to be. Often it must speak as a solitary voice, championing truth against the clamor of outraged opinion and prejudice.

The language in the first passage is colloquial and suggests the informality of a living room or office conversation. Most of the words in the second passage are colloquial too, and the sentences are simple. But it is evident that the style has been refined and elevated for the public platform. It is not a question of which style is better—the formal or informal. Each is suited to its setting. In general, audiences expect the language of public speech to have tone and distinction that lifts it above the level of casual, off-the-cuff conversation.

AVOID WORDS THAT VIOLATE GOOD TASTE

Some words are plainly taboo. Public disapproval of such words is spelled out, for example, in radio and television codes. These are not the decrees of self-appointed censors; they are reflections of our social mores. It is risky to skirt the boundaries of good taste, and it is suicidal to flout public standards.

Slang should be used cautiously and sparingly. When it is picturesque and earthy, it spices conversation and public address. But slang quickly loses its freshness and appeal. It is seldom appropriate for formal occasions, and a slangy tone debases style on any occasion.

POINTS TO KEEP IN MIND

1. Clarity is the first requirement of a good speaking style.
   a) Treat words as symbols that may have different meanings for different people.
   b) Anchor your words to reality.
   c) Practice good language usage and strengthen your vocabulary.
   d) Be direct and unpretentious in your style. Avoid saying things the hard way.

2. Use vivid and energetic language.
   a) Specific words and phrases etch impressions on your listeners' minds.
   b) Concrete words recreate experience.
   c) Good figurative speech dramatizes relationships.
   d) Make your speech direct and personal through the use of dialogue, rhetorical questions, and personal pronouns.
   e) Speak in short, crisp, sturdy sentences.

3. Suit the degree of formality or informality of your language to the audience and the occasion.

EXERCISES

1. Choose a concept that is unfamiliar to your listeners or about which they have imprecise ideas. Examples are: humanism, existentialism, nationalism, the poetic attitude, the American way of life, psychosomatic medicine. Make your concept the subject of a report. Develop your talk with specificity and concreteness.

2. Take a stand on a controversial issue. Be as precise as you can in outlining your position. As you speak, keep checking on the reactions of your audience. Respond to signs of disagreement or misunderstanding by putting your thoughts in other words. If the signs keep coming, don't hesitate to stop and clear up possible misunderstandings. Determine whether the disagreement is verbal or substantive. The object here is not "smooth talk" but to experiment in reaching a meeting of minds on what is being said.

3. Prepare a two-minute descriptive talk on a topic such as one of these: a sunset, an airplane ride through a thunderstorm, a horse race, landing a salmon, the Golden Gate Bridge, the New York skyline, Niagara Falls, a quaint village, an impressive monument or painting, Main Street on Saturday night, sailing a boat, a locker room between halves. Through vivid language recreate the scene or event for your listeners.

4. Rework a speech you have given before. Clarify and brighten your language and style in ways that will win a new interest for your subject.

5. Select a short speech that has appeared in print—one that falls short of the standards of good speech style. Revise it. Read portions of the original speech and of your revision to the class.

6. Arrange a group discussion on a controversial question. Most of the class will take part in the discussion, but appoint four or five members as observers to take notes on the language behavior of the speakers. Have the observers look especially for these things.
   a) Instances of remarkably clear and precise statements of a point.
   b) Instances when the discussion bogged down because of cloudy or rambling "contributions."

c) Language that blocked or sidetracked the discussion.

d) Instances when members spotted and clarified misunderstandings; instances when misunderstanding went unchecked.

e) Differences that sprang directly from opposing convictions rather than from confusions in language.

7. Take note of unfamiliar words in the sample speeches at the end of this book. Look up their meanings. Underline the familiar words that are not now part of your speaking vocabulary. First use some of these words in sentences, and then make a point of introducing some of them into your next speech.

twelve

Motivated Listening

We listen to many sounds from many sources, but none has greater potential than the spoken word—the sound that admits us to the thinking and feeling of our fellow men. The ultimate rewards of all speech are realized through listening. We want people to listen to what we have to say, and we want to get something out of what others say. In this chapter we shall examine the nature of listening and the means by which both speaker and audience may contribute creatively to good listening.

WHAT IS GOOD LISTENING?

The fact that people are within hearing range of your voice does not necessarily mean that they are listening to you. They may close their ears to you, wander away, or switch the dial on their radio or television set. You may have a captive audience—such as the members of your speech class—but you can't force them to listen to you. And the minute listening stops, communication ceases—even though your voice goes on and on.

KINDS OF LISTENING

As you gain experience as a speaker, you will discover that audiences listen in different ways. Although any listening may be better than none at all, certain kinds of listening get the best results.

VOLUNTARY VS. INVOLUNTARY LISTENING

Some sounds we listen to by choice; others we hear whether we want to or not. Involuntary listeners seldom make a good audience. You may win an initial hearing from listeners simply by talking loudly enough for them to hear. They listen at first without really choosing to listen. But unless you succeed very quickly in capturing their interest and in making them *want* to listen, chances are they will tune you out.

CASUAL VS. PURPOSEFUL LISTENING

A casual listener is one who gives offhand, careless, or irregular attention to what you say. He is likely to drift off unless you provide him with some good purpose for hearing you out. A purposeful listener may soon become a casual listener if you fail to recognize his purpose and help him carry it out. Casual listening is a very short step from no listening at all.

DISCIPLINED VS. MOTIVATED LISTENING

Fortunately for dull speakers, some people force themselves to listen out of courtesy, or habit, or in the hope that they may get something worthwhile if they work hard enough at it. And sometimes these self-disciplined listeners reap a fine harvest, because poor speakers may be able men. But much more comes through to listeners when they listen because they want to and when they find pleasure in doing so. Motivated listening takes place when the promise of reward is great enough to command the listener's attention without his having to exercise great self-discipline.

CRITICAL VS. UNCRITICAL LISTENING

The critical listener follows the speaker's ideas carefully and thoughtfully and tries to evaluate them objectively. He is alert and keeps all his mental faculties at work. A critical audience is the best kind of audience for a speaker who knows what he is talking about and who is willing to enter his ideas in a free, competitive market where they must stand or fall on their own merits. Speakers with less confidence may be better off with less discerning listeners. In fact, some speakers even try to create an atmosphere that invites un-critical acceptance of their ideas. The motives of such speakers may be either good or bad, but the listener who yields to their efforts does so at his own risk. Uncritical acceptance may imply indifference or poor critical acumen.

COOPERATIVE VS. HOSTILE LISTENING

The cooperative listener hopes for the best from the speaker and gives him friendly attention; the hostile listener dislikes the speaker or his ideas, and will not cooperate with him.

THE RESPONSIBILITY FOR LISTENING

A quick review of the kinds of listening will show that people are more likely to give close attention to a speaker when they *want* to hear what he has to say—when they believe he has a message of value to them. This simple fact provides a very practical criterion for determining who is responsible for good listening. If a person has some information you want very badly, you will listen when he speaks and gladly assume the responsibility for doing so. On the other hand, if the speaker is very anxious to get something across in which you are not especially interested, the burden of commanding your attention rests on him. In other words, the primary responsibility for good listening lies with the party to communication—the speaker or the listener—who stands to reap the greater gain.

Fortunately, there are many situations in which the speaker and his audience have a mutual interest in the outcome—where *both* stand to gain. Here the responsibility of good listening is shared. The speaker does his best to maintain interest, and the listener does his best to follow what is being said. Mutual interest and shared responsibility are desirable goals in all communication.

PRINCIPLES OF GOOD LISTENING

What are the principles of good listening? Perhaps the best way of getting at these principles is to examine several situations that invite good communication. As you read the following examples, imagine yourself first as the speaker and then as the listener.

1. The day before a final examination, the professor summarizes for his class what he regards as the highlights of the course.

2. A successful writer of mystery stories explains to a group of hopeful writers how to plot a marketable "whodunit."

3. A judge gives final instructions to conscientious jurymen who are about to bring in a verdict in a case where a man's life hinges on their decision.

4. A technician reports to other technicians the phenomenal results of an experiment that has made old methods obsolete and that will determine future procedure.

5. Alert, intelligent parents attend a popular lecture given by a professor who has favorably altered the course of their sons' or daughters' lives.

6. Men in the club car of a train pull their chairs closer as one man says, "I just heard a good one."

7. A builder explains to his carpenters a new construction method he expects to use in several homes under contract.

8. A doctor explains to a cardiac patient the adjustments he must make in order to prolong his years of usefulness.

9. Following a disastrous flood that has stripped the topsoil from miles of farmland, an engineer suggests to the owners methods of restoring fertility and of preventing another flood.

10. In a strike-threatened factory, the manager calls in a respected foreman and asks him to explain and interpret the causes of the workers' grievances as he understands them.

11. A month before an important election, the candidate of a major party speaks for the first time in your home town.

The three principles of good listening implicit in these examples are (1) the more rewarding the outcome promises to be, the higher the quality of the listening will be; (2) listening is best when both speaker and audience have a stake in the communication; and (3) the person who stands to make the greater gain from the communication has the primary responsibility for promoting good listening.

Review the eleven examples with these three principles in mind. Answer the following questions in each case. What opportunities for a useful or pleasurable experience are there? What does the listener stand to gain? What does the speaker stand to gain? Who is likely to have the greater interest? What might the speaker and listeners do to improve communication? The following pages will help you answer the last question.

WHAT CAN THE SPEAKER DO TO
ACHIEVE GOOD LISTENING?

No one is going to listen for long unless he starts out with a good reason for listening, or unless the speaker is skillful enough to provide him with such a reason. This means that the speaker must know his audience and must accommodate his remarks to it. In short, analyzing the audience and adapting to it are the speaker's best approach to good listening.

ANALYZE YOUR AUDIENCE

The same group of people may behave as an entirely different audience from day to day. When the President of the United States delivers his State of the Union message, the public's reaction will depend in part on what the state of the nation really is. Although the same congressmen may be present day after day, their attitudes toward speeches and the quality of their listening will vary with the topic, with domestic and international moods and circumstances, as well as with the speaker's ability. What seems to be the same audience will react quite differently to different subjects and occasions.

Outside your speech class—now and in the years ahead—you will encounter an almost infinite variety of audiences. No two audiences are exactly alike. And the characteristics of the particular audience you happen to be addressing will guide you in adapting your speech to your listeners. Audiences differ in five important characteristics: *composition, information, attitude, participation,* and *homogeneity.*

Composition refers to the membership of your audience. How large is it—one, two, or a hundred people? What age? What sex? What is the educational level, religion, occupation, economic status, political outlook? In any given situation, you will be interested in those factors that appear to affect the receptivity of your listeners. The economic status of your audience, for example, need not even enter into your thinking if you are discussing what we know about the moon. But it would be critically important if you were proposing a hike in corporation income taxes. The political attitudes of your listeners would obviously be important if you were campaigning for public office but would be of little significance if you were describing the plight of our migratory waterfowl.

How much *information* do your listeners have about your subject, about you, and about the occasion? A member of a research team investigating a problem will not report his findings to his colleagues as he would address a group of people who know little or nothing about the subject. A speaker has a major advantage if he knows in advance whether his audience is informed, uninformed, or misinformed about his subject matter.

What is the *attitude* of your audience? How do your listeners regard you as a person? How do they feel toward one another? What interest do they have in what you plan to talk about? And what is their attitude toward your purpose and your stand on this subject? The attitude of your listeners may range from deep respect for you, strong group cohesiveness, keen interest in your subject, and complete acceptance of your ideas, to open hostility, rejection, disinterest, and complete disagreement.

How much opportunity does your audience have for *participation* in the proceedings? Audience participation may be overt or covert, but the audience must participate if there is to be any kind of listening at all. If the physical setting makes it difficult or impossible for your audience to see or hear you, there will be little or no participation—and little or no communication. Most of the remedies for this barrier to communication are within the power of the speaker to control. But audience participation may go well beyond silent responses. It may reveal itself in the form of applause, expressions of disapproval, or questions, replies, and remarks that place a member of the audience at least temporarily in the role of speaker. This kind of overt behavior may seem disruptive at the moment, but it may also lead to a dramatic improvement in the quality of listening.

Is your audience composed of people who are essentially alike or of people who have almost nothing in common? An audience of like composition, information, and attitude and with equal opportunities for participation is known as a *homogeneous* group. Such an audience may or may not be a good audience, but at least its members are likely to respond in a fairly similar way to what you say.

A *mixed* audience presents special problems, however. Should you

United Auto Workers President Walter Reuther. *(Wide World Photos)*

try to appeal to what appears to be the majority? Should you give special attention to a minority? Should you diversify your approach in an attempt to hold the entire group? The answers depend mostly on your purpose and the occasion. But the wise speaker makes some decisions at the outset and sets some goals. Otherwise he will find himself appealing to no one at all.

ADAPT TO THE AUDIENCE

Almost everything you say and do as a speaker can be adapted to your audience—your choice of subject, your purpose, the structure and materials of your speech, your language and style, your manner of speaking, and sometimes even the time and place of your speech. These and many other choices are usually the speaker's. But how can you know what the best choice will be in each case? We know that the best listening takes place when an audience thinks it is going to get something of value out of what is said. The speaker's job, then, is to make the audience want to listen. This is where analysis of the audience comes into play. The better you know your audience and the circumstances under which you are going to talk to them, the easier it is to command their interest and attention. The basic purpose of audience adaptation is to develop motivated listening. There are, of course, other obvious accommodations—speaking loud enough to be heard, using language that can be understood, providing necessary information, and so forth—but the subtlety of achieving audience adaptation consists in making an audience feel that it has an important stake in the proceedings.

We all act in response to needs, wants, desires, drives, or urges. And we listen in response to the same basic motivations, because listening is a kind of action. True, we respond to different motives in different situations, and certain motives operate more strongly in some of us than in others. That is why knowing your listeners helps you to enlist their interest. But a working knowledge of the more basic motives that affect human behavior—listening included—is part of the equipment of every effective speaker.

Other things being equal, audiences are more likely to listen if their *security, status, ambitions, affections,* and *pleasures* are related or appear to be related to the speaker's purpose.

Security

Some of the most powerful motives are those that spring from our desire to preserve and perpetuate ourselves. These involve both physical and psychic security—health, comfort, and freedom from danger, care, and fear. Most people identify their happiness and well-being with security. Anything that threatens their security is a matter of concern, and anything that promises them greater security is a matter of interest. By capitalizing on these concerns and interests, effective speakers command the attention of their listeners.

Status

Many of our real and fancied needs spring from our desire for social approval. What others think of us is often more important to us than we care to admit. We strive for a reputation that will give us satisfaction, compete with others for social recognition, and conform to custom in order not to lose caste. Even the nonconformist is lonesome if his aberrant behavior goes unnoticed. Many of the beliefs we profess and many of the things we want have their greatest value to us as status symbols. A pat on the back, an approving comment, or any token of recognition sincerely given will help you enlist the interest of the people to whom you speak.

Ambitions

Most people have goals, objectives, and values that they seek as a means to self-realization and personal growth. These goals represent what we want to be and what we want to accomplish with our lives. They may be low and crass, but they may also be high and worthy. The desire to realize one's potentialities, to make something out of oneself, continues to be a strong drive in our culture. Our hopes, dreams, and ambitions may be dulled by cynicism or frustration, but the skillful speaker can energize them into powerful motives for listening.

Affections

Strong emotional attachments control our behavior in many situations. We develop these emotional bonds with people, institutions, traditions, ideals, and even with some of our material possessions.

These affections explain many of our loyalties and many of our defensive and protective attitudes. They are usually rooted in long associations, familiar conditions and circumstances, and often are surrounded by nostalgic memories. Whenever the speaker's message impinges on the strong affective ties of his listeners, he will soon discover that he has to work with these ties or work around them. Our affections seldom yield to a frontal attack.

Pleasure

The desire for pleasure—relaxation, release, escape—is a primary reason for listening in many situations. We often listen to be entertained, and we are held by speakers whose recommendations give promise of pleasurable rewards.

You have probably noticed that motives never exist in pure form but are always modified and affected by countless influences. Most of the things you want for yourself are things that you also want for others—for your family, your friends, your church, your school, or your town, state, or country. These group-centered motives are often even stronger than self-centered motives. A father will risk his life to save his child, people will make sacrifices to build a new church or synagogue, and fanatical loyalties grow up around group symbols.

To add to the complication, motives are usually *mixed*—compounded of several of the motivations we have discussed. And these mixed motives often contain competing elements that pull in different directions. The expression "I have mixed feelings about that" is usually an indication that conflicting motives are at work.

In many cases, the motives for listening are already present in your audience. Your job is to recognize the interests at work and to make the most of them. If these interests do not exist, your job is to discover the motives that can best be enlisted in your cause and to involve them in the development of your subject. In either case, you face a task that must be handled subtly and adroitly. Any obvious or overly contrived attempt to capitalize on the motives of your listeners is likely to alienate them rather than win favorable attention.

Ask yourself this question: Why should this audience want to listen to me discuss this subject? If there is no good answer, you had better look for another audience or another subject. If you find the answer, you have found the motives that will serve you best.

Always remember, though, that adapting your speech to your listeners is not the same as capitulating to them. The customer is *not* always right, and you may need to tell him so point-blank at times. A speaker who sacrifices his integrity for the sake of expediency betrays both himself and his listeners.

WHAT CAN THE AUDIENCE DO TO ACHIEVE GOOD LISTENING?

The final decision on all listening is necessarily made by the listener. We can resist the best efforts of any speaker if we choose to do so. We face two questions as potential listeners: *When* should we listen? And what are the *best ways* to listen if we decide to listen at all?

WHEN SHOULD YOU LISTEN?

Almost every waking minute of every day someone is demanding that you listen to him. You should, and usually will, give your attention to the speakers who seem to have the most to offer. Apart from observing common courtesies, you are under no obligation to listen to every speaker in search of an audience. Choose wisely, for much of the wisdom and pleasure of life is transmitted through the spoken word. And remember that in many cases good listening is much more important to you than it is to the speaker. You may have more to gain than he has.

You will be exposed to many speeches in your course in speech. You will be the listener today and the speaker tomorrow. If you want the attention of your classmates when you speak, they have a right to expect the same of you. Not all good speakers are good listeners and not all good listeners are good speakers. Use your speech class as a means of improving both your speaking and listening skills.

HOW SHOULD YOU LISTEN?

There are two answers to this question. First, listen in ways that will encourage the speaker to give you his best. Second, listen in ways that will enable you to profit by the best the speaker gives you. Both efforts contribute to the same result—the best communication possible, no matter how effective or ineffective the speaker may be.

An attentive audience is an incentive to any speaker. Under most circumstances, if a speaker is worth listening to at all, it will pay you to give him a fair hearing. This does not mean that you have to make serious compromises with your own values and convictions; nor does it mean that you have to put up with incompetence. If and when your best listening efforts fail to bring rewards, then is the time to direct your attention elsewhere.

In listening to a speaker for the first time, try to gauge him as a person and assess his ideas carefully. Guard against being deceived by a superficially attractive manner, but keep in mind the possibility that a speaker whose manner does not immediately appeal to you may have valuable counsel.

Critical listening also demands skill in analysis—the ability to perceive a speaker's purpose, his main points, and how he develops them. Here is the first test of critical listening: Do you know *what* has been said? Then ask yourself this question: Does it *make sense?* This second test involves judgment, interpretation, and evaluation. Whatever leads to proficiency in speaking also develops competency in listening. If you know what makes good speech, you will be a far more intelligent consumer of speech.

Listening to speech is much like reading a book or article. The principal difference is in the immediacy of the spoken word. Unless speech is recorded, you have to get it here and now or it may be gone forever. You can put a book aside and come back to it at your leisure. As a reader you have an opportunity to study and ponder a matter and return to the writer's words for further reference. The speaker's message must be received and, very often, interpreted and reacted to without benefit of long reflection. A good speaker accommodates his remarks to these exigencies of oral communication, but opportunities for misunderstanding, misinterpretation, and even exploitation are undeniably present. Their presence imposes a responsibility on the audience to listen carefully and sometimes even cautiously. The next chapter analyzes a few of the stratagems that overzealous speakers may use with unwary listeners.

POINTS TO KEEP IN MIND

1. The best listening is *voluntary, purposeful, motivated, critical,* and *cooperative.*

2. The best listening is achieved when (a) the speech promises a rewarding outcome, (b) both speaker and listener have a stake in the communication, and (c) the person who stands to make the greater gain assumes active responsibility for good listening.

3. The speaker can help to achieve good listening by analyzing his audience and adapting to it in ways that motivate listening.

4. The listener can promote good communication by giving the speaker thoughtful attention.

EXERCISES

1. Plan a group discussion on a question that has evoked great public interest: a trial, a strike, a prison riot, a crime, a legislative proposal. Find out all you can about the event beforehand. But in the discussion concentrate on the *people* who are involved in it. Try to see through their eyes what happened. Try to find out all you can about the backgrounds and conditions that motivated them. Your purpose here is not to evaluate their motives but to understand them.

2. Bring to class two or three "human interest" news-items—stories about people who caught the public eye for a moment because they did something unusually kind, amusing, stupid, or bizarre. Tell or read the stories and analyze *why* the behavior of these people attracted attention. Can you find any clues to the motives that led the people to act as they did?

3. Select two speeches directed to a nationwide audience by a public official. Have all members of the class analyze them. What did the speaker try to accomplish? What motives did he appeal to? Did he appeal to them directly or obliquely? Did he choose the right appeals for his purpose? Organize a class discussion based on the analyses.

4. Prepare a five-minute speech explaining a complicated process. Try to teach the class to master the process. When you finish, question the audience to see how well they grasp what you have said.

5. Think of an audience that you know well. Prepare a speech for this audience that will impose heavy demands on you if you are to capture its interest and win it over to your point of view. Deliver your talk to the class; but before you speak, ask the class members to "become" the audience you have in mind. Describe your hypothetical listeners in detail. Let members of the class ask you further questions so that they will have a clear idea of the audience you are aiming at. After you have given your talk, have the class members discuss how well they think you have succeeded.

thirteen

Critical
Listening

Speech is a bilateral or multilateral process in which both speakers and listeners participate. A speaker one moment, you become a listener the next. As a broad framework, the principles of good speech are guides to listening just as they are to speaking.

Our special purpose in this chapter is to issue a few warnings against speakers who misapply or ignore the principles of good speech in ways that lead to distortion and deception. If speech is to achieve its highest social purposes, it is imperative that listeners hold speakers responsible for what they say. And the more vital the subject is to our personal and collective well-being, the more important it is that we listen critically.

Here are some of the more common fallacies, stratagems, and obstacles to communication that may mislead listeners. The sensible listener will remember the marketplace warning *caveat emptor* (let the buyer beware) when he is invited to accept another man's ideas.

PERSON AND MANNER

We all know that the person and manner of the speaker affect our acceptance of his ideas. Although ideas should be able to stand on their own two feet, the means for assessing these ideas are not always immediately available, and we necessarily rely on our impression of the competence and honesty of the speaker.

Pretensions

The best credentials a speaker can submit to his listeners are those he reveals by competent treatment of his subject. A speaker who finds it necessary to resort to adventitious claims in his own behalf is at least suspect. It is notorious that persons introducing speakers to an audience will often embarrass everyone, including the speaker, with exaggerated accounts of the speaker's achievements. Few speakers are tactless enough to parade their own credentials blatantly, but many resort to devices designed to build their reputation. Listeners should be aware of these devices and wary of speakers who abuse them.

Most of us have encountered the *name-dropper*. He sprinkles his speech with apparently casual references to famous people—authors, artists, executives, politicians, and the like—in an attempt to suggest familiarity with these people and thereby enhance his own prestige. The names dropped may be familiar to the audience: "The last time I talked with the President . . . ," "The boss dropped in to get my advice on . . . ;" or the names may be completely unfamiliar to the audience (and not much more familiar to the speaker). But who wants to admit he does not know the world-renowned Mr. X or Madame Y or the Right Reverend Mr. Z?

Technical or pseudotechnical jargon may be applied to impress, to confound, or to cover up one's own inadequacies. Some discussions demand a specialized vocabulary; even so, the speaker should make every effort to make himself clear. If you suspect that the speaker's "professional" vocabulary is impeding communication unnecessarily, you may wish to withdraw your attention or to force him to make himself understood.

Nothing is more disarming to the pretentious speaker than utter frankness and honesty on the part of the listener. You may say very frankly that you never heard of Mr. X, that you haven't the slightest idea what the speaker is talking about, or that you have a few questions for him. If you have misjudged the speaker's pretensions, he will set you right in a hurry. If your suspicion was well founded, communication may be considerably improved.

Simulation

We place confidence in speakers whose personal qualifications we respect. A speaker may pretend to be something he is not, to win favor with the audience. If the suggestions in Chapter 4 for improving the speaker's relations with his listeners are misapplied, one of two things is likely to happen: If the speaker succeeds in passing himself off as someone to be trusted and respected, his listeners may be seriously misled; if he fails, he is discredited as a person, and the cause he is pleading suffers, sometimes undeservedly.

What protection do you have against imposters? Fortunately, bad currency has a false ring. Even the cleverest actor usually gives himself away. It is hard for a speaker to feign intellectual, emotional, moral, and social qualities. Critical listeners—who must have considerable sophistication in human relations—are an imposter's severest enemies. A speech course affords experience for both speakers and listeners; both learn that their stake in communication is shared and their efforts are reciprocal.

Contrived motivation

If a speaker praises his listeners, they may impute to him insight, sympathy, and understanding that may not exist. It is heartwarming to find someone who appreciates us and who appears to see in us what we would like to be, but it pays to be objective in assessing flattery. A speaker has every right to present his cause in terms of the wants, desires, and needs of his listeners as he preceives them, but this kind of motivation is dangerously contrived when the listener is regarded as a potential victim to be taken in by exploitation of his personal weaknesses and vanities.

Ask yourself these questions as a listener: What is the speaker's motivation? Does he stand to gain more than I do? Does the praise he accords me have anything to do with the decision he is asking me to make? Has he made a sound case for his proposal, quite apart from any personal involvements I may have in the matter?

DIVERSION AND DISTRACTION

In decorating a room when you suffer from limited resources, it is a common practice to place the most worthy furnishing or *objet d'art* where it will attract attention to itself and accord relative inconspicuousness to more vulnerable objects. Speakers are not above this kind of arrangement in presenting their ideas.

Slanting

A slanted speech mingles truths, half-truths, and falsehoods in a subtle mosaic that attempts to pass for the whole truth and nothing but the truth. All of the techniques of slanting may be reduced to *selection* and *arrangement*. The speaker goes as far as he thinks he can in selecting just those materials that appear to support his position, and adroitly sidesteps damaging facts and interpretations. He then arranges these materials in ways that emphasize his strengths and conceal his weaknesses. The careless or gullible listener is thus diverted from objective analysis.

Slanted discourse results from censorship exercised by the speaker to achieve specious plausibility. The unwary listener is led astray by errors of omission and commission infiltrated into a speech that seems honest and authentic. Truth and falsehood seldom come in wholly separate packages. A completely false report is much easier to spot than one that stretches the truth, tells only part of the story, or glosses over sticky facts. The listener who wants to believe, who is predisposed toward the speaker, is especially vulnerable to this kind of concealment.

Extension

Setting up straw men and knocking them down is the essence of diversion by extension. Vulnerable statements may be cleverly substituted for defensible or relatively defensible statements to which they bear some resemblance, in an attempt to shift the discussion to the speaker's advantage. Who has not had the experience of taking a reasonable position only to have it seriously misrepresented and then attacked in its distorted form?

There are variations of diversion by extension. The strategy may be used against a speaker by an opponent who deliberately misinterprets his views; or it may be used positively by a speaker who substitutes a more defensible position for the relatively weak motion he is trying to win approval for. The subtlety of the technique lies in a superficial resemblance among statements that may range from sense to nonsense. Thus, a man who does not like cats because

Evangelist Billy Graham speaks in Wall Street. *(Wide World Photos)*

he is allergic to them may find himself attacked as an animal hater who in all probability is unkind to his children. Or an advocate of some modest social reform of limited usefulness may lay claim to the larger values of more substantial action that he surreptitiously identifies with his own proposal.

The obvious remedy in all such cases is to identify the proposition under discussion and insist as best you can that the speaker stay with it.

Side issues and irrelevancies

This kind of diversion is caused by unsound analysis, intentional or otherwise. The speaker concentrates on some minor point and presses the matter in an attempt to sidetrack the discussion. The result may be a victory on the side issue with the appearance of victory on the real issues. In any case, the vital points on which the question should be settled are obscured and may go unchallenged. Any resolution so determined can hardly be expected to yield good results.

MANIPULATION

All of the stratagems of diversion discussed above attempt to draw attention away from the real issues. It often happens, however, that a speaker will stay with the issues but argue in ways that obstruct sound reasoning. We call these tactics *manipulation.*

Black-and-white reasoning

The most pervasive of the manipulative stratagems arises from failure to understand that most of the phenomena we talk about are variable and difficult to classify without making arbitrary distinctions. Scientists can sometimes devise rigid categories for the things they wish to describe. But in ordinary conversation, whatever we wish to describe probably falls into a *continuum* or group of things that share a fundamental characteristic yet differ in degree from one another. A continuum exists between black and white; if an object is gray, are we justified in classifying it as black or white? Black-and-white reasoning attempts to categorize things in just that way, and may achieve specious plausibility by using classifications and definitions that ignore degrees of difference.

The essential fallacy involved in black-and-white reasoning is *hasty generalization*, imputing to all members of a given species, class, or category what may be true of only some or even of most members, or what may be true of all but only to a certain degree. Discussion of racial distinctions among mankind is frequently hampered by hasty generalization that results in black-and white thinking. What generalizations can we safely and honestly make about any group without doing an injustice to individuals? Yet, when action is required and policies must be determined, some distinctions must be made. Any speaker may find himself in a dilemma: If he offers no hard and fast definitions and classifications, he may be charged with confused thinking; if he does attempt to make distinctions for purposes of clarity and precision, he may be accused of dogmatism.

What we might call the *gray thinker* can be just as perverse as his black-and-white comrade. This man decries any attempt at classification and orderly arrangement and complains about generalizations of any kind no matter how carefully qualified.

Both the black-and-white speaker and the gray speaker are guilty of manipulation when they deploy their reasoning to gain strategic advantage by promoting a cause of their own or defeating a motion proposed by someone else.

The mean between two extremes

This variety of manipulation attempts to exploit a preference most of us have for moderation. A speaker may show that his position occupies mid-ground between two extremes—not too cautious or conservative and not too radical, daring, or different—to suggest that his proposal is moderate and reasonable.

There is nothing wrong in claiming moderation as one of the virtues of a proposal, but such a claim is *not* established by merely suggesting that the recommendation in question is neatly in the middle of two more extreme positions. The fact of the matter is that any conceivable proposal can be presented as a mean between two extremes by simply constructing the so-called extremes. An expenditure of a thousand dollars is comfortably in the middle between the extravagance of fifteen hundred dollars and the penuriousness of five hundred, but this fact in and of itself proves nothing. If this means moderation, then any amount can be shown to be moderate by resort to the same expedient.

A careful listener will insist that any proposition be argued on its own merits. If moderation is claimed, then it should be established by a reasoned analysis of the problem in relation to the available means of dealing with it.

The logical next step

If a man were to build a house and stop short of putting a roof on it, it could be argued with considerable cogency that a roof of some kind would be the logical next step. In any given situation, there are almost always further steps that might and perhaps should be taken. This line of argument carried to its logical conclusion, however, would mean that we are always committed to future action by the very fact that certain steps have already been taken. You buy a new car and then you are pressed to buy innumerable extra gadgets with the argument that since you have spent three thousand dollars already you might as well throw in another five hundred to make the car presentable.

You may already have recognized that we often use this "logical next step" thinking to rationalize our own desires. It is not at all surprising, therefore, that speakers try to exploit this weakness by encouraging us to take steps to which we are in no way committed, by the simple stratagem of suggesting that these additional steps merely complement action already taken.

Any action may or may not be a logical next step. A careful listener will insist that these further commitments be argued on their own merits. And it is sometimes worth considering that a so-called logical next step may mean putting good money after bad. If you have made a mistake, certainly nothing is gained by taking steps that compound it.

POINTS TO KEEP IN MIND

1. Listeners may be led astray by:
   a) Stratagems that involve the person and manner of the speaker.
   b) Diversionary tactics.
   c) Deceptive devices that are made to pass for sound reasoning.
2. Defense against these tactics requires:
   a) The full exercise of your critical capacities in listening.
   b) Knowledge of the ways in which these common tactics are employed.

3. Supplement this list of special devices by drawing upon other chapters in this book; e.g., "The Personal Equation in Speech," "The Content of Speech," and "Language and Style."

EXERCISES

1. Discuss in class the following questions about acting (playing a role in a drama) and speechmaking.

    a) What are important differences between acting and speaking to an audience?

    b) Do you think that training in acting is helpful or harmful to a public speaker? Why?

    c) Is role playing ever proper and useful in public speaking? What are the advantages and disadvantages?

2. Discuss in class the following questions about definition.

    a) Is it ever possible to define a term or a concept so that the definition admits no exceptions? Give examples.

    b) Can you distinguish: *work* and *play; sane* and *insane; black* and *white; friends* and *enemies; kind* and *unkind; like* and *dislike; now* and *later; old* and *new; good* and *bad?*

    c) What is meant by a *continuum?* How does this concept enter into definition and classification?

3. Bring to class two or three examples of *slanted reporting.* Examine the news columns of newspapers for these examples. Be prepared to demonstrate that the reporting you select is slanted and to show how this slanting was accomplished. Consider these questions in relation to your examples: Can a reporter ever achieve complete objectivity in reporting? How objective should a report be?

4. Try your hand at slanted writing by producing two or three paragraphs on some controversial issue. Then rewrite these paragraphs to avoid slanting. Compare the two compositions.

5. Test your understanding of the stratagems discussed in this chapter by preparing and presenting a short speech on a controversial subject about which you feel deeply. Take a stand and make strong recommendations; so far as possible get into areas where you might expect to encounter these stratagems, but do *not* employ them.

Listen to these speeches carefully and critically. Discuss both delivery and composition.

6. You can have fun with this exercise: Prepare and present a speech that employs as many of the stratagems discussed in this chapter as possible; don't be too obvious; use them subtly. Then give members of the class a chance to test their listening by exposing and identifying the stratagems.

fourteen

Voice and Diction

A good speaking voice is expressive, well projected, and pleasant. Expressiveness calls for vocal flexibility to convey meaning and register feeling. Projection is achieved through control of force and enunciation. A pleasant voice has a warm, sympathetic quality; it is unobtrusive, effortless, and free from disagreeable qualities. Good articulation shapes voice into clear and recognizable sounds; good pronunciation complies with prevailing standards. These aspects of your vocal process merit analysis.

WHY YOU SPEAK AS YOU DO

The way you speak is largely determined by organic, environmental, and personality influences.

ORGANIC FACTORS

If you are healthy and robust, you are more likely to have a strong, vibrant voice than if you are frail and weak. A small larynx with short vocal cords produces a higher-pitched voice than a large larynx with long vocal cords. A cleft palate or poorly aligned teeth may cause a lisp. Chronic hoarseness is frequently caused by malformation of the larynx. Adenoids impair nasal resonance. A hearing deficiency may result in blurred speech or vocal monotony.

If your trouble springs from organic problems, arrange for a medical examination before you undertake voice training.

ENVIRONMENTAL FACTORS

A child's environment furnishes models for his own speech. By trial and error, he perfects the form of speech that meets with surest acceptance. We talk very much like the people with whom we communicated while our speech habits were being formed.

Geographic environment influences the rate of our speech, tonal patterns, our articulation and pronunciation. Even an untrained ear can detect differences between speech that is indigenous to the Deep South and speech that is indigenous to parts of New England. Skilled linguists can detect dialectal differences within relatively small geographical areas.

Home and community environment may affect our speech for good or bad. A child who is reared in a discordant home may speak in a voice that reflects tension. A child surrounded by people who speak English with a foreign accent may learn to speak English with the same accent.

Speech patterns determined by environment are learned and therefore can be unlearned. New and more desirable habits can be substituted through directed exercises.

PERSONALITY FACTORS

Your voice is a mirror of your personality. A person who talks loudly and with exaggerated heartiness or who gushes over trivialities is probably insecure in his relations with others, is overcompensating for his timidity, and is overanxious to please. We recognize a whining, complaining voice as belonging to a person who feels mistreated, abused, and discriminated against. And we can spot the flat, impersonal tone and the monotonous lack of inflection of the inhibited person who tries to shield himself from the intrusion of outsiders.

If you recognize that your voice lacks confidence, warmth, vibrancy, or expressiveness because of poor personal adjustment, you have taken the first step toward improvement. Your speech course offers a favorable environment for re-evaluation of yourself and redirection of your vocal habits.

EFFECTIVE USE OF THE VOICE

The source of energy for the voice is the breath stream, which sets into vibration the vocal folds (also called cords or bands) that are housed in the larynx. Since speech occurs as the breath is exhaled, exhalation needs to be controlled, steady, and adequate. Inhalation needs to be quick enough not to interrupt continuity, silent, and accomplished without tension in the neck and throat. The vocal folds, then, are the vibrator. Vibrations are built up or resonated principally by the pharynx, mouth, and nasal cavities—all located above the larynx.

With this equipment we produce sounds of varying degrees of loudness, at different pitches, with distinctive qualities, and of varying durations. Breathing (the source of energy) is particularly important in loudness and duration; phonation (the vibration of the vocal bands) is the most important factor in pitch and a determining factor in vocal quality; and the resonators are of great importance in bringing out qualities of tone.

The human voice, like other sounds, has four physical characteristics—force, pitch, quality, and time. Properly controlled, these four elements contribute to effective use of the voice.

FORCE

Talk loudly enough to be heard easily and quietly enough to be heard without annoyance. With attention and practice you can bring force under control. If people do not hear you, it may be that you need, not just more volume, but finer control.

Varying the force of your voice to convey meaning and feeling is a much more subtle matter. Stress—making a word, sentence, or point "stand out"—is an important part of it. Added loudness serves to underline what you say; so does reduced loudness. Any notable departure from your normal level of loudness serves to draw attention. This means that you can use variations in loudness to mark anything that you want to emphasize. Such variations also help to reduce monotony in speaking.

PITCH

Is your habitual pitch level the best pitch level for you? In what ways can you use variations in pitch sensitively and meaningfully?

Each person uses one pitch level more frequently than any other. This is the level on which he most often begins speaking and to which he returns after shifting up or down the scale. It is his *habitual* pitch level.

For each voice there is one pitch level or a small band of pitch levels at which the voice operates most easily and most effectively. This is called the *optimum* pitch level. To achieve best results, try

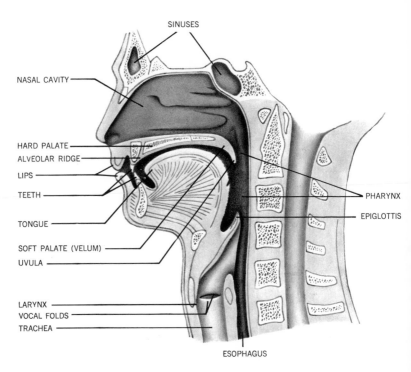

SINUSES

NASAL CAVITY

HARD PALATE

ALVEOLAR RIDGE

LIPS

TEETH

TONGUE

SOFT PALATE (VELUM)

UVULA

LARYNX

VOCAL FOLDS

TRACHEA

PHARYNX

EPIGLOTTIS

ESOPHAGUS

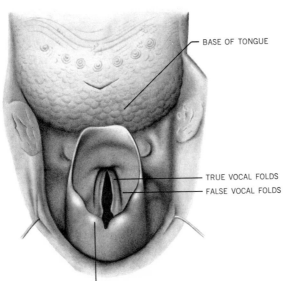

BASE OF TONGUE

TRUE VOCAL FOLDS

FALSE VOCAL FOLDS

CORNICULATE TUBERCLE
(ARYTENOID CARTILAGE BENEATH)

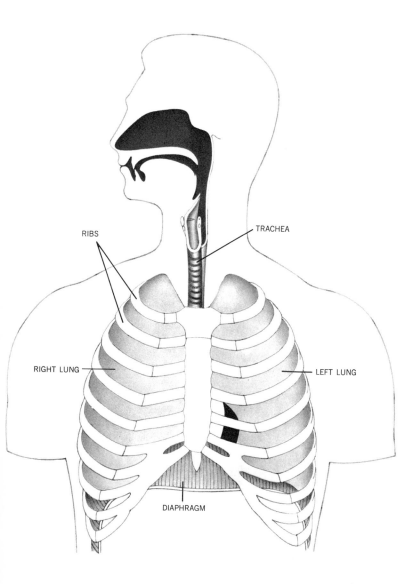

RIBS

TRACHEA

RIGHT LUNG

LEFT LUNG

DIAPHRAGM

Above: The respiratory mechanism. On facing page: (top) Sagittal section of the head and neck. (bottom) Superior view of the vocal folds. *(Drawings by Lorelle Raboni)* to make your habitual pitch level the same as your optimum pitch level.

Many people begin speech training with a notion that they would like to "lower their voices," because they admire low-pitched voices. Whether this is a realistic purpose depends on the capacity of a particular person's vocal mechanism. If you owned a fine violin, people would think you foolish if you tried to make it sound like a cello. The two instruments operate in the same fashion, just as two voices do. But the cello has larger and longer strings and a larger and differently shaped resonating cavity. The violin's most beautiful tones are considerably higher than the best tones of the cello. A young man who attempts to force his pitch down to the level used by a public speaker or actor whom he admires may be sacrificing tonal beauty in the process. Even though his father's voice is a bass-baritone, his may be a tenor. On the other hand, some people continue to talk at a childish or early-adolescent pitch level long after their matured vocal mechanism has become suited to a lower pitch.

Listen to yourself and see if you detect a harsh, gravelly quality, especially when your voice moves down the scale (as at the ends of sentences). If you do, it may mean that you are forcing the pitch of your voice uncomfortably low. On the other hand, do your high pitch levels (as when you accent a word) sound thin, sharp, or strained? If so, your habitual pitch level may be too high.

An expressive voice moves up and down the musical scale continuously in an infinite variety of patterns. This variation in pitch, which we call *melody*, is one of the most important factors in conveying emotions and meanings. Consider this sentence: "You are not going out of the house today." Say it with a continuous downward inflection, and it has the authority and finality of an order. Use a rising inflection, and it becomes a simple question. Leap to a high pitch on the word *not*, and it takes on a threatening tone. Use a gliding inflection upward and then downward on the word *you*, and it becomes contemptuous. For greatest effectiveness, melody should be combined with variations in force and rate, but melody itself permits more subtlety of expression than does either force or rate.

Monotony in melody is of several types. The true *monotone*, who literally does not vary from a single pitch level, is comparatively rare. A more common offender is the speaker who shifts back and forth among three or four notes in a repeated pitch pattern that is quite unrelated to the meaning of what he is saying. Such a pattern seems colorless and dull. The person who ends every sentence on a rising inflection seems indecisive and lacking in self-confidence. A speaker who repeatedly uses heavy downward inflections seems dogmatic and aggressive. True melody demands the use of changes in pitch to supplement and emphasize the intellectual and emotional content of speech.

QUALITY

Vocal quality is the most sensitive indicator of emotion in speaking, and it is the least subject to direct control by the speaker. The *quality* of a sound is determined by the relations between the overtones and the fundamental tone (the basic pitch).[1] These relations are determined by the vibrating mechanism and the resonators. The muscles involved in voice production respond to the emotion of the speaker. This response is almost involuntary—it is largely beyond the speaker's control, except as he is able to control his emotions.

It is very hard to disguise or simulate emotion, because vocal quality always gives clues to one's real feelings. A mechanical approach to varying vocal quality produces artificial effects. Sincerity of emotional expression stems from sincere involvement in the emotion itself.

TIME

We have all heard speakers who rattled along at a rate far too fast to be understood, and others who spoke so slowly you could almost take a nap between words and phrases. These extremes are both undesirable, and yet there is no one ideal rate of speaking. What is good for one speaker in one environment, in one situation, for one subject, will not necessarily be good if one of these factors is altered. How, then, can you find a good rate of speaking?

The speaker's temperament and personality

The speaking rate of a slow-moving person will naturally vary from that of an excitable, high-strung person. Follow your individual

---

[1] Do not confuse *pitch* and *quality*. Sound the identical pitch on the piano and the violin and note the differences in the sound. These are differences in *quality*.

pattern, so long as it does not hamper intelligibility, annoy your listeners, or seem inappropriate to what you are saying.

The speaker's environment

As we have seen, speech habits (including our rate of speaking), are formed on the basis of models provided for us early in life. In some sections of the United States, people speak more rapidly than in other sections. Your speaking rate should be largely determined by what your listeners are used to.

The situation

Use a slower rate in addressing a large audience than in intimate conversation.

The content of the speech

Complex ideas, statistics, or problems that the audience has not previously considered take longer to grasp than more simple or more familiar statements. In expressing some emotions, such as joy and excitement, we usually speak more rapidly than when we are expressing grief or reverence.

Duration is the time spent in pronouncing a single word or phrase. *Pause* is the space of silence between words or phrases. The two combine to determine the over-all rate of speech.

Pauses are the punctuation marks in speech. Use them:

1. To separate ideas and to set them apart as units of thought. "He rose awkwardly, / looked about furtively, / cleared his throat, / shifted his weight once or twice, / and finally began to speak."

2. To point up an important idea that you are about to express. "The most dangerous force operating today to undermine our political structure is / apathy of the electorate."

3. To give yourself time to organize your thoughts. But don't use too many pauses for this purpose, or prolong them excessively. Be especially careful to avoid the vocalized pause "er."

Pauses provide a natural opportunity to inhale. If you find yourself interrupting phrases by gasping for breath, practice deeper breathing and give more attention to spacing your inhalations so that they come at logical stopping places. If you talk on and on without pausing for breath, your audience will wonder whether you will make it to the end. Practice phrasing your thoughts to allow for more frequent pauses, and avoid trying to talk on the last molecule of air you can squeeze from your lungs.

ARTICULATION

Articulation means the adjustments and movements of the organs involved in producing speech sounds and in joining these sounds to form words and phrases. As we use it here, the term has about the same meaning as *enunciation.*

The sounds of spoken English include vowels, diphthongs, and consonants. Four actions are essential in producing *vowel sounds:* The vocal folds vibrate, producing voice; the opening into the nasal passage is closed or reduced; the tip of the tongue is held down behind the lower front teeth; and the mouth is opened to permit the sound to come out. How widely you open your mouth varies with different vowels, as do the shape of the lips and the position of the tongue.

A *diphthong* is a continuous blending of two vowel sounds to form one syllable. For example, say these two sounds rapidly, one after the other: the *ah* in *father* and the *oo* in *hoot.* The resulting sound is the diphthong *ow* in *cow.*

Consonant sounds are formed by interrupting or restricting the breath stream. For example, say the word *up.* Notice that you produce the consonant *p* by closing your lips and stopping the breath stream. Then say the word *his.* Here the consonant *s* is produced by forcing air through a narrow aperture formed by tongue and teeth.

ARTICULATING VOWELS AND DIPHTHONGS

Whether your voice is pleasant may be determined by the way you produce vowels and diphthongs. Let your ear be your guide. Try for clear, mellow, resonant intonation. Avoid harsh, guttural, strident tones.

If you are careless about producing vowels and diphthongs, you will also impair intelligibility. Poor production of these sounds will cause listeners to confuse your words and thus mistake your meaning. If you say *tar* when you mean *tower,* you can hardly expect your listeners to know what you are talking about.

ARTICULATING CONSONANTS

The consonants are most important in giving distinctness and clarity to speech. Poor enunciation results largely from a failure to produce consonants with precision. Improvement depends upon finer control over the action of tongue and lips in relation to the gum ridge and teeth. If this contact is not sharply made, the sound produced by releasing the contact is weak. Poor enunciation can usually be improved by more active, precise formulation of consonant sounds.

ASSIMILATION OF SOUNDS

We seldom give speech sounds their full value as we talk. This is all right so long as we do not seriously impair our vocal quality and so long as we identify sounds clearly enough for listeners to understand us. Stilted speech that results from loving attention to each individual sound is either an affectation or a bad habit.

Speech sounds are affected by their neighbors. Omissions and glides and carry-overs from one sound to another are inevitable in free-flowing, easy speech. This sort of natural adjustment is called *assimilation*. Say this sentence: "Pat takes science." Notice that one *t* serves for both *Pat* and *takes,* and one *s* for both *takes* and *science*. More assimilation is admissible, of course, in conversation and informal speech than on occasions where considerable volume is required.

PRONUNCIATION

Good pronunciation depends on the speech sounds you choose in saying a word and the syllable or syllables you choose to accent in a word. Suppose you use the same vowel sound in *pour* and *poor,* or in *but* and *full;* or suppose you use the final consonant sound of *rage* in *garage,* or the initial consonant sound of *chill* in *charade,* or say *bus* exactly like *buzz;* or suppose you accent the wrong syllable in *pretense, cigarette, infamous.* These are examples of errors in pronunciation. They are failures to conform to good usage in sound or accent, and they may occur even though your articulation is perfect.

STANDARD PRONUNCIATION

If you have traveled through the United States, you were probably impressed by the variety of pronunciation patterns you heard. Even within a single large city, varying patterns of pronunciation are noticeable. Pronunciations in the various sections of the United States, and at different social levels within any one section, differ in many particulars.

The greatest uniformity in pronunciation occurs among educated speakers. Less uniformity exists at lower cultural levels. When a given pronunciation becomes the predominant usage of educated speakers over a large area, it is accepted as a *standard* pronunciation. A pronunciation that is limited to less-educated speakers or to a very small area is termed *substandard.*

DIALECTS OF THE UNITED STATES

By far the largest number of words in English have one "correct" pronunciation—i.e., one pronunciation that all cultivated speakers of English prefer. There are, however, certain groups of words that are pronounced with a slight difference in various large geographical areas.

A *dialect* is any pattern of pronunciation that is commonly used in one geographical area, but that differs somewhat from the usage of other areas.

A *provincial dialect* is a pattern of pronunciation that is limited to a narrow geographical region and that is not accepted by good speakers over a large area.

A *standard dialect* is a pattern of pronunciation that is used by most good speakers in a large geographical area, but that differs somewhat from the predominant good speech of another large area.

In the United States there are *three standard dialects:* (1) *Standard Eastern,* which is used in eastern New England and in New York City; (2) *Standard Southern,* which is used in the states that roughly made up the Confederacy; and (3) *Standard General American,* which is used in the rest of the United States.

The General American dialect is spreading in usage, because it is the most common form of pronunciation in radio, television, and movies. The Eastern dialect most closely resembles standard British pronunciation, which is the model for stage diction.

Each of the three major dialects has a beauty of its own, and none is superior to another. All are standard and entirely correct. The criterion of good pronunciation is what is preferred by the majority of educated, careful speakers in a large geographical area. The best choice for an individual is the best speech of his own area.

USE OF THE DICTIONARY

You can improve your pronunciation if you get in the habit of using a good dictionary. Referring to a dictionary is futile, though, unless you know how to interpret what you find there.

Many people think that a dictionary's function is to *prescribe* pronunciation. But if you read the preface of several dictionaries, you will discover that the editors have attempted rather to *describe* the pronunciation used by most good speakers.

Other people think that when a dictionary lists more than one pronunciation for a word, the first is the "preferred" pronunciation. Actually, when several pronunciations of a word are used by large numbers of good speakers, the dictionary lists all of them. The order of listing is simply an attempt to indicate their relative popularity. It does not mean that any one pronunciation is superior to the others.

But how can you decide which pronunciation is "preferred"? When you have pronounced the word in each of the ways listed, choose the one that sounds most familiar to you. That pronunciation is likely to be the one most frequently used by good speakers in your dialect area. It is, therefore, the preferred pronunciation for your dialect.

In using a dictionary to improve your pronunciation, be sure you understand the symbols it uses. Mispronunciation of the key words cited by the dictionary to identify sounds will result in mispronunciation of the words you are checking. It will do you no good to know that the *a* in *any* is pronounced like the *e* in *end* if you pronounce *end* as *ind* (a substandard pronunciation common in some areas). Although the key-word system of indicating pronunciation is always open to this misunderstanding, an awareness of the problem and care in identifying the pronunciation of the key words will help you to avoid most mistakes.

SUGGESTIONS FOR SELF-IMPROVEMENT

1. Find out how others react to your speech

Ask for frank opinions. What is good and what is bad? Do you project your voice? Is your vocal quality pleasant, jarring, or distracting? Do you speak distinctly? Is your pronunciation accurate? Sampling the reactions of others enables you to judge how well you communicate.

2. Learn to listen objectively to yourself

This is difficult but essential. Frequent recordings of your voice on a disc, tape, or wire recorder will help. If the result seems unflattering, don't jump to the conclusion that the recording is bad. It is more likely that you are getting the full impact of some defect in your voice for the first time.

3. Listen analytically

Casual listening, however objective, won't help you spot problems that need attention. Analytical listening means the ability to isolate your individual characteristics of volume, quality, pitch, and rate, and the elements of your articulation and pronunciation. You will need the ability to detect fine distinctions. This may require ear training.

4. Draw upon visual, tactual, and kinaesthetic impressions

Some parts of your vocal mechanism are hidden from view, but you can observe the functioning of others with the aid of a mirror as you perform exercises. The sense of touch will help you identify and reshape your articulatory habits. For example, you can feel the point where your tongue tip touches to form a *t* or where your lower lip comes against your teeth in forming an *f*. Through kinaesthetic impressions you can acquire the *feel* of a relaxed pharynx, the degree of tension in the tongue when a particular vowel sound is formed, or the relaxation of throat muscles not needed in phonation.

5. Practice

A finer control over voice, articulation, and pronunciation is possible through daily work-outs. Start with the exercises at the end of this chapter and collect others to meet your needs. If your problem is relatively minor, it can usually be cleared up quickly. Should your problem be deep-seated, then patience, time, and work will be required to reform your speaking habits.

POINTS TO KEEP IN MIND

1. A good speaking voice is expressive, well projected, and pleasant. It should be accompanied by distinct articulation and accurate pronunciation.

2. Speech is shaped by organic, environmental, and personality influences.

3. Voice is produced through a sequence of breathing, phonation, and resonation. Like other sounds, the human voice has four characteristics—force, pitch, quality, and time.

4. Articulation means the adjustments and movements of the organs involved in producing speech sounds and in joining these sounds to form words and phrases.

5. Standards of pronunciation are determined by the predominant usage of educated speakers within a large geographical area.

EXERCISES

1. Stand erect before a full-length mirror. Support your weight on both feet, with the center of support toward the front of each foot. Imagine that one string is tied to the top of your head, and that another is tied to your breastbone; imagine that you are being held up by these two strings. Try to "grow upward" in the line of these imaginary strings. Be sure your shoulders and neck are relaxed; your body should be erect but not stiff. Now your lungs are free to fill with air. Remember that slouching crowds the chest cavity and hampers breathing.

2. Place your left hand lightly on your breastbone, and your right hand across your abdomen between the navel and lower ribs. Take a quick, silent breath. Watch your two hands; the left one should remain steady, for the breastbone should not move (nor should the shoulders

rise); the right hand should be forced outward, since the abdominal wall is forced against it when the diaphragm pulls downward against the viscera. Watch the lower ribs also. Do you see the lower chest expanding? Now you have inhaled in an easy, natural manner for speech, "packing the breath against your belt."

Remaining erect and keeping the breastbone steady, *gradually* force the breath from your body by pulling inward with the abdominal muscles. Your left hand on the breastbone should remain steady; your right hand should pull inward as the abdominal muscles contract. As you exhale, say the vowel *ah*. Prolong it, keeping the tone smooth and steady.

3. Slowly repeat the question, "Who are you?" five times per breath. The first time, use a small inhalation and control the exhalation so that the words are loud enough to carry to a person five feet away. Next, imagine you are speaking to someone ten feet away; then twenty; then forty. Beware of tightening the throat or raising the pitch level as you increase your strength of tone. Make each successive question louder by taking a slightly deeper inhalation than the time before, and, on exhalation, by pulling inward more firmly with your abdominal muscles.

4. In the following selection, underline the words that need greater force to carry emphasis. Practice reading the poem as you marked it.

> Teach me to feel another's woe,
>   To hide the fault I see;
> That mercy I to others show
>   That mercy show to me.
>   —*Alexander Pope*

5. Each of the following sentences has an obvious mood. Read each one aloud, pausing and varying the rate of your speech to convey the particular mood.

> Life is a narrow vale between the cold and barren peaks of two eternities. (*Robert Green Ingersoll*)
>
> I wish I knew what to do about it.
>
> Let me tell you the wonderful news!
>
> Will you tell me how to get to Vine Street?
>
> Why don't you look where you're going?
>
> I'm too tired to go another step.

6. Hold your head erect. Now let the neck muscles relax until your head drops forward on your chest. Be sure you don't pull it forward, but let it drop of its own weight. Rotate your head slowly toward the right shoulder, then to the back, to the left shoulder, and front again, letting it fall of its own weight, relaxed. Keeping your muscles relaxed, read the following sentences. Then read the three lines from Matthew Arnold and listen critically to your tone to detect any return of tension.

Ah, how easy this is!

I will relax and relax and relax.

The sea is calm to-night.
The tide is full, the moon lies fair
Upon the straits—
          —*Matthew Arnold*

7. Using various melody patterns, discover how many different meanings and emotional shades you can express with each of the following sentences.

I don't know why you want me to go to the movies with you.

How would you like to move to the moon?

I've always been polite to Tom.

I should change my attitude toward mathematics.

8. Read the following sentences. There should be no nasal sounds.
This is the house that Jack built.

She goes to school every day.

Who left a light gray hat by that chair?

Now read these sentences, giving full nasal resonance to the *m, n,* and *ng,* none to the other sounds.

Nobody expects him to come home.

Turn left at the next corner.

His name must be in the telephone book.

9. Practice reading the following selection aloud, paying particular attention to the way you produce the vowels and diphthongs.

If thou must love me, let it be for naught
Except for love's sake only. Do not say,
'I love her for her smile—her look—her way
Of speaking gently,—for a trick of thought
That falls in well with mine, and certes brought
  A sense of pleasant ease on such a day'—
  For these things in themselves, Beloved, may
Be changed, or change for thee—and love, so wrought,
May be unwrought so. Neither love me for
  Thine own dear pity's wiping my cheeks dry:
A creature might forget to weep, who bore
  Thy comfort long, and lose thy love thereby!
But love me for love's sake, that evermore
  Thou mayst love on, through love's eternity.
          —*Elizabeth Barrett Browning*

10. Practice reading the following selection aloud, paying particular attention to the way you articulate the consonants.

Trust thou thy Love: if she be proud, is she not sweet?
Trust thou thy Love: if she be mute, is she not pure?
Lay thou thy soul full in her hands, low at her feet;
  Fail, Sun and Breath!—yet, for they peace, She shall endure.
                    —John Ruskin

11. During the next five days, listen for the mispronunciations that other people make. List all that you hear.

fifteen

Bodily Action

Bodily action is the visible code of speech. As long as you are in sight of an audience, you are communicating with it, even though you aren't saying a word. Your eyes, facial expressions, the tone of your muscles, your posture—all reveal something about you whether you want them to or not. And if words and actions say conflicting things, the audience will intuitively take their cues from your actions. A speaker's manner can make us feel unwanted even though he speaks words of welcome. Bodily actions carry meaning in their own right, and they can reinforce or defeat your words.

SOME COMMON MISCONCEPTIONS

CONFINING BODILY ACTION TO GROSS MOVEMENT

Some people think that bodily action refers only to big movements of the entire body or sweeping gestures made with arms and hands. They are suspicious of instruction in bodily action, for they have watched persons who behaved like acrobats rather than speakers intent on communicating ideas.

Eloquent gestures need not involve big movements. The body has hundreds of muscles, and all of them contract and relax. These voluntary and involuntary muscle movements *are* bodily action. An expressive face, a thrust of the jaw, a toss of the head, a shrug of the shoulders—these and dozens of other small movements constitute bodily action.

Big movements are not taboo. Far from it! But bodily action includes more than the gross movements of arms, legs, or the whole
body.

TREATING BODILY ACTION AS MECHANICAL

Mechanical gestures, like mechanical phrases, say very little to your
audience—except that you have spent a lot of time practicing how
to turn them out. Old-time elocutionists often charted elaborate
classifications of gestures and worked out precise instructions for
making each one. The result was a mechanical speaker whose
puppet-like movements had little to do with his thought or mood,
but who felt he had to make gestures even when there was no
good reason for them.

CONFUSING NATURAL WITH
HABITUAL MOVEMENT

Sometimes people insist that good bodily action is whatever "comes
naturally." They confuse natural behavior with habitual behavior.
We often hold nature responsible for what really is the product of
habit, and call something natural only because it is familiar.

This confusion gets us into trouble when we excuse bad habits
as being natural. People whose unfortunate habits of posture or
gesturing interfere with communication need new habits, no matter how natural the old ones seem. Bad habits are changed by
objective self-study followed by corrective exercises.

HOW BODILY ACTION WORKS
FOR OR AGAINST YOU

ACTION WINS AND HOLDS ATTENTION

A listener can rivet his attention to a fixed point for only a few
seconds. You must constantly adapt your matter and manner to his
shifting energies. You can catch his ear by keeping your ideas and
language lively; you can catch his eye by matching your physical
movements to your marching ideas.

An animated window display attracts more attention than a stationary one. A physically active speaker excites more interest than
a "stationary" one. A vital speaker stimulates listeners to empathize
with him. Listeners respond to a lively speaker much as a fan in
the bleachers responds to the backfield in action. When you stir

your listeners to participate in communication, you win their active interest.

ACTION COMMUNICATES MEANING

Look about you. Out of earshot but within eyesight you see two people lounging on the lawn. One leans forward in a confidential manner. The other throws back his head and slaps his leg. Both seem to laugh uproariously. You see two other people standing on the sidewalk. Their bodies quiver; one gestures menacingly at the other. Without hearing a single word, you reach conclusions about each conversation, the moods of the participants, and their attitudes toward each other. Action is loaded with meaning.

Physical behavior is an index to personality

Our impressions of a speaker come from his total behavior, from many cooperating cues so faint and fleeting that we can seldom isolate them. For instance, our initial confidence—or lack of it—in a speaker's ability depends upon "something" we sense in his general manner. Not that we actually sit back and muse, "Here's a fellow who walks energetically, has a bright eye, has an easy, comfortable manner, and for these and other reasons warrants my confidence." Still we sense these things without realizing it, and we respond favorably to him. In the same way, we respond unfavorably to a speaker whose facial muscles are taut, who shuffles about, and who darts furtive glances here and there as if seeking to escape. His anxiety transfers itself to his audience.

Certain patterns of physical behavior lead us to make snap judgments. Mincing movements suggest a prissy person. A scowling face and a jutting jaw send us off to a neutral corner for safety. The man who descends upon us, gives us a bone-crushing handshake, and flashes smiles on and off like a neon sign puts us on guard and stimulates our sales resistance. Whenever you speak, your listener responds to your mannerisms as well as to your words. He is sizing you up. We may deplore snap judgments, but people go right on making them. The man who totters onto the platform like Casper Milquetoast may have nerves of steel and the courage of a lion, but unless his listeners have a chance to test these qualities on the spot, many of them will never revise their first impressions of him.

Gestures aid in description, narration, and exposition

Gestures supplement words and fill in gaps. A traveler excitedly describes the volcanic eruption of Mt. Parícutin, in Mexico. His arms and hands begin to speak, suggesting clouds of billowing smoke and a flood of white-hot lava. His actions help you to create the scene in your own imagination. Or you are lost and ask a farmer for directions. As the farmer talks, he points north and west to help you get your bearings; his arms cross to suggest an intersection; he moves hand and arm in a sweeping curve to indicate a bend in the road. Indeed, it is difficult to instruct—either formally or informally —without gestures that indicate location, space, size, speed, force, and procedure.

Gestures express conviction and feeling

We speak forcefully with our entire body when we are under the influence of strong convictions and feelings. Even someone who is usually shy and reserved becomes a person transformed. His face becomes mobile; there is a new set to his shoulders; and his arms and hands suddenly go to work without any conscious effort on his part. Unless a person's emotions get out of control, he is at his best when he speaks for a cause that means a great deal to him. His mind and body cooperate in an accent and rhythm of expression that the audience quickly detects and respects. Any one of his gesture—a shrug of the shoulders, a clenched fist, an expression of scorn—may be ambiguous in itself; but in the full context of his unmistakable attitudes and feelings, it will move the audience to give undivided attention and to react correspondingly, with laughter, vexation, or indignation.

ACTION RELIEVES TENSION

Some tension, though we may scarcely be aware of it, is normal even in our day-to-day speaking. Heightened tension is inevitable when you are on the spot—whether you are participating in a conference or giving a public reading or speech. From autobiographies and biographies of great speakers, we learn that before each speech they too built up tensions bordering on stage fright, even after years and years of experience. Norman Thomas, himself a brilliant and seasoned speaker, describes this universal reaction:

> Some degree of nervous tension one must expect before an important speech. At least before certain speeches, especially in a debate or symposium, one shivers on the brink of speech as before diving into cold water. But once in, the speech, like the water, is bracing.[1]

As tensions mount, some speakers freeze in their shoes, unable to think clearly and to find the right words. If this happens to you, take deliberate steps to break the cycle of tensions. Change your position. Move about. Make some gestures. Clearly these are only temporary expedients to use in emergency situations. But it is important to shake off your immobility and to loosen up. Physical activity is your best way to gain freedom and relaxation, no matter how awkward it makes you feel at first.

If you don't find some way to relieve dammed-up tensions, they may spill over into random, nervous movements. In effect, these are the body's involuntary and uncontrolled attempts to relieve itself of strain. You have seen a speaker move about the platform in a distracted manner, shifting his weight from one foot to the other, clenching and unclenching his hands, forcing a ring up and down a finger, stretching his neck to relieve the pressure of his collar. Actually this distraught behavior doesn't really relieve the tension; and once the speaker becomes aware of it, he responds to it as a further distraction. And so does his audience.

The way to break up random behavior is to focus sharply on what you are saying, then *induce* some purposeful activity that will enforce your statements. The gestures you make may not be the best, but they will help to re-direct your energies. With increased poise and self-control, your body will begin to speak purposefully without conscious direction.

CHARACTERISTICS OF GOOD BODILY ACTION

1. Vitality

Energized speech keeps the listener listening. A person who is alive from head to foot relays his vitality. A droopy, lethargic speaker

[1] *Mr. Chairman, Ladies and Gentlemen* . . . (New York: Hermitage House, 1955), pp. 80-81.

suggests, in effect, "I'm sorry to take your time. I'll be through soon." A vital speaker mobilizes his audience.

2. Variety

Physical flexibility is the key to variety. Unrelieved action wearies an audience. Overworked gestures, no matter how well they are executed, are monotonous. Still worse are unvaried and meaningless gestures, such as the perpetual motion of a bobbing head or chopping the air with an arm and hand. Tension or poor habits usually account for this monotony. Variety is achieved through self-appraisal, a keener appreciation of purposeful movement, and exercises that induce flexibility.

3. Coordination

Though varied, gestures may be awkward and disjointed. Any single gesture should mesh smoothly with all parts of a totally responding body. A speaker who bobs his head around but holds his shoulders stiff reminds his viewers of a poorly manipulated puppet. And if he thrusts out his arm and hand mechanically, he calls to mind a badly adjusted mechanism of wheels and springs. When all movements are well coordinated, no single gesture is conspicuous as a detached action.

4. Integration

Effective action springs from the meanings a speaker is trying to convey. He shrugs, smiles, scowls, points, draws himself up because he is responding to an inner impulse to do so. Action is integrated when it is keyed to a speaker's mind and emotions.

5. Timing

A good gesture is timed to fit the word or phrase it is intended to enforce. An arm or hand gesture is ludicrous when it precedes the essential word or phrase it is supposed to emphasize, or when it comes as an afterbeat. Poor timing is the result of uncoordinated activity, weak integration between action and meaning, or "canned" gestures.

6. Reserve

Expend energy freely in speaking, but don't squander it all at once. If you unwind with a terrific burst of gestures, you will soon dissipate your initial impact. Give your listeners the feeling they have when they are driving a high-powered automobile—that there is plenty of power left if it's needed. Listeners grow uneasy when a speaker strains or wilts. End your speech as you begin it, with energy to spare.

7. Appropriateness

Adapt your action to both the audience and the occasion. A pep rally calls for abundant action from a cheer leader. But exaggerated gestures at a dinner party or in a small group suggest that the speaker is either an exhibitionist or that he suffers from an overheated mind.

HOW TO IMPROVE YOUR BODILY ACTION

1. Study other people's physical behavior

Observe the part bodily action plays in the speech that goes on around you—in lectures, movies, TV programs, and your classmates' talks. Sensitize yourself to the role of bodily action in communication. Note how bodily action works for or against the people you observe. How would you advise those with poor bodily action to improve?

2. Get an image of your own characteristic physical behavior in speech

This may not be easy. You can get some visual glimpses from candid camera shots, or, better yet, from home movies. But the image also includes a feeling for what you're doing when you're doing it.

Welcome your classmates' descriptions of your physical behavior. Try to see yourself objectively through their eyes. Then check their descriptions by talking before a full-length mirror. If you see an unrelieved deadpan expression or an unbroken frown, remember this is what your audience has to look at each time you speak.

3. Form a clear idea of how to correct your problems

Once you have pinpointed your problems, let your instructor and classmates help you find procedures for correcting them. Short workout programs in class are particularly helpful. Experiment on the spot with the suggestions that are made and get your classmates' reactions to the results. If you don't understand a suggestion, ask someone else to demonstrate it for you.

4. Devise a specific plan and practice privately

Follow through on helpful suggestions made in class. A posture problem has to be worked at every day, not just when you speak before a group. Devise special exercises for work-outs at home to deal with persistent problems. If your bodily action is inhibited, stiff, and awkward, use pantomime exercises in which you imagine yourself as a tennis player on the courts or a swimmer in a pool. Or read aloud excerpts from dramatic literature that stir up muscular responses in you. Now and then, practice these exercises before a full-length mirror to check the results. After a time, you will acquire the new sense of physical freedom that you need in reading and speaking.

5. Choose subjects for your class speeches that call for physical action

Demonstration talks in which you show how to build a piece of furniture, assemble an apparatus, or execute a dance step—are especially helpful. Or recall some exciting event you have witnessed; then re-create the event with actions as well as words. Speeches on subjects about which you have especially strong convictions induce action.

SOME SPECIAL PROBLEMS THAT PLAGUE PUBLIC SPEAKERS

How should I walk to and from the platform?

The important thing is to make the trip without calling unfavorable attention to yourself. A hesitant manner suggests timidity, and a hurried, nervous walk marks you as overanxious. Shuffling feet suggest indifference. A stilted, strutting, or lilting entry leads to speculation about your personality and makes listeners more interested in proving their hunches than in listening to what you have to say.

Simply walk to your place in a firm, easy manner that tells your audience you have business with them. Once you have finished speaking, make your exit in the same easy, unhurried manner.

Where and how should I stand?

Stand where it will be easiest for you to establish the best contact with all your listeners. Normally, this is at the front and toward the center of the group. Stand as close to your audience as you can without seeming to press in on them or crowd them. Avoid turning your back on any of them. If your listeners are scattered, ask them to move together. This will reduce the strain on you and will give you better contact with them.

Good posture improves appearance and contributes to bodily action. Stand upright but not stiffly. Avoid both the slouch of a bum and the strut of a drill sergeant. And don't drape yourself over the lectern, lean carelessly against the wall, or dangle one leg in midair. The Napoleonic stance, with legs spread far apart, or the oratorical pose, with feet planted at studied angles, is conspicuous and contrived. Make good posture habitual, and you will be free to direct your attention to more important matters.

Should I move around while speaking?

By all means, if you have some place to go. Moving around may help maintain contact with all your listeners. A few steps break the monotony of one position, indicate a transition in thought, and also relieve tension. Roaming restlessly like a caged tiger distracts the audience.

What should I do with my hands?

When you make your first few speeches, you may discover that your hands have suddenly become as large as violin cases hanging at your side. This is just one sign of exaggerated self-consciousness.

Beginning speakers are often told to drop their hands to their sides when they are not gesturing. But this may look artificial and may make them seem more conspicuous. There's nothing wrong with thrusting a hand into your pocket—but don't forget where you left it. If you are standing near a lectern, feel free to rest your hands on it naturally, without clutching it like a shipwrecked passenger clinging to a floating log. After you get into your speech, your hands will stop being a problem and you will find good use for them.

How should I use the speaker's stand?

During the first few minutes of a talk, it's comforting and reassuring to have a good, solid speaker's stand as a base of operations. It can, however, become an obstacle instead of an aid. Speakers who grimly attach themselves to the lectern, hide behind it, or drape themselves over it are a familiar and dismal sight. Make a point of moving to one side or out in front from time to time. You will find that your audience is much more interested in you once you come out of hiding.

Sometimes, of course, you have to stay close to the speaker's stand, as when you read from a manuscript. And when you are talking into a microphone fixed to the stand, you must remain relatively stationary. But it is still possible to gesture without pounding the lectern or rattling the mechanism.

POINTS TO KEEP IN MIND

1. Develop and control your physical behavior in speech to:
    a) Capture and hold your audience's attention.
    b) Lodge favorable impression of yourself as a person.
    c) Supplement your words in narrative, descriptive, and expository discourse.
    d) Give added impact to your convictions and feelings.
    e) Reduce muscular tensions.
2. Work especially for action that is:
    a) Vital and stirs up responses.
    b) Flexible and varied.
    c) Coordinated.
    d) Integrated with thoughts and feeling.
    e) Timed to fit the point you are making.
    f) Under control.
    g) Appropriate to the occasion.
3. In conducting yourself on the platform, try to:
    a) Walk easily and firmly to and from the platform.
    b) Stand where it is easiest to communicate with your audience.
    c) Make natural and comfortable adaptations that will relieve initial strain.

EXERCISES

1. Select two sites, one a building on campus, the other a building in your home town or city. Devise a one or two-minute report to instruct a stranger on how to get from one building to the other. Use bodily action and blackboard sketches to supplement verbal description.

2. Prepare a how-to-do-it talk on directing an orchestra, interpreting the gestures of football officials, or administering aid at the scene of an accident. Use bodily action as an aid to communication.

3. Prepare a report on a process, an operation, or an institution. Tell how stage sets are built; explain the structure of the United Nations organization; describe the layout of your college library; report on prospecting for oil. Use visual aids, but also use gestures to suggest height, width, distance, direction, movement, relationships.

4. Recall an exciting event you witnessed firsthand—the finals of a tennis match, a rescue, a parachute jump, fighting a fire or a swollen river, climbing a mountain, a mock political convention. Try to recover the excitement you felt at the time. Make use of bodily action to depict the event and to communicate your excitement.

5. Pick a short story with lots of action in it. Read part of it to the class. Make it come alive.

6. Choose a subject about which you have strong feelings. Make up your mind that the time has come to speak out. Deliver your talk with force and energy that do justice to your convictions.

7. Listen to comments about other people. Do any of them express stereotyped judgments based on appearance and physical behavior? Write up the results of your observations and present them to the class.

sixteen

Inquiry

All speech is communication designed to elicit response, but effective speakers adapt their approach to serve the purpose at hand. We now begin four chapters dealing with the special methods associated with the four primary purposes of speech—inquiry, reporting, advocacy, and evocation. Logically the method of inquiry comes first.

THE ROLE OF INQUIRY

Inquiry is a search for meaning, understanding, and guidance. In this respect it is unique among the purposes and methods of speech. In our other capacities as speakers we make use of insights and understandings, but first we must discover them. Speech performs one of its most important services in aiding in this search and discovery.

We are impelled toward inquiry by the problems we face in our daily lives and the larger problems of the society in which we live. But sensitive, thoughtful people raise questions in all areas of human experience, even to the nature of man and his ultimate destiny. The will and the capacity to explore these questions reflectively and creatively are among the highest marks of maturity.

THE NATURE OF INQUIRY

Inquiry may be a solitary venture, or it may take place when two or more people meet to think together. There is no such thing as "group thinking," of course, except in a metaphorical sense. Only individuals think. But individuals within a group do think, and often they think more gainfully than they would if each were by himself. By sharing information, exchanging views, and trying out ideas, we find our way to new vantage points and to a higher level of creative thinking.

An everyday conversation with a friend may contain some, most, or all of the elements of organized inquiry. You tell him about a problem that is worrying you. He responds with interest. He draws you out. He asks questions that focus on aspects of the problem you haven't considered. Together you ponder various answers, discard some, and ultimately settle on the one that seems to fit the case. This is inquiry in its simplest form.

The most favorable setting for inquiry is a small group of interested, congenial people. Even large conferences and legislative assemblies refer most questions to committees for preliminary study. In small groups, everyone has a chance to participate. Roles shift from speaker to listener and back again. In large meetings, this kind of give and take usually yields to public speeches of inquiry followed by an open forum. Even in small groups, though, it is often wise to let a person talk himself out on a point without interrupting him. Such miniature speeches contribute most when they fit the spirit and pattern of inquiry.

THE PATTERN OF INQUIRY

Inquiry is both an analytical and a creative process. At its best, it combines rigor and freedom. Sometimes it resembles loosely organized chaos but there is much to be said for letting ideas tumble forth before trying to sort them out. Inquiry should be relatively uninhibited, but must not degenerate to aimless conversation.

What pattern of thinking leads most readily to the answers to a problem? People who have studied this question have identified six steps in *reflective thinking*. Used flexibly and imaginatively, these steps provide a sound guide for inquiry.

1. Identify the problem

Reflective thinking is triggered by a problem. Begin by stating and describing the problem as specifically as you can.

Phrase the problem as an open question that will invite a variety of answers. It is better to ask "How should I invest my savings?" than "Should I buy Goods, Inc.?" The second question tends to limit answers to a simple "Yes" or "No." Put your question objectively. "How may we get rid of our worthless physical education requirement?" is a loaded question that is likely to block discussion at the outset. "How may we best insure a student's physical fitness?" opens the question objectively.

Explain the problem so that others can identify it. Then get them to share your concern so they will seek the answer as eagerly as you do.

2. Analyze the causes

Most important problems have numerous and complex causes, some close at hand and others deep-seated and obscure. The reflective thinker must detect those causes that seem most vulnerable to attack and most intimately related to an ultimate solution of the problem.

Product analysis may indicate that one reason for an item's failure to sell is its unappealing package design. This might be the root of the problem. But before jumping to such a conclusion a marketing executive would probably ask whether the firm's advertising campaign was appropriate, whether some deficiency was inherent in the product, and other questions to determine possible further causes for the problem.

3. Clarify your values

Before you consider various solutions to the problem, you must establish standards by which to judge them. These standards or criteria are your values—what you want the solution to do, the specifications that it must meet. Faced with the question "How may we improve our college newspaper?" students might agree that any forthcoming suggestions will have to fit within the fixed budget, be consistent with a balanced coverage of college news, and not make excessive time demands on the student staff.

4. Suggest solutions

Try to develop one or more solutions and then judge each proposal on its merits. Spare no effort at this stage to draw forth as many suggestions as possible. Even seemingly farfetched ideas should be welcomed and given a hearing, for no one can be sure in advance that a novel approach might not turn out to be the best.

5. Weigh the alternatives

Treat each proposal as a working hypothesis, as a guide to further exploration. Discuss its pros and cons, but avoid committing yourself prematurely. Superficially attractive answers may not stand up under exposure. Ask questions such as these: Does this proposal get to the root of the problem? Does it fit our criteria? Can it be made to work? Will it cost too much? If it solves the problem at hand, will it introduce new problems in the future? The solution that you ultimately agree on may be one of the suggested solutions, an integration of two or more of them, or a compromise.

6. Test the solution

Once you reach consensus, re-check your thinking before you make the decision binding. This is imperative if the decision is to be irrevocable. Often it is wise to keep the decision tentative until everyone has had a chance to ponder it or to talk it over with others. Or you may decide to experiment with the proposal on a limited scale.

INQUIRY THROUGH GROUP DISCUSSION

Preparing yourself

Nothing is gained by pooling ignorance and misinformation. Most of the suggestions given in Chapter 7 will help you explore your subject in preparation for discussion. Following the six steps in reflective thinking, work up a discussion outline that records your information, organizes your thinking, and directs your questions. You may or may not refer to your outline during the discussion. Under no circumstances should you try to force the discussion to follow the outline. Good discussion combines the thinking of all. Your outline should merely sharpen your own preparation and enable you to apply your best efforts.

Cast your discussion outline in the topical or logical pattern or some combination of the two (see Chapter 8). Present your topics or premises as questions designed to bring about a full and satisfying exploration of the problem.

The sample discussion outline that follows does not record the facts and expert opinions that you would consult and use, but it does trace out the lines of thought in each phase of the reflective thinking process. The facts, quotations, and examples that undergird your thinking may be included in your outline, recorded on file cards, or stored away in your head.

HOW SHOULD OUR COLLEGES HANDLE FINANCIAL AID TO STUDENTS?

I. *What is the problem?*
   A. What is meant by financial aid?
      1. Are scholarships included?
      2. Are student loans included?
      3. Are grants-in-aid without specific grade requirements included?
      4. How about tuition rebates?
      5. Should board, jobs, and the like, provided by the college, be regarded as a form of financial aid?
   B. What are the present provisions for financial aid to college students?
      1. How much aid is given?
      2. What kinds of aid are given?
      3. Who gets this aid?
      4. On what basis is it granted?
      5. What are the sources of the funds?
   C. How adequate are the present provisions for financial aid to students?
      1. Are worthy students denied a college education because they cannot afford it?
      2. Are needy students in our colleges forced to give too much time to jobs in order to stay in college?
      3. Are colleges using financial aid funds to best advantage?

II. *What are the principal causes of the problem?*
   A. Do the colleges face increasing demands for financial aid? From what sources? Why?
   B. Is financial aid more easily obtained in certain educational fields than others?
   C. Are the budgetary provisions for financial aid too limited?

III. *What should our objectives be in granting financial aid?*
   A. A college education for every worthy student regardless of financial resources?
   B. An equitable distribution of the available funds?

IV. *How can this problem be solved?*
   A. Should colleges appropriate larger sums for student aid in their operating budgets from the sources now available to them?

B. Should colleges seek aid from outside sources: private foundations; the federal government; industry?

C. On what bases should aid be given: scholastic ability; need; service to the college?

V. *What are the merits of these proposals?*

    A. Is it wise for colleges to appropriate more money for student aid?
        1. Do they have the money to use for this purpose?
        2. How would an increase in funds for student aid affect other items in the budget?

    B. Should colleges seek student-aid funds from outside sources?
        1. How available are funds from these outside sources?
        2. Is there any danger that these outside agencies would exercise objectionable control over these funds?
        3. Will student-aid funds from outside sources force the colleges to pay hidden costs not covered by these funds?

    C. Should student-aid funds be granted on the basis of scholarship, need, or service?
        1. Should good students be denied scholarships because their parents can pay the bills?
        2. Whose need should determine the assistance: the student's need; society's needs? And what constitutes need?
        3. Should students work for the financial assistance they receive from the college?

VI. *How sound is the proposed solution to the problem?*

    A. Does it attack the causes of the problem?
    B. How well does it achieve the objectives?
    C. Is it workable?

Taking part in group discussion

Inquiry at its best is "thinking out loud." You submit your ideas in a spirit that encourages others to assess their merits, to agree or disagree, and to point out why they agree or disagree. Sometimes you are not at all certain just where your inquiry will lead you. Other times, you will have formulated a tentative conclusion and will invite others to examine the thinking that has led you to it. You ask your listeners questions such as these: How do you react to this idea? Am I right? Where have I gone wrong? Your listeners may answer you with an account of their own thinking. Out of these exchanges emerge a clarification of the problem and new insights that enable you to progress.

The spirit of inquiry is essential to the success of inquiry. You are engaged in a cooperative undertaking to find the best answer. If special interests come into play, or if participants become more

Astronaut John H. Glenn, Jr. *(United Press International)*

concerned with private gain than with group purpose, the level of inquiry quickly sinks. Inquiry demands *cooperation among people* and *competition among ideas.* Ideas need to stand on their merits —not on the personality or prestige of their defenders.

Inquiry, then, calls for ideal attitudes—attitudes that are seldom perfectly realized. People have special interests and prejudices but they can learn to act maturely. Those who do are able to engage profitably in group discussion.

In an informal discussion of your college's plan to increase the mathematics requirement from one to two years, you might favor the new policy by stating your real reasons or by giving reasons that simply sound good, or you might assert your opinion without giving reasons. If you realize during the discussion that your enthusiasm for mathematics is due mainly to your success in the subject, your opinion might waver when you consider that not everyone has had the same happy experience. But if you reverse your opinion, you fear that you will be suspected of retreating under fire. So you continue to defend an opinion you no longer wholeheartedly believe. This behavior denies you the full benefit of discussion. If you persist in such behavior, you may find yourself unwelcome in serious conversation.

An objective attitude toward people and their ideas leads to the most rewarding inquiry. People with an objective attitude show a lively interest in ideas; they are willing to suspend judgment until they have heard the whole case for the other side; they can accept fair criticism of their ideas without taking it as a personal affront; they are willing to give up or modify ideas that have proved untenable; they can criticize poor ideas without attacking the person who proposed them; they assume that others are acting in good faith until they prove otherwise; they try to make it easy for people to back down from weak positions.

How to lead discussion

The leader of a discussion may be someone who is formally appointed or elected, or someone who assumes the job with the approval of the group. In fact, leadership often shifts as one person after another temporarily assumes the responsibility.

The essential duties of the leader are to stimulate, guide, and integrate the group. He *stimulates* the members of the group by arousing their interest, by focusing their attention on relevant matters, and by encouraging them to contribute their ideas. He *guides* the members of the group by helping them think through the problem together, but without forcing them to follow any preconceived pattern. And he *integrates* the group by helping members resolve differences, recognize areas of agreement, and come to some kind of understanding. These duties are best performed by a democratic leader who helps each participant to make his greatest contribution.

The two most useful skills in leading discussion are the ability to ask good questions and the capacity to summarize matters clearly and succinctly. Skillfully worded questions, asked at the right time and directed to the right people, are the leader's first responsibility. He builds his questions around the words *what, why,* and *how.* What is the problem? Why is it a problem? How can it be solved? Such questions help the group to identify the problem, to discover its causes and effects, and to work out a solution.

If you are leading a discussion, try to ask questions that will draw out the members of the group—What is your position? Why do you feel that way? How would you handle the matter? Keep the discussion moving along by raising a new question as soon as each successive point has been handled adequately. Use questions to probe into important aspects of the problem, to introduce phases of the problem that might otherwise be overlooked, and to explore the bases of agreement and disagreement.

Questions evoke discussion, and summaries pull together what has been said. Make short, tentative summaries when agreements have been reached and when disagreements have been fully explored. Use summaries to rephrase a position that needs clarification, to state the points at issue, to remind the group of the ground that has been covered, and to pin down conclusions. If your summary is acceptable, the group can move on to new ground; if it is not, it will open the way to further discussions of a controversial point.

INQUIRY THROUGH PUBLIC SPEECH

Public speech as a vehicle of inquiry

Public speeches of inquiry are *open-ended,* and in this respect they differ from other forms of public address. A report transmits information. A speech of advocacy urges acceptance of a predetermined conclusion. An evocative talk inspires or entertains. But in an inquiry the speaker remains a seeker whose goal is to find a solution to a problem by enlisting others to join in the search. If circumstances permit, his audience may enter into the discussion after he has finished his talk. Otherwise, the most he can do is to send his listeners away intent on continuing the search he has initiated. But whether or not the audience has an opportunity to think aloud, the speaker achieves his purpose only if he can induce his listeners to think with him.

Here are typical examples. A president confronts his board of directors with the unhappy news that the company's business is slipping. Why? He explains the reasons as he sees them. Then he goes on to suggest alternative ways of recovering the lost business. His speech sets the stage for a general discussion by members of the board of directors. At a chapter meeting, a sorority girl analyzes rush methods, raises doubts about the efficacy of present practices, and stirs other members to consider new ones. An instructor in philosophy analyzes the moral issues of war, discloses various ethical theories that come to grips with these issues, and challenges the class to assess the merits of the theories.

Speeches of inquiry don't make their way into anthologies much oftener than pictures of a house under construction are placed among photographs of model homes. Such speeches are thought in process rather than the product of thought. And they should always be judged by standards appropriate to their unique purpose.

Developing a speech of inquiry

The six steps in reflective thinking offer a natural sequence for a speech of inquiry. Just how many of the steps you should try to take depends on the situation. Under some circumstances, it is enough to establish the validity and urgency of the problem itself. Here is an actual instance in which most of the speeches were properly limited to problem analysis.

A community grew up around an airbase that was originally planned for small military training planes and later was converted into a base for jet planes. Many residents felt threatened by the switchover and called a mass meeting. Anyone who wanted to speak was given the opportunity. Some speeches called for immediate action, but most were exploratory. The speakers addressed themselves to questions such as these: Does the conversion to jet planes threaten lives and property? What is the magnitude of the threat? Do we have a problem that is serious enough to investigate further? Out of such probing, consensus was reached that a problem did exist and that a committee of citizens should plan an extended study of all possible ways to deal with it.

Whether you choose to develop your talk through some or all of the steps in reflective thinking depends upon the nature of the problem, your present knowledge and insights, the time at your disposal, and the background of your listeners. Student speakers often are challenged by topics that are too big and complicated to be carried through all the six steps in reflective thinking. They may perform a distinct service, however, simply by creating an awareness of the topic *as a problem* and by stimulating thinking where there has been none before.

Private inquiry may lead you to a tentative conclusion. When you speak, invite your audience to examine the steps that led you to your conclusion. This should not be an *ex post facto* report of your private struggles with a problem. Remain open-minded and be prepared to modify or abandon your conclusion if the thinking you provoke in others justifies a revision in your own thinking. The sample outline on financial aid for students is applicable to a six-step speech of inquiry as well as to group discussion. If you have tentatively concluded that federal funds provide the best source for extending aid to worthy college students and you know that this conclusion is highly controversial, you will wish to share the thinking that led you to this conclusion—the same thinking you would introduce if this were a group discussion. Such a speech might then become the basis for an open forum or group discussion.

The skeletal outline below suggests the general framework for a speech of inquiry on the question "How can scientists communicate with the public?"

THE SCIENTIST AND THE PUBLIC

Introduction

I. Dr. Albert H. Crews, Director of the Argonne National Laboratory, warns that unless scientists learn to communicate with the public, the country is in danger of splitting into two cultures—one of *science,* the other of *magic*. He puts it this way: "Those who practice science will be able to communicate effectively only with other scientists. The rest of the population will live in a world of magic—a world of devices, gadgets, appliances, and structures that are not understood by them and that are provided by the other culture. . . ."

II. If Dr. Crews is correct in his view, it is useful to ask: How can we establish better communication between the scientists and the public?

Discussion

I. How wide is the gap between the scientist and the general public?
   A. Have scientists lost touch with the general public?
   B. How literate is the public in the realm of science?

II. What factors are operating to produce this schism?
   A. How communicable are modern scientific data and their applications?
   B. Is our educational system at fault?
      1. Is our scientific education too specialized?
      2. Is the exposure of nonscientists to scientific training too limited?

III. Would our society gain by closer communication between the scientific community and the public?
   A. To what extent do policy decisions in our society require scientific knowledge?
   B. Who should make these decisions: the scientists; our elected representatives?

IV. How might communication between scientists and the public be improved?
   A. Should we provide scientific training for all?
   B. Should the education of scientists be strengthened in the humanities and the social sciences?
   C. At what level of scientific sophistication should this communication take place?
   D. Should we look to the scientists for more social leadership?

Conclusion

I. Communication is a two-way street. If we are to close the gap between the scientific community and Dr. Crews's "world of magic," it would seem essential that some common ground be established where the people who populate these two worlds can meet and talk together.

II. I invite your consideration of ways and means of achieving this common ground.

POINTS TO KEEP IN MIND

1. Speech that serves the purpose of inquiry is investigative and exploratory in nature.

2. The six steps in reflective thinking provide a useful pattern for speech of inquiry: *Identify the problem; assess the causes; clarify your values; suggest solutions; weigh alternatives; test the solution agreed upon.*

3. Good discussion results from careful preparation, effective participation, and skillful leadership—all accompanied by objective attitudes, reflective thinking, and speech that complements and reveals the thinking of the group.

4. A public speech can serve the purposes of inquiry in large groups if it takes one or more of the steps in reflective thinking in the same spirit that motivates the best discussion. Such speeches may be given to stimulate the private inquiry of others or to lay the basis for cooperative group deliberation.

EXERCISES

1. Adopt a question worthy of discussion during two or more class meetings. Develop discussion outlines and come to class prepared to work through the six steps in reflective thinking. Take up each step systematically and carefully. Your main purpose here is to gain mastery of the reflective thinking process and experience in applying the process in discussion.

2. Use the subject you selected for Exercise 1, or some other problem of your own choice, for a speech of inquiry. Read the sample speeches of inquiry on pages 303-10 before tackling this assignment.

3. Plan a discussion in which each member of the class comes prepared to act as leader. Appoint someone to begin as leader and then pass this responsibility around to others as the discussion progresses. Be prepared to ask questions that evoke discussion and to provide short, terse summaries that pull the discussion together.

4. Divide the class into groups of five or six, adopt questions for discussion, appoint a leader for each group, and prepare discussion outlines. Then seat the panel in front of the class. The audience may be invited to present questions at the conclusion of the panel discussion. The leader of the panel may preside over this question period.

5. One way of conducting an inquiry is through interviews. Choose a person you would like to interview, select a problem, and prepare questions that follow the six steps of inquiry. Conduct your interview on the basis of these questions.

seventeen

Reporting

The reporter's job is to find relevant information, to communicate it with maximum accuracy, clarity, and economy, and to do this in ways that invite the interest of listeners. Most of us do not expect to become professional reporters, yet hardly a day passes without our making or hearing reports. As our life experiences broaden, more and more we are cast into the role of reporter. How well we acquit ourselves depends primarily on how well we understand the job.

KINDS OF REPORTS

Perhaps the most useful way to classify reports is on the basis of the audience to whom you are reporting: learning groups, policy-determining groups, the general public, your friends and associates, or people to whom you want to give directions or other instruction.

The oral report is a familiar aid to learning. A teacher gives such reports when he lectures to his class. And you, as a student, may be asked to report on your own studies, a special investigation, or on research that you have conducted. When you give such a report your purpose is basically the same as that of the teacher: to increase your listeners' knowledge and understanding of the subject.

Many reports are given to policy-determining groups such as boards of directors, councils, and legislative bodies. Such groups usually have standing committees to make reports at regular intervals and special committees to make reports on problems as they arise. In either case, your job as a reporter is to provide dependable information on which decision and action may be based. At a later date, you may be called on to survey the results of a policy thus determined and report your findings back to the group for review. If you make a career as a consulting engineer, a legal investigator, an auditor, or a diagnostician, reports of this kind will be an important part of your professional duties.

Other reports are made to the general public by news reporters and commentators. Most people who listen to radio and television have their favorite reporters, men and women who can be depended on to report reliably, clearly, and interestingly. Any report designed for the general public must necessarily take into account the broader interests of this audience and the many other sources of information competing for their time and attention.

Much of the reporting you do consists of conversation with friends, neighbors, and other close associates. You report experiences, give explanations and directions, and pass along news. There is no reason why this informal reporting should not be entertaining. But if your primary purpose is to inform rather than entertain, your first responsibility is to meet your obligations as a reporter.

QUALITIES OF A GOOD REPORT

RELEVANCE

"Who does not know fellows," asks Oliver Wendell Holmes, the Autocrat of the Breakfast Table, "that always have an ill-conditioned fact or two which they lead after them into decent company like so many bulldogs . . .?" Holmes' quarrel is not with facts as such, the hard core of knowledge, but with people who turn their minds into almanacs and then proceed to abuse the privileges of discourse. They use facts to intimidate others or kill off the free play of minds; they grab or create openings and unload everything they know about hi-fi apparatus, the intricacies of missile construction gained from *Popular Science*, the relative merits of various types of lawn fertilizers, and other ill-assorted items. Such people are bores—if not boors—utterly insensitive to the possibilities of satisfying conversation and oblivious to the truth that information is seldom welcomed if it is not really wanted.

Since formal reports are usually commissioned in advance, their relevance may be presumed. Even so, formal reports often fail because they are burdened with unnecessary materials that obscure essential information and tire the listeners. We respond affirmatively to information when we need it and to speakers who stay on the track. Always ask yourself: "Have I properly analyzed the informational needs of my listeners? Does my report stick to the point? Are all details pertinent? Is my report well within the time limits?" The speaker who flounders in a sea of irrelevancies is likely to be dismayed when he sees listeners furtively looking for some inconspicuous exit.

CLARITY

Clarity is dependent upon a number of things. The speaker must have a good grasp of his materials, have a purpose and plan, and make adaptations to his audience. Audience adaptations are particularly important; it is a common failing among reporters to concentrate exclusively on their subjects.

Granted, not every subject can be made intelligible to everyone who happens to be within earshot. If you must talk of highly technical matters in technical language, then you are bound to overshoot the uninitiated. More typically, though, you are likely to be called upon to report about matters of mutual concern to people with different backgrounds, interests, and capacities. Somehow you must link what you have to say with listeners as you find them.

Begin where your listeners are, and relate the new to the old. Learning proceeds from the known to the unknown, from the perceived to the unperceived, from the understood to the less well understood. Some of the best adaptive devices are examples, comparisons and contrasts, illustrations, and stories. Such devices translate the general into the specific, the abstract into the concrete. They serve as bridges from the familiar to the unfamiliar. In reports that involve statistical analyses, you will discover that charts, diagrams, graphs, maps, and pictures are invaluable aids to clarity.

A speaker should be full of his subject, but clarity demands that we think through our subjects imaginatively in relation to the particular audience we shall face.

DEPENDABILITY

A report stands or falls on the dependability of its information. It is completely useless if it misleads because of insufficient, inaccurate, or misinterpreted data, and sometimes its consequences prove downright vicious. The point hardly needs to be labored for anyone who has wandered aimlessly in a strange city because he was given incorrect or inadequate directions on how to find a particular address. You want assurances that the insulation for your house is as good as the claims that are made for it, that the milk you drink is pure, that the ice is safe for skating, and that the legislator's record justifies your vote.

Since the ostensible purpose of many reports is to lay the basis for belief and perhaps action, the reporter is under obligation to render a true and faithful account of his investigations. He may take it for granted, therefore, that in any matter of serious interest to his listeners, his report will be subjected to scrutiny, that its credibility will be judged by its concurrence with information listeners have on hand and by verification they may undertake later. Inevitably, too, the audience will judge the dependability of the report by what they already know about the reporter's reputation for competence and integrity and by impressions they gain about him while he speaks.

INTEREST

Oral reports seem particularly susceptible to dullness. Even people with a keen and vested interest in the information often complain bitterly of being bored. Speakers are often so completely dominated by their material that they neglect the normal, human requirements that must be satisfied to sustain good listening. Conventions of learned and professional societies offer many examples of speakers who assume that all they need to do is dish up facts for listeners eager to lap them up. Not so. And at least one group, the American Chemical Society, has felt impelled to issue injunctions against the more common of the dreary faults, urging speakers to use short sentences, refrain from using a manuscript, and keep up their interest in what they are saying as a way of sustaining the interest of the audience. Oversimplified and insufficient as are these bits of advice, they underscore the problem that provokes these admonitions. Many of the suggestions we offered in behalf of clarity will also enliven your report.

If in effect you dismiss your listeners *as listeners*, then it is well not to impose on them as a speaker. It will be far better for everyone if you simply write up your report, have it duplicated, and distribute it for people to read at their leisure. But if you choose to report orally, then a vivid sense of your listening audience should manifest itself in attributes of oral style and in the expressiveness of your delivery.

REQUISITES OF A GOOD REPORTER

HEALTHY SKEPTICISM

Facts seldom lie exposed like driftwood on a beach. They are often hard to discover, identify, and isolate. Because things are not always what they seem to be or what they are represented to be, the reporter must dig facts from a world of appearances.

Our legal system demonstrates the difficulty of distinguishing between facts and nonfacts, between truths and half-truths when people's interests are in conflict and must be adjudicated. Advertisements may conceal more than they reveal. Claims made for a drug say nothing about the possibility of harmful side effects. Travel advertisements that tempt us with exotic palm trees near blue, blue water never caution against insects, infectious fungi, or high pollen counts. Exceptions to the protective provisions of a contract are often written in print so fine that it requires a reading glass.

Healthy skepticism cautions the reporter in search of facts to evaluate sources and to distinguish between verifiable data and special pleading. He knows that anyone with a commitment to a point of view will present only those facts that support it.

Healthy skepticism is the *sine qua non* of the good investigator.

OBJECTIVITY

Objectivity comes hard, for we are human beings first, reporters second. All of us carry around preconceived notions that guide our perception of things. Each of us is forever threatened by his gullibility and by his private herd of sacred cows. But a good reporter has a cultivated awareness of these susceptibilities that is his first line of protection against them.

It is easy, of course, to be objective about matters that seem remote from our immediate interests. We can be coolheaded about the bookbinding business, tariff schedules, the tide tables for Hong Kong, and the history of the dye industry in Germany, so long as they do not significantly touch our lives. But objectivity is more difficult when we deal with topics that involve our personal interests—topics, possibly, such as federal aid to schools, the pesticide and pollution controversy, civil rights, real estate taxes, the population explosion, and divorce laws.

Even though he may be tempted to do so, the reporter who is worthy of his craft does not grind axes. He tries honestly to see the facts for what they are and to present them as he finds them, not as he or anyone else wishes they were. He resists short cuts, doctored information, and slanted statements. The reporter with integrity seeks the truth and reports it with dispassionate accuracy, letting the chips fall where they may.

PERSPECTIVE

Perspective involves discriminating awareness of what is important, what is of lesser importance, and what is unimportant. It expresses itself in focus and proportion. Without perspective we may be accurate in everything we say without saying anything of consequence. For example, a reporter who pretends to cover a musical event actually commits a travesty if all that he offers are tidbits taken from program notes, interspersed with social notes on celebrities in the audience. What about the success of the music itself?

METHODS FOR COMPOSING YOUR REPORT

Exposition, description, and narration are your principal tools in reporting. Exposition gives an explanation, description paints a picture, and narration tells a story. You will find that most of your reports are primarily expository, with description and narration playing supporting roles.

Exposition classifies the data you wish to report and then identifies the more significant items in each category. For example, you might report the operations of a corporation by explaining the several departments of the corporation and the essential activities of each. The short exposition below reduces the principles of elephant stalking to a few simple steps and then tells you how to perform each of these steps—at your own peril.

As an expert elephant stalker of 72 hours' experience, I now elucidate to you the principles of elephant stalking.

First you must do it in a motor vehicle of instantaneous acceleration. You will find no difficulty in stalking by automobile, for the elephants like to walk on roads and frequently stay on or near them.

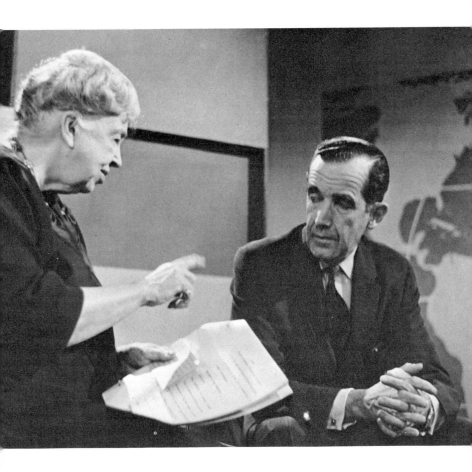

Mrs. Franklin D. Roosevelt and Edward R. Murrow meet to make plans for a television program. *(Wide World Photos)*

Next you spot your elephant, knocking down trees or dallying in a water hole. You find which way the wind is blowing by throwing a handful of dust into the air. You want to approach him in such direction that the wind blows from him to you. For if it is the opposite, it will carry your obnoxious odor to him and he will either charge you or run away in nausea.

The next thing to know is that the elephant has very bad eyesight. There is a legend that bull elephants sometimes show off in front of large boulders for hours on the mistaken assumption that the latter are potential mates. If you remain stock still, an elephant cannot see you at thirty yards distance. Even when you are moving, he loses sight of you at fifty yards distance.

Now . . . you spot your elephant, get the wind on the right side of you, then you back your vehicle up to the pachyderm slowly, the cameraman on the back shooting pictures. This is so that when he gets sight of you and charges, you can move forward, away from him, at top speed. Since he becomes blind to you at fifty yards distance, when you have put that space between you and him, you are safe, and the elephant will thrash around in the bush blindly and never find you.[1]

Description gives your listeners a picture of your subject by dividing it *spatially* and then listing the qualities—size, shape, color, texture, smell, feel, taste—of the significant items in this division. When you focus your camera on a landscape, you can capture the entire picture with one click of the shutter. But if you want to describe the same scene in words, you have to begin with the cottage in the foreground, or the hills that form the backdrop, or the sunset, or the sheep grazing on the slopes. These spatial relations give your listeners perspective and provide you with topics for description that you can put into clear, vivid word pictures.

Narration tells how something happened, usually by giving the details of the event in chronological order. Here, *time* rather than *space* is the guiding principle in organizing your report. Description stops the clock and takes a still picture; narration keeps the clock running and takes a motion picture. For example, one speaker used narration in making a report on shipping by freight. He gave a narrative account of the travels of a freight car in a single month—where it was loaded, the freight it carried, the switching terminals it passed through, the tracks it traveled, and the stops it made. He

---

[1] Reproduced by permission from a CBS broadcast made by Howard K. Smith on November 17, 1954.

told a story, but in telling it he gave an informative report on the car pool maintained by American railroads and the purposeful wanderings of freight cars from one line to another.

Edward R. Murrow's report on Hurricane Edna, one of the Sample Speeches that follow the text, combines exposition, description, and narration, but the basic plan is narration.

ORGANIZING YOUR REPORT

Of the two general patterns for organizing speech, the topical and the logical patterns, the topical is better suited to reporting because it is a process of analysis and synthesis. It breaks a subject into its parts and exhibits the relationships between the *whole* and its *parts*. These parts or components might be steps in a process or operation, in an explanation of how to make out your income tax, how to treat the common cold, or how to use the library; they might be the working parts of a machine you are trying to explain, a classification of the parking regulations in your community, the formations most commonly used in professional football, the leading characters in a play; or they might be a list of trends, causes, historical periods, or basic principles. Actually, you may divide your subject into its parts on any conceivable basis or principle, so long as the division provides a useful organization for your report.

In a report on the accident problem in masonry construction, for example, the speaker began by discussing the most dangerous operations in masonry construction. Next he considered the most common types of injury; then he explained the incidence of accidents among workers of different age and experience; and he concluded with an explanation of a three-step plan of attack to reduce accidents. He discussed each of these topics in terms of the "parts" provided by the division: the *operations,* the *types,* the *incidences,* and the *steps.*[2]

No matter how you organize your report, always work for accurate, concise, sharp divisions. Mixed lists, long, unclassified lists, overlapping topics, fuzzy distinctions, and intrusions of unrelated items are signs of faulty analysis.

The sample outline that follows is an example of topical organization suitable for reporting. Such outlines may be tight and rigorous

[2] A report by Howard H. Warzyn, Senior Engineer, Construction section, National Safety Council.

or relatively relaxed and informal, depending on the subject and
needs of the occasion.

Introduction

I. The woman voter is important in this election year.
   A. Over 110 million people in the United States are eligible to vote.
   B. Over 63 per cent of the eligible voters cast ballots in the last
      presidential election year.
   C. More than half (approximately 56 million) of the eligible voters
      are women.
II. I wish to analyze the woman's use of the vote, factors influencing
    the woman's vote, and some of the effects of the woman's vote.

Discussion

I. To what extent do women value the franchise?
   A. Voting records show that women are becoming increasingly ac-
      tive in political life.
   B. What women vote?
      1. A larger percentage in upper-income brackets vote.
      2. There are more voters in the upper educational brackets.
      3. A larger percentage vote in metropolitan areas than in rural
         areas.
II. These factors influence the woman's vote.
   A. Women vote more according to their interests than men do, and
      with more of an awareness of issues.
   B. There is greater conservatism among women voters.
   C. Family influences affect their vote.
      1. In one case in twenty, the husband and wife vote for different
         political parties.
      2. Parents and children vote differently in one case out of ten.
      3. The proportion of disagreement among in-laws is one in five.
III. What are the effects of the woman's vote?
   A. What is its impact on political parties?
      1. Control remains in hands of men.
      2. Women are active on the precinct level.
      3. Women are given modest positions in party organizations.
   B. Women have greater influence on local elections and local issues
      than at the national level.
   C. There is enough difference between distribution of men's votes
      and women's votes to make women's votes crucial in close elec-
      tions.

Conclusion

I. Women are making progress in using the franchise.
   A. They were given the ballot in 1920.

B. The percentage of women casting the ballot is increasing.

C. The development of organizations such as the League of Women Voters tends to increase their influence.

II. Parties and candidates cannot afford to neglect the woman voter.

POINTS TO KEEP IN MIND

1. The tests of a good report are relevancy and dependability of its information, and the clarity and interest with which it is presented.

2. To be an effective reporter, you need to acquire a capacity for critical inquiry, a commitment to objectivity, and a keen sense of discrimination for sorting out what is important in any particular case.

3. The compositional tools of the reporter are exposition, description, and narration.

4. The topical outline affords the appropriate structure for your report.

EXERCISES

1. Make a report on some process—how something is made, how something operates, how something is marketed, how you use a product. Try to reduce the process to a series of steps. These will be your main points. Amplify each main point with specific, concrete materials. Make your report interesting as well as informative. In preparing this report, be certain to draw up a careful topical outline as a basis for your speech. Discuss this kind of outline in class until you are sure you understand it.

2. Plan a short biographical report on a historical figure, a contemporary person, or an interesting fictional character. Make the subject of your report come alive for your listeners. Deal with two or three of the most interesting facets of the man's life. Here is a chance to use vivid description and narration.

3. Choose an important event that genuinely interests you—either a recent event or one that took place long ago. Steep yourself in information about it. Report it to your audience so that the event will live for them. Give your report the color and life and suspense that marked the event itself.

4. Plan a review of a book you have read or a play or movie that you have attended. Your primary purpose here is to report rather than evaluate. Make the review interesting and vivid, but remain impartial and objective. We are interested here in *learning about* the book, play, or motion picture, rather than in your opinion of its merits.

eighteen

Advocacy

The president of the Student Council is speaking to the student body: "As you know, the Council has voted to uphold the Board of Publications in their decision to replace Jim Meyers as editor of the *Daily Reporter*. Several of us sat in on the Board's discussion of the case. Later we took it up in Council meetings. Professor Smith, who has been chairman of the Board of Publications for years, gave us an unbiased report on the whole incident leading to Meyers' dismissal. Now, we've got nothing against Jim. We like him, and we respect his position. At the same time we're convinced that the Board's decision is right. We think you should support the action of the Board and Council because. . . ."

Here is an introduction to a speech of advocacy. The president of the Council has made an inquiry into a problem and has studied a report on it. He has reached a conclusion. He has committed himself to a position, and he now speaks to win support for it. This is advocacy in action.

KINDS OF ADVOCACY

Some people are professional advocates—lawyers, salesmen, and public relations men, to name a few. Men and women in many other occupations—clergymen, executives, and legislators, for example—often speak as advocates. But advocacy is not limited to these occupations. All of us speak to convince and persuade in family councils, community meetings, and even in the most informal social gatherings.

Advocacy may be presented in public speech or in conversation. And, in either case, other speakers may or may not be moved to express opposing views. If such opposition does develop, we have all the necessary ingredients of debate, no matter how public or private, formal or informal the occasion may be.

THE METHODS OF ADVOCACY

An understanding of the methods of advocacy will enable you to present your views convincingly and persuasively. Basically, these methods consist of five clear-cut steps. But how closely you follow these steps in any particular situation will depend on your specific purpose, the nature of the occasion, and the presence or absence of others who argue against your views.

1. DETERMINE WHAT IT IS YOU ARE PROPOSING OR ATTACKING

In the parlance of the debater, your proposal is your *proposition*. But whether you call it a proposition, a motion, a bill, or simply a statement of position, both you and your listeners need to know what it is. You should always be able to state your proposition in clear, concise, unambiguous terms.

The matters you propose or attack will appear as statements of *fact, value,* or *policy*. Your proposition may be a *factual* judgment: "Air travel is the safest means of transportation." "Television reduces attendance at sports events." Or a *value* judgment: "The new Plymouth is the best buy in the low-priced field." "Alaska is the land of opportunity." Or a *policy* judgment: "State University should build a guest house for parents." "The voting age should be reduced to eighteen years."

2. DETERMINE THE ISSUES

Once you have phrased your proposition, you are faced with this question: What do I have to do to get my proposal accepted, endorsed, or favorably acted on? Or, if you are on the other side of the fence: What do I have to do to defeat the proposal? Whenever you are under some obligation to *prove* your proposition, you must look to the issues for the answer to this question. And you will always be on safer grounds if you know what the issues are. Otherwise you may deceive yourself as well as your audience.

The issues are the *inherent* and *vital* points on which the truth or falsity of a proposition hinges. The words *inherent* and *vital* are the keys to the matter.

The issues are *inherent* because they exist or inhere in the proposition quite apart from anyone's personal wishes or predilections. You discover issues. You don't invent them or make them up. Two or more persons analyzing a proposition independently should discover the same issues. If they do not, either their analysis is faulty or else the proposition is ambiguous.

The issues are *vital* because the life of the proposition depends upon them. If any one of them is opposed successfully, the proposition is lost, just as death results when a single vital organ is destroyed. No point may be regarded as an issue simply because it is interesting, or even because it is important. To qualify as an issue it must be vital.

Suppose we say that the Jones farm, now up for sale, is a good investment. Here is a proposition of value. How do you know the farm is a good investment? In other words, what are the issues? First, is the farm *a good value*—in terms of agricultural production, future subdivision, or any other uses to which it might be put? Second, is the asking price *a fair price* on the current market? And third, are *real estate prices likely to rise* so that the investment will yield a significant inflationary increment?

Let's take our example one step further. Suppose a real estate agent offers the Jones farm to Mr. Davis as an investment. Now we have gone beyond a proposition of value—we have a proposition of policy. In addition to the first three issues, we now have three new ones: Does Davis have *the financial resources* to swing this deal? Will he get *a fair return* for his time and trouble in making the transaction? Is this the *best investment* he can make?

The problem of finding the issues may be simple or complex. In many propositions the issues are fairly obvious; in others, considerable study and analysis is required. The following steps may help to direct your search: (1) Be certain that you know exactly what your proposition means (define all terms); (2) study both sides of the question; (3) array the leading arguments pro and con; and (4) test the points believed to be issues.

By an "array" we mean a written list of the arguments for and against the proposition arranged in parallel columns. After you have prepared such a list, consolidate the arguments in each list under main headings. Then compare the affirmative and negative lists and note where the main affirmative and negative arguments clash. These points of clash are likely to be the issues—or, at least, a close approximation of the issues.

After the issues have been phrased tentatively, the following tests should be applied: (1) Is *each* proposed issue vital to the proposition? (2) Do the proposed issues include *all* the vital points necessary to establish the proposition? (3) Are the issues as proposed *mutually exclusive?* Does each issue operate as a single, independent factor or variable? (4) Are the issues so phrased that the affirmative answers "Yes" to each issue and the negative answers "No"?

3. PLAN YOUR CASE

Your case is the sum of the arguments, evidence, and any other inducements you offer to secure acceptance of your proposition. You stand or fall on how your case is regarded by the people you are trying to get to accept your proposition. You may present your case in a public speech. You may develop it in conversations with other interested parties. In any event, whenever circumstances permit, it is wise to plan your case carefully.

The main points

These are the principal divisions or lines of argument in your case. They may or may not coincide with the issues.

Let's say that a village council is discussing the advisability of drilling a well to provide a central water supply. Up to now the villagers have had to secure their own water by means of private wells, cisterns, or rain barrels.

There appear to be four issues involved here: (1) Will the proposed well reduce significantly *the inconveniences* imposed by the present arrangement? (2) Will the new well produce water in *sufficient quantity* to meet the needs of the village? (3) Will the new well deliver water of *good quality?* (4) Are *the costs* of this project reasonable?

Assuming these to be the issues, the case *for* the new well might be organized around four main points—convenience, quantity, quality, and cost. And the case *against* the well might be organized around these same points. In both cases, the main points would coincide exactly with the issues.

There is no compelling reason, however, for organizing either case in just this way. A speaker favoring the new well, for example, might decide to break the issue of inconvenience down into two main points, then handle the issues of quantity and quality under a single main point, and conclude with a final point based on the issue of cost. Or he might omit one or more of the issues completely. Or he might, for reasons of strategy, even introduce main points that have little or nothing to do with the issues.

Any advocate, whether he is for or against a proposition, should build his case with full knowledge of the issues. But how he *plans* his case—how he *uses* the issues—will depend on his analysis of his listeners and the known or potential opposition. The issues are impersonal logical considerations. The main points of the case represent the speaker's appraisal of the issues in terms of the occasion. A contention does not become an issue simply because some speaker chooses to make it one of the main points in his argument.

The burden of proof

The burden of proof in any argument always lies with the advocate who is dissatisfied with things as they are. For example, if you propose a new high-school building for your community, you have the burden of proof. This simply means that you must initiate the argument and make a convincing case for your proposal before you can expect action on your proposal. Let's say your next-door neighbor is perfectly happy with the present high-school building. In these circumstances, there is no reason for him to offer a defense of the present building until you have made a case for a new building. And even then, it may be sufficient for him merely to refute your arguments.

Any proposition you choose to discuss, whether it is a proposition of fact, value, or policy, will fall into one of two categories: It will propose some *new* idea, policy, or way of looking at things—some *change* in the status quo. Or it will argue for the preservation of the status quo—for things *as they are now,* for our *present* institutions, values, and convictions. The burden of proof always rests on the speaker who is advocating change. He is the dissatisfied party. He is the one who stands to lose if nothing is done.

In advocacy of any kind, it always pays to know whether you have the burden of proof. This burden imposes two responsibilities: that of initiating the argument, and that of making a case that supports the issues. If you advocate any proposition that involves a change in existing policies, attitudes, and beliefs, these responsibilities are yours. On the other hand, if you support existing policies or attitudes and beliefs generally held, you have no reason to make a case for them until they are effectively challenged. And when you do make your stand, it is sufficient, if you choose, to defeat your opponent on any *one* issue—on any matter that is vital to his proposal.

This doctrine is simple common sense. Our example of the village council illustrates all its points. When the council is in session, quite obviously the people who want the new well will have to present their proposition and defend it. If they say nothing—make no motion and no case—the meeting will adjourn without even considering the matter. Certainly the people who oppose the new well aren't going to mention it. Why should they? They are satisfied with the present water facilities.

But let's say a motion is made that the new well be approved and a strong case is made in its behalf. Such a case, of course, calls for an answer from those who oppose the new well, because it threatens their position. They can no longer remain silent. They must counter this threat with a case that defeats the proposal on at least one vital count, at least one issue. The issues involved here, as we have seen, appear to be convenience, quantity, quality, and cost. The attack would be completely devastating if all issues were opposed successfully. Here the opposition would contend that the present water facilities are adequate, that the proposed well would not deliver enough water anyway, that what water it did produce would be of poor quality, and finally that the costs were prohibitive.

Actually any one of these points would logically defeat the motion. Why seek a new water supply if the present supply is fully adequate? Why drill a new well if it won't produce enough water? Why turn to a well that will deliver water of such poor quality that no one wants to use it? Or why give serious consideration to a proposal that you can't pay for?

W. P. Gullander, President of the National Association of Manufacturers, makes a speech. Listening is George Meany, President of the AFL-CIO. *(Wide World Photos)*

The point is simply this: Wherever and whenever you speak as an advocate, you either have the burden of proof or you don't have it. If you understand the duties and the privileges that are yours in these different circumstances, you are in a position to behave much more persuasively and much more strategically than you would otherwise be able to do. The issues and the burden of proof prescribe your *logical* responsibilities in planning a case. You *may* win an argument without discharging these responsibilities, but critical listeners and informed opponents are likely to hold you to them.

Refutation

When you are planning a case, try to take care of arguments that may be used against you or that may exist in the minds of your listeners. This is what *refutation* means—replying to arguments that oppose your position. You may include a scheme for refutation as part of your planned case, or you may devise it to be used in replying to another speaker.

Your refutation may take the form of an *objection*—you may point out flaws in the other speaker's argument. Or it may take the form of a counterargument—you may present an argument of your own to support a conclusion that is inconsistent with the one you are trying to refute. For example, your opponent declares that Latin should be a required subject because a knowledge of Latin enables students to speak and write English more competently. You might offer the *objection* that he has presented no convincing evidence for his proposition. Or you might *counter* by showing that if the time given to Latin were spent on the study of English, better results would be achieved in the students' use of English.

There are four ways of dealing with arguments that are raised in opposition to your position:

1. Ignore them if they are unimportant.
2. Admit them if you can show that they do not damage your case.
3. Show that they are irrelevant.
4. Refute them: First state them clearly and correctly; then show why they won't hold up.

4. PREPARE A CASE OUTLINE

The outline you prepare for a speech of advocacy should reveal the structure of your case. It gives you a chance to organize all the materials—facts, expert opinions, and inferences—that you plan to present.

The logical outline (see Chapter 8) is ideally suited for speeches of advocacy, for here you present your main points as reasons in support of your proposition. You buttress your main points, in turn, with subpoints that serve as reasons to support the main points. You can carry this reasoning process down to points that can be supported directly by evidence (facts and expert opinions) or to points you believe will be accepted without further support.

This kind of rigorous, logical organization is useful in close argument, but you may find that it denies you the freedom to develop your case persuasively. And it is true that this organization, methodical and logical though it is, may be heavy-footed and dull if it is not brightened by description, narration, and exposition. Consequently the most skillful advocate combines logical and topical outlining in whatever pattern best serves his purpose.

Here is a tightly drawn logical outline. Notice that complete sentences are used and that all subpoints, except those in the introduction, serve as direct support for the points under which they appear.

A HEDGE AGAINST INFLATION
Introduction
I. I should like to propose that now is the time to invest in common stocks.
   A. If you have any surplus funds to invest, I am convinced that common stocks are your best investment at this time.
   B. If you don't have funds to invest, you may know somebody who does.
II. The distinction between stocks and bonds is essential to an understanding of my argument.
   A. A stock certificate is evidence of ownership of one or more shares in a corporation.
   B. A bond is a certificate of ownership of a specified portion of the *debt* of a corporation.

Discussion
I. We face an inflationary period in the years immediately ahead, because
   A. Strong inflationary forces are at work, because
      1. There are heavy consumer demands, because
         a. There is a shortage of residential units.
         b. We are not keeping up with the demand in many commodity lines.

  2. Heavy expansion of manufacturing plant and equipment is in prospect.
  3. Government spending is increasing, because
      a. The international situation calls for heavy military expenditures.
      b. The philosophy of the present administration favors large governmental expenditures.
  B. The evidences of inflation are already at hand, for
     1. Prices have started up again.
     2. We have strong demands from labor.
II. Common stocks increase in value during periods of inflation, because
    A. The tangible assets of the corporation increase in value, because
       1. Plant and equipment are worth more.
       2. Commodity inventories on hand increase in price.
    B. The corporations are able to pay larger dividends out of increased profits.
III. The real value of bonds decreases during inflation, because
     A. They are paid off in cheaper dollars.
     B. The interest rate is fixed.

Conclusion

  I. Investments with fixed returns suffer in an inflationary period.
 II. Common stocks are your best hedge against inflation.

This next sample is another example of a logical outline. Here the speaker is urging action, and he develops his case with this purpose in view. Notice that he also includes some refutation.

VOTE FOR THE CITY MANAGER PLAN

Introduction

  I. I should like to open this meeting with a message from Mayor Brown.
 II. I join the mayor in urging you to go to the polls tomorrow and vote for the city manager plan.

Discussion

  I. The old mayor-council form of city government has outlived its usefulness, because
     A. The system can't handle the growing complexities of city government.
     B. It makes a political football out of city government.
     C. The argument that the mayor-council system is more responsive to the will of the people is a myth.
 II. More progressive cities everywhere are adopting the city manager plan—over a thousand of them—because
     A. It streamlines city government—it is more efficient, because

      1. It places a professional manager in charge.
      2. It fixes responsibility.
      3. It reduces the size of the council.
  B. It takes corruption out of city government.
  C. The contention that we will be unable to get a good city manager for the salary we propose is groundless, because
      1. We already have two applicants.
      2. We know where we can go for a man with an established record as a city manager.
III. Now is the time for us to act, because
  A. Mayor Brown, the best mayor we have had in decades, is retiring.
  B. Mayor Brown supports the new plan.
  C. With few exceptions, our community leaders are behind the plan.

Conclusion

  I. I am not going to promise you that your taxes will be reduced, but I think I can promise more for your tax dollar.
  A. We'll get our garbage collected on time!
  B. We'll get the snow cleaned off the streets!
  C. We'll get better fire and police protection!
  D. And last, but not least, we'll let a little fresh air blow through the city hall!
 II. These things are worth voting for!

5. DEVELOP YOUR CASE PERSUASIVELY

Persuasion rests squarely on four basic concepts: attention, motivation, suggestion, and implication.

Attention

Listeners respond favorably to speakers who capture their attention and hold it at a high level. An audience that listens only grudgingly and halfheartedly is unlikely to be stirred into action or into acceptance of a proposition. In giving speeches of advocacy, put to work what you learned about developing your ideas in Chapter 10 and what you learned about motivated listening in Chapter 12.

Plan an exciting opening. Make your listeners feel that you are talking to each of them as an individual. State your proposition arrestingly. Make abundant use of illustrative materials so that the bony structure of your case will be endowed with flesh and blood. Fresh language ignites interest; tired language snuffs it out. Show directness and vitality in your delivery. It is easy to accept the conclusions of an interesting speaker and just as easy to reject the conclusions of a dull one.

Motivation

Make your listeners feel that their needs or desires will be satisfied by what you are recommending. Offer them a reward for buying your proposition. Some people respond most readily when the rewards are concrete and immediate. As they listen to you, they are asking, "What's in it for me?" But don't assume that everyone acts only for selfish purposes. Every day people are moved by calls to greatness. Every day they make personal sacrifices for the sake of justice, compassion, and the common good.

Effective motivation is not accomplished by working a few purple patches into your speech or by making a few isolated appeals. It must be part of the warp and woof of your argument. The reasons you use to prove your case should motivate your listeners to accept your conclusion. Ask yourself *two* questions about each reason before you use it in developing your case: Does it advance my argument logically and convincingly? And does it offer an incentive to my listeners to believe or act as I want them to believe or act?

In short, the key to effective motivation is first to identify the needs, interests, wants, and desires of your listeners and then to show them how your proposition will help satisfy those needs.

Suggestion

Sometimes you can persuade listeners by dropping hints rather than by giving them a developed argument. You let them come around to your conclusion in their own way. In short, you don't spell everything out, although you should be able to do so if you have to. Present your listeners with an attitude, a word, an example, a story, or a gesture, and then let them interpret it for themselves.

A speaker who was urging a bond issue for a new school once said, "I'm going to vote for this bond issue even though I'm a taxpayer and haven't any children in school. And I'm not wholly altruistic in doing so either." He didn't have to spin out his argument. He simply suggested that if he was willing to pay higher taxes even though he didn't have children, those who had children should be much more interested. He merely hinted at the benefits the new school would bring to the community and the general increase in property values that would accompany it.

Another speaker, confronted with an incredibly stupid argument, simply shook his head slowly and said, "I pass." This action was more tactful and perhaps more eloquent than an extended reply would have been. It simply suggested that the silly argument had refuted itself. In effect, the speaker said, "Why go into it? We all see its weakness. Let's get on with the business."

Implication

In using implication, you lead your audience to draw the conclusion that you want them to draw by explaining a matter to them, by describing a situation, or by telling a story. You use description, narration, and exposition—the tools of the reporter—to present a picture that implies your conclusion. The argument is implicit in your explanation, but you don't state it outright.

Let's say you want to persuade a friend to accompany you on a short vacation to New Hampshire. You describe the brilliant foliage, the hills, the "Old Man of the Mountain," inviting trails, streams and lakes teeming with fish. You tell him about a lodge off the beaten path where interesting people sit around a huge fireplace on cool evenings. You have certainly used this technique at one time or another, whether or not you called it development by implication.

The outline below is for a speech that is persuasive in purpose and implicative in development. The talk is designed to involve the audience psychologically and stimulate the "vagabond spirit." The topical outline is appropriate since the talk proceeds along descriptive, narrative, and expository lines, and key phrases are sufficient because of the highly personal and informal nature of the material and occasion.

A SUMMER ON TIPTOE

Introduction

  I. Traveling to Europe in a vagabond spirit
    A. The high adventure of planning the trip
    B. Joining the green passport club
 II. Watching the New York skyline recede from the deck of the Queen Mary

Discussion

I. First stop is Britain
  A. Glimpses of the countryside from the window of a boat train
  B. This is London
    1. City of medieval towns
    2. Excellent transportation plus the courtesy of the people make it easy to get around
    3. Queuing up for a day in Parliament
  C. Short journeys out of London
    1. The spires of Oxford
    2. On the banks of the River Cam
    3. The swans of Avon
  D. The moors of Scotland
II. From Dunkirk to the Riviera
  A. Making your fractured French work in the provinces
  B. Left Bank—Right Bank
    1. The live-and-let-live attitudes of the Parisians
    2. A city of art, superb cuisine, and gaiety
  C. A week end at Villefranche
III. The trek north from Rome to Amsterdam
  A. Crisis on the crest of the Apennines
  B. The tinkle of cow bells at St. Gotthard Pass
  C. Twilight specters in the historic city of Worms
  D. The land of green canals
    1. From the terrace of the Hotel Grand Gooiland
    2. Rembrandt's "Night Watch"
    3. The Peace Palace of the Hague
IV. Some quick glimpses of Belgium

Conclusion

I. Goodbye to the White Cliffs
II. Europe is within your reach

POINTS TO KEEP IN MIND

1. Know what it is you are proposing or attacking and be prepared to phrase it as a concise proposition of fact, value, or policy.

2. Analyze your proposition to discover the issues.

3. Plan your case: Build it around main points calculated to win the response you are after; build it with full awareness of the responsibilities and opportunities arising out of the burden of proof; build it to counter arguments that may be used against you.

4. Prepare a case outline—a logical outline or some adaptation of it.

5. Develop your case persuasively by using attention, motivation, suggestion, and implication.

EXERCISES

1. Phrase five propositions of policy that you would like to defend or oppose in speeches of advocacy. State the issues in each proposition and be prepared to defend your analysis.

2. Plan a speech of advocacy on any one of the propositions you devised in Exercise 1. Make this a tight, logical speech in which your main points coincide exactly with the issues. Give special attention to cogency of argument and adequacy of evidence.

3. Plan a persuasive speech in which you urge your listeners to take a specific action. Make sure that the action is reasonable and that they are capable of taking it. For instance: Join an organization; read a particular book; eat at a certain restaurant; buy something. Give your speech with conviction and sincerity.

4. Divide the class into groups of five. Let each group adopt a proposition of policy that lends itself to debate. Two people will defend the proposition and two will oppose it. The fifth person will act as chairman and moderator. Then conduct a debate in which the positions of the several speakers are developed through conversation. Do *not* work as teams. Each speaker is on his own and it is up to him to get his ideas accepted as best he can. The moderator's job is to hold the reins on the debate, to draw speakers out, to give each speaker a fair chance, and to invite questions and comments from the class when the debate is concluded.

nineteen

Evocation

The purpose of evocative speaking is to inspire or entertain. It rewards listeners with emotional satisfactions ranging from the sublime to the ridiculous. Mind and emotions combine in all speech, but evocative talk gives *priority* to man's emotional needs.

Inspirational talk engenders a feeling of fulfillment, energizes hopes, reaffirms loyalties, stirs sympathy, stimulates appreciation. Its purpose is to awaken, quicken, and excite us. Entertaining speech, on the other hand, diverts and relaxes us. Listening to a pun, a joke, or a bizarre experience releases us from tension and tedium.

Although evocative speaking is commonly associated with sermons, lectures, ceremonial talks, and after-dinner speeches, it is by no means limited to public occasions. We seek diversion and fellowship through informal conversation with our friends. Inspiration and entertainment find their way into interviews, conferences, and all sorts of group meetings. The term *evocative speaking*, then, applies to all situations in which either emotional stimulation or relaxation is appropriate.

ELEMENTS COMMON TO EVOCATIVE SPEAKING

A high degree of speaker sensitivity

All good speaking calls for sensitivity, but evocative speaking requires a particularly fine awareness of what is appropriate. A report or a logical demonstration of a proposition invites objectivity. Evocative speaking, on the other hand, ventures into intimate areas of personal experience around which we ordinarily throw a protective cloak—our fears, hopes, failures, whims, ideals, and caprices. Our guards are up until the speaker satisfies us that he is a sensitive and perceptive person. We need to feel confident of his sense of taste and propriety. We want assurance that he knows the difference between sentiment and sentimentality, between wry humor and boorish jokes.

To say that evocative speaking calls for high sensitivity is not to suggest that only a few, rare mortal beings are endowed with this capacity. Everyone, as he grows up, learns to draw upon his accumulated experiences and make judgments of what is fitting. You learn when to stifle an impulse to laugh, and when to let go. If you're talking to someone who is in a panic over his grades, you withhold the joke about the fellow who was booted out of school. You don't make sport out of your interest in the obituary columns in the local newspaper when talking with someone who has recently lost a close relative. You choose the friends with whom you are willing to share your deepest personal feelings involving love, ambition, and fears.

The point is this: In evocative speaking, you must make full use of your sensitivities. No two situations are identical. Factors such as age, sex, and religion may be critical. Moods are evanescent. Never assume that a joke or appeal that was successful in one situation will be suitable to the next.

A high degree of audience involvement

You want your listeners to do more than agree with you. You want them to empathize with you and what you are saying. You must create or recreate *specific experiences* with which your listeners can identify their own emotions.

Our minds assent to praise for Albert Schweitzer, the great humanitarian, but the winsome story of a boy's admiration for Schweitzer *moved* thousands to follow his lead. When thirteen-year-old Robert Hill, son of an army sergeant stationed in Italy, read of Schweitzer's hospital in Africa and its continuing need for medical supplies, he wanted to help out. He bought a bottle of aspirins and then asked an Allied Air Force Commander if he would drop it off when he flew over the hospital. By chance an Italian radio station carried the story. It caught on, and donations of $400,000 poured in. Subsequently, Robert and four and a half tons of medical supplies were flown to Africa in planes provided by the Italian and

French governments. Said a grateful and astonished Dr. Schweitzer, "I never thought a child could do so much for my hospital." The point here is that someone at the Italian radio station discerned the evocative elements implicit in this human interest story and recognized its possibilities for creating audience sympathy and empathy. No doubt, though, the results exceeded his expectations.

A high degree of creative imagination

Do you cringe a little when you hear the word *inspiration?* You have been drenched with corn-soaked exhortations to "buck up, old boy" and to strive upwards and onwards. Does "speaking to entertain" seem fatuous to you? You're probably still groaning at musty after-dinner jokes of the Pat and Mike variety. We all borrow ideas and materials, of course, but we should never be tempted by embalmed platitudes and decayed jokes. Some approaches have been worked to death. "When I was a boy, I walked five miles through snowdrifts to get an education"—however honest and sincere the speaker is, this opening probably leaves you a bit cold too.

Avoid hackneyed formulas. Inject fresh insights and your own individuality into what you say. Nobody else has had exactly the same experiences as you. No matter how ancient your theme, your listeners will find new inspiration and new delight if you endow it with authentic freshness and individuality. And match the freshness of your approach with freshness of language. Use words that are rich in associations, words that conjure up images. Observe how Carl Sandburg evokes appreciation for the character of Lincoln through images that suggest antithetical qualities he embodied and held in tension.

Not often in the story of mankind does a man arrive on earth who is both steel and velvet, who is as hard as rock and soft as drifting fog, who holds in his heart and mind the paradox of terrible storm and peace unspeakable and perfect.[1]

SPEAKING TO INSPIRE

Although there is no single, all-purpose method for you to follow in speaking to inspire, you will find that you can choose one of four

[1] Carl Sandburg's tribute to Lincoln before a joint session of Congress, February 12, 1959. *Vital Speeches of the Day*, March 1, 1959, p. 293.

master-plans, and perhaps use one or more of the others in sub-sidiary ways.

THE IMPLICATIVE METHOD

To understand and appreciate the essential characteristic of the implicative approach, we suggest you first read Eric Sevareid's radio talk entitled "The Dark of the Moon."

Good evening . . . This is not only Friday night, thank goodness, but the first warm and balmy night of the year in these parts; the first frogs are singing; altogether this is hardly the night for whispering sweet sentiments about the reciprocal trade act, the extension thereof. But since we are confined, by tradition to the contemplation of public themes and issues, let us contemplate the moon. The lovely and luminous moon has become a public issue; for quite a few thousand years it was a private issue; it figured in purely bilateral negotiations between lovers; in the incantations of jungle witchdoctors and Indian corn planters; poets from attic windows issued the statements about the moon, and they made better reading than the mimeographed handouts now being issued by assistant secretaries of defense.

The moon was always measured in terms of hope and reassurance and the heart pangs of youth on such a night as this; it is now measured in terms of mileage and foot-pounds of rocket thrust; children sent sharp, sweet wishes to the moon; now they dream of blunt nosed missiles.

There must come a time, in every generation, when those who are older secretly get off the train of progress, willing to walk back to where they came from, if they can find the way. We're afraid we're getting off now. Cheer, if you wish, the first general or Ph.D. who splatters something on the kindly face of the moon. We shall grieve for him, for ourself, for the young lovers and poets and dreamers to come, for the ancient moon will never be the same again. Therefore, we suspect, the heart of man will never be the same.

We find it very easy to wait for the first photographs of the other side of the moon; for we have not yet seen the other side of Lake Louise or the Blue Ridge peak that shows through the cabin window.

We find ourself quite undisturbed about the front page talk of "controlling the earth from the moon," because we do not believe it. If neither men nor gadgets nor both combined can control the earth from the earth, we fail to see how they will do so from the moon.

It is exciting talk, indeed, the talk of man's advance toward space. But one little step in man's advance toward man—that, we think, would be truly exciting; let those who wish try to discover the composition of a lunar crater; we would settle for discovering the true mind of a Russian commissar or the inner heart of a delinquent child.

There is, after all, another side, a dark side to the human spirit, too. Men have hardly begun to explore these regions; and it is going to be a very great pity, if we advance upon the bright side of the moon with the dark side of ourselves, if the cargo in the first rockets to reach there consists of fear and chauvinism and suspicion. Surely, we ought to have our credentials in order, our hands very clean and perhaps a prayer for forgiveness on our lips as we prepare to open the ancient vault of the shining moon.[2]

What elements emerge from your reading of Sevareid's remarks that are common to the implicative development? Thematically, the speech focuses upon values by which people live. Symbolical in tone rather than literal, the talk is developed by means of hints and suggestion rather than by argument or didactic exposition.

Quietly speculative, the talk unfolds through juxtaposition of ideas that provide new insight and by a succession of subtle images that stimulate the listener's imagination. It affords an example of what Lew Sarett called the discovery of poetic implications in the prose facts of life. In short, the success of the implicative method as applied to evocative discourse turns on some problem in human values, on originality in the juxtaposition of ideas, and on stylistic deftness.

THE METHOD OF COMPARISON AND CONTRAST

You can create a mood and heighten appreciation by pointing out dramatic similarities and differences between ideas, events, people. You might spark a new response to our rich, diversified heritage, for example, by contrasting the stark, crude frontier life suggested by the restoration of New Salem, Illinois, with the gentility and elegance of Mount Vernon, Virginia. In his speech "The New South," given in 1886, Henry Grady developed his theme by unfolding a succession of comparisons and contrasts. He opened with, "There is a South of slavery and secession—that South is dead. There is a South of union and freedom—that South, thank God, is living, breathing, growing every hour." As Grady continued, he used con-

---

[2] CBS News broadcast presented over the CBS Radio Network, March 28, 1958. Reprinted by permission.

trast and comparison to soften the bitterness between the sections and to emphasize their common culture and common ideals.

THE CHRONOLOGICAL METHOD

Carrying your audience through successive periods of time is particularly appropriate on occasions that call for tribute, dedication, and commemoration—speeches in which you evaluate human experience. A notable example is the Gettysburg Address. Lincoln opened with a reference to the past ("Fourscore and seven years ago . . ."), moved on to the immediate occasion ("We are met on a great battlefield of that war. We have come to dedicate . . ."), and ended by holding up the goals of the future (". . . that this nation, under God, shall have a new birth of freedom—and that government of the people, by the people, and for the people, shall not perish from the earth.").

Naturally you don't have to stick slavishly to one order of events. You might want to open with the present, look ahead to the future, or flash back to the past.

THE METHOD OF CUMULATIVE DEVELOPMENT

You give an idea impact by restating it in new contexts. You impress the idea on your audience by weaving together example after example, illustration after illustration, quotation after quotation.

Suppose you speak to affirm some principle drawn from human experience, such as "The only thing constant is change itself" or "Imagination is the power behind all creative effort." You might open by stating your theme and then give examples and illustrations that reveal the range of its truth and applications. But your speech will be even more arresting if you open with a well-chosen example that suggests the theme, and then offer additional instances that carry your thought forward into ever widening circles of human experience. Note this emerging pattern in the introductory passage of a sermon by Ernest Fremont Tittle:

> Once there was a young man in Anathoth, a small town not far from Jerusalem, who was called of God to be a preacher. He began his ministry in his home town and was not well received. Quite the contrary. A group of influential people, taking umbrage at the things he was saying, determined to get rid of him. In fact, they

went even so far as to plot against his life. When the young preacher learned of this, not unnaturally he was upset. In his anxiety he turned to God for some word of

Opening example suggesting the universal principle to be developed

encouragement, and the word that came was this: "If you have run with men on foot, and they have tired you out, then how will you keep up with horses?" Strange comfort! Like the whimsical admonition: "Cheer up, the worst is yet to come." Yet in Jeremiah's case it availed. Life for him did become more strenuous, more difficult and dangerous. But learning to run with men on foot and not get all tired out, he won the power to keep up with horses.

That life's demands increase with the years is a fact of human experience. In high school you may think the assignments are pretty stiff, and so they are; but how relatively easy in comparison with what is required of you if and when you get into college! When the first

Application of principle to a variety of personal situations

baby comes, you may think: Oh my! What would I do if I had two or more to care for? And presently you may find out. When you try to get started in business or in a professional career, you may take comfort from the belief that the first years are the hardest. You will, however, be mistaken. The first will presently appear easy in comparison with what you are now up against. You may even look back upon them with a feeling of nostalgia, wishing that life were now as relatively simple and undemanding as it then was. It is indeed a fact that burdens and responsibilities increase with the years.

This holds true of human history as well as of the individual life. Life for us is easier in some ways than it was for those who came before us. Streets are lighted and paved. Houses have bathrooms, electric lighting, central heating. . . .

But technological advance, if it in some respects made

Extension of principle to wider areas of human experience

life easier, has at the same time created new problems and dangers. Those who came before us knew the meaning of privation and hardship but not the meaning of mass unemployment or of widespread want in the midst of plenty. They were confronted with the problem of winning fundamental freedoms from reluctant kings, emperors, and czars, but knew nothing of the problem of how to *preserve* freedom in a world situation become so complex as to make necessary an increasing measure of government control. They knew the meaning of war but not of total war waged with absolute weapons against whole populations. Science and technology have brought it to pass that, whereas those who came before us ran with men on foot, we have got to keep up with horses.[3]

OUTLINING INSPIRATIONAL SPEECH

In working up an inspirational speech, use the topical outline. Organize and state your points with finesse lest you blunt the fine edge of your purpose. The following outline is drawn from a speech by Raymond Fosdick, "The Challenge to Knowledge," delivered at the dedication of the giant telescope on Mount Palomar, California.[4]

Introduction

I. In 1843, John Quincy Adams helped dedicate the Cincinnati Astronomical Observatory.
   A. He deplored the neglect of science in the United States.
   B. His speech did not foreshadow today's gap between advancing science and social control of it.
II. Today, knowledge and destruction have joined in a Grand Alliance.

Discussion

I. Our dilemma is that we can't foresee the uses to which knowledge will be put.
   A. Knowledge itself can't be classified into safe and unsafe categories.
   B. We can't predict how the instruments of knowledge will be used.
      1. The University of California's cyclotron, which was used to further the atomic bomb, was originally conceived of as an instrument of pure research.
      2. Who knows to what purposes this telescope may be converted?
   C. We may elect to use any segment of knowledge for destructive purposes.
II. How should we deal with our modern dilemma?
   A. We can't fix the boundaries of intellectual adventure.
      1. This would certainly lead to retrogression.
      2. We can't suppress man's innate and insatiable desire to know things.

[3] *A Mighty Fortress* (New York: Harper & Row, Publishers, 1950), pp. 19-21. Reprinted by permission.
[4] See *Vital Speeches of the Day,* July 15, 1948, pp. 586-87.

    B. We need to anchor knowledge to sound moral purposes.
      1. Man's towering enemy is his own moral inadequacy.
      2. Man's survival hinges on the moral use he makes of his new
        knowledge.
III. Modern man may well face his final choice.
    A. He can use his knowledge to build a rational world.
    B. Or he can put his knowledge at the disposal of his untamed
      passions.

Conclusion

  I. This telescope holds the promise of a healing perspective.
    A. Through it man confronts the order and beauty of the universe.
    B. It will dramatize the unsolved mysteries of his universe and ex-
      istence.
    C. It will help man to see himself in proportion.
 II. There is a real sense in which Mount Palomar is Mount Everest.

SPEAKING TO ENTERTAIN

The range of topics suitable for an entertaining talk is almost unlimited. The subjects grow out of your experiences, interests, observations, and imagination. On the surface, this statement may not
strike you as very helpful. But there are no categories of entertaining talk as such. Almost anything can be treated entertainingly if
you have an intimate acquaintance with it, look at it from a fresh
point of view, and present it engagingly.

Call to mind experiences and interests your listeners might consider unusual. Recall out-of-the-way places where you have lived
or visited, extraordinary events you have witnessed, a novel hobby
you pursue, a curious institution you know about, a cult you have
studied, a celebrity you have met, a harrowing experience. Here are
some examples of novel subjects that students have used successfully
for entertaining talks.

    Life in a ghost town
    My fractured French in Quebec
    Face-to-face with a bear in the woods
    My interview with the Vice-President
    My summer as a ballet dancer
    A restaurant where you pay what you think the meal is worth
    Working my way through Europe
    Fighting a forest fire

Outwitting a thief
A parrot that talked too much
Playing in a bagpipe band
Hurricane panic
I was there when my father was married
A summer on a sheep ranch
The deepfreeze I won

But novelty is not a requisite. You know from your own listening that people talk engagingly on ordinary, prosaic matters. They give these everyday occurrences a unique twist, a wry interpretation, a comic slant, or a suspenseful development. Remember too that a subject may seem ordinary to one audience and extraordinary to another. These subjects, for example, have yielded delightful speeches.

A night on a day coach
An acre of tri-levels
Pets that have known me
Mannerisms of teachers
A TV commentator who speaks as the Voice of Destiny
Frantic behavior during exam week
Traffic snarls
The ideal parent
My thirty seconds of play in a football game
A broken fiddle string
Summer brings poison ivy and Aunt Maud
Profile of a Good Humor man
Blind dates
A fifty-year-old teen-ager

KEYS TO EFFECTIVE ENTERTAINING TALK

1. Re-creation

As you plan your talk, re-create it in your imagination so vividly that once again you hear, see, touch, taste; so realistically that once again you feel fear, panic, rhythm, or whatever sensation you wish to convey.

2. Sequence

Line up your steps or points so that you won't stumble or backtrack. Avoid interrupting yourself with, "Oh, I forgot to mention. . . ."

True, you need to keep your material flexible enough for easy adaptation to your audience. But you can plan without putting your speech into a straitjacket.

3. Suspense

An element of suspense and surprise picks up interest. Don't model every speech after a whodunit, but keep your audience guessing whenever you can. This calls for close attention to details that build toward your punch line or climax. Suspense depends on subtle blending of composition and delivery.

4. Vividness

Give enough detail to establish mood and action—but don't use a dump truck. Let concrete language and images work for you. "The man dressed oddly" doesn't help us to see him. But suppose you say he wore a Homburg hat, a rumpled plaid shirt, a dinner jacket, gray flannel slacks, and a pair of sneakers. Now we see what you mean.

5. Dramatization

If it is conversation you are recounting, let the participants speak for themselves. Use actual dialogue. If you have a knack for mimicry, go right ahead. Suggest mood and action through posture, gestures, and pantomime.

6. Timing

This is tricky. Droll incidents can be annihilated by machine-gun delivery. On the other hand, action-loaded material needs to be presented at a good tempo. Fit the pace to the nature of the materials and the mood of the occasion. Bear in mind too that subtle touches are conveyed by well-placed pauses and skillful phrasing.

HUMOR

Humor is useful (1) in helping you to get on good terms with your audience quickly, (2) in making serious points painlessly, (3) in providing comic relief from concentrated mental effort and tension, and (4) in affording mutual delight by uttering and hearing nonsense.

Humor arises out of a spirit of play and out of a surprising or incongruous turn of events.

CHARACTERISTIC FORMS OF HUMOR

1. Plays on words

These include boners, slips-of-the-tongue, misused words leading to confusion, and puns. A lawyer is questioning a witness in police court. "Will you testify to the driver's sobriety?" asks the lawyer. "Well, now I dunno," replies the witness, "but my guess is that he ain't so bright."

A pun is more likely to be intentional. If it is perfectly timed and tuned to the situation, it will get the laugh it deserves. Two men driving along barely miss a collision when a Cadillac cuts sharply into their traffic lane. One of the men says, "You never know how a cad'll act." Whether or not you find this pun funny, remember that it takes its humor from the event and emotions of the moment. But a pun can never be quite sure of itself. One man's pun may be another man's punishment.

2. Overstatement and understatement

Overstatement leads to a broad, open kind of humor. Work in some element of plausibility, though, unless you can put your story across with such dexterity that your listeners will delight in your ingenuity. Usually exaggeration succeeds best when your manner underplays your words. The comic effect of Will Rogers' outrageous comments was heightened by his dry, mischievous manner. Mark Twain perfected a deadpan delivery.

Understatement is a more sophisticated form of humor. "Waiting to be whipped," said Josh Billings, "is the most uninteresting period of boyhood life." *Uninteresting*, as any boy who knows will testify, is hardly the word. It surprises by saying too little. Mark Twain was a master at combining overstatement and understatement. Note the abrupt switch in this passage from a speech on widespread property damage, injuries, and death caused by Fourth of July celebrations.

I have suffered in that way myself. I have had a relative killed in that way. One was in Chicago years ago—an uncle of mine, just as good an uncle as I have ever had, and I had lots of them—yes, uncles to burn, uncles to spare. This poor uncle, full of patriotism, opened his mouth to hurrah, and a rocket went down his throat. Before that man could ask

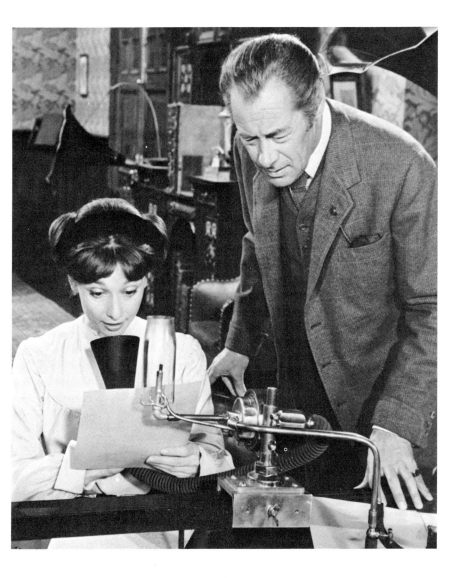

Rex Harrison and Audrey Hepburn, in a scene from My Fair Lady. Miss Hepburn, as Eliza Doolittle, is learning the proper use of aspirates: each time she pronounces an initial "h," the flame in the burner flickers. Hence the refrain "In Hertford, Hereford, and Hampshire, hurricanes hardly ever happen." (© *Warner Brothers Pictures, Inc.*)

for a drink of water to quench that thing, it blew up and scattered him all over the forty-five states, and—really, now this is true. I know about it myself—twenty-four hours after that it was raining buttons, recognizable as his, on the Atlantic seaboard. A person cannot have a disaster like that and be entirely cheerful the rest of his life.[5]

3. Caricature

This is humor through distortion. A ridiculous subject is treated with mock seriousness; a serious subject becomes absurd. Under suitable circumstances, almost anything may be caricatured—individuals, events, groups, manners, and customs. As one of America's most popular lecturers, John Mason Brown knows well the types of people who live to be heard.

. . . Before the hall has been cleared and the chairman has asked for any questions, their full lungs have ballooned them to their feet. When they do leap up, they do so with the vigor of salmon headed upstream.

"Mr. Chairman!" they call, their eyes rolling with frenzy, their voices a cross between Daniel Webster's and Willie Stevens', and their notes tucked behind their backs. "Mr. Chairman!"

But the chairman, knowing them all too well from previous sessions, looks the other way. To him they seem not men and women but dreaded ectoplasms. He no more sees them than Macbeth's guests spied Banquo at the banquet. "Mr. Chairman," they continue, eyeing the audience as Danton must have surveyed the Convention. The audience mutters, sometime going so far in its forgetfulness of Emily Post and the Bill of Rights as to cry, "Sit down," "Throw him out," "Shut up."

"Mr. Chairman, is this the United States of America or is it not?"

The chairman, well aware of his Rand McNally, is sorrowfully compelled to admit it is.

"Oh, you, Mr. Ventrelibre," he says, much as a judge might recognize an old offender. His tones would have chilled anyone else, but not Mr. Ventrelibre.

"Mr. Chairman," continues Mr. Ventrelibre, whose name is legion, "as an American citizen I demand the right to be heard."

And heard he is, while you and the chairman get so tired of standing that finally you have to sit down, and while those in the audience who

---

[5] *Mark Twain's Speeches* (New York: Harper & Row, Publishers, 1923), p. 347. Reprinted by permission.

have remained for the question period begin to run, not walk, to the nearest exits.[6]

4. Satire and irony

Although not identical, these two forms of humor are closely related. *Satire,* which often bears a trace of irony, is trenchant wit laced with a spirit of ridicule. Commonly this ridicule is directed against specific human blunders, stupidities, vanities, and vices. In *irony,* we say one thing and mean another. We poke fun by intimating meanings that are in opposition to or at least at variance with the literal sense of our statements if taken at face value.

Both satire and irony backfire if their barbs are so sharp that they puncture the spirit of play and create sympathy for the victims. After long suffering at the hands of maladroit program chairmen, Stephen Leacock had won the right to satirize them:

When any lecturer goes across to England from this side of the water there is naturally a tendency on the part of the chairman to play upon this fact. This is especially true in the case of a Canadian like myself. The chairman feels that the moment is fitting for one of those great imperial thoughts that bind the British Empire together. But sometimes the expression of the thought falls short of the full glory of the conception.

Witness this (word for word) introduction that was used against me by a clerical chairman in a quiet spot in the south of England.

"Not so long ago, ladies and gentlemen," said the vicar, "we used to send out to Canada various classes of our community to help build up that country. We sent out our laborers, we sent out our scholars and professors. Indeed, we even sent out our criminals. And now," with a wave of his hand towards me, "they are coming back."

There was no laughter. An English audience is nothing if not literal; and they are as polite as they are literal. They understood that I was a reformed criminal and as such, they gave me a hearty burst of applause.[7]

Note the vein of irony in this passage from a speech by Mark Twain. After commenting on the great number of people killed in railroad accidents, he added:

[6] *Accustomed As I Am* (New York: W. W. Norton & Company, 1942), pp. 52-54. Reprinted by permission.

[7] Reprinted by permission of Dodd, Mead & Company from *Laugh With Leacock.* Copyright 1930 by Dodd, Mead & Company, Inc.

. . . But, thank Heaven, the railway companies are generally disposed to do the right and kindly thing without compulsion. I know of an instance which greatly touched me at the time. After an accident, the company sent home the remains of a dear distant relative of mine in a basket, with the remark, "Please state what figure you hold him at—and return the basket." Now there couldn't be anything friendlier than that.[8]

SUGGESTIONS ON YOUR OWN USE OF HUMOR

1. Original humor is best

Don't hesitate to try your own brand. You may have more ability than you have yet discovered. Given a mellow mood, listeners enjoy the sly comment, the quick comeback, banter, raillery, a play on words. Remember, you don't always have to work for the big laugh. There are many states of amusement short of the guffaw.

2. Be sure the humor is appropriate

Adapt your humor to the sophistication of your listeners and the tone of the occasion. Humor may be too subtle or not subtle enough. Low humor is dubious.

3. Plan humor when it is integral to your speech

Good humor may be spontaneous or it may only appear to be so. If you are forewarned that your audience will be expecting you to talk with a light touch, you will want to make careful preparation just as you do for any other type of speaking. Experienced humorists seldom depend on the inspiration of the moment.

4. Handle humor effortlessly

You can't drive an audience to laughter. You have to lead it. It's pretty painful to watch a speaker struggling with his audience to make them laugh.

5. Don't advertise your humor

Avoid comments such as "You'll die laughing at this one," or "Let me tell you a very funny story." If it's funny, your listener will discover it for himself.

[8] *Mark Twain's Speeches* (New York: Harper & Row, Publishers, 1910), p. 415. Reprinted by permission.

OUTLINING ENTERTAINING SPEECH

In outlining a speech of entertainment, use the topical form. Your outline need not be so detailed or tightly drawn as outlines for other types of speaking. The example below is based on a speech Mark Twain gave to the students of Barnard College, called "Morals and Memory." [9] Though a casual speech with a light touch, it has a design and order of its own.

Introduction

I. Here are two things common to our human experience.
   A. Everyone has a memory, however capricious.
   B. Everyone has morals though I won't inquire into yours.
II. I want to tell you about some freaks of my own memory that may teach you some kind of a lesson.

Discussion

I. I always considered myself a model boy.
   A. Oddly, I seemed to be alone in this opinion of myself.
      1. People around me seemed to think this estimate lacked something.
      2. Even my mother in her old age had forgotten everything about me except this youthful self-prejudice.
   B. There's a moral here if you search for it.
II. Once I "extracted" a watermelon from a farmer's wagon.
   A. I was overcome with remorse—when I discovered the melon was green.
      1. I returned it to the farmer and made him replace it with a ripe one.
      2. I also upbraided him for peddling green melons.
   B. My timely action helped to reform this farmer.
III. I learned something from another boyhood event I can vividly recall.
   A. This is what happened one day when I went fishing without my parents' knowledge or consent.
      1. A stranger in town was killed in a brawl.
      2. My father, who was the coroner, laid out the corpse in our living room.
   B. I came home after dark, not knowing what had happened.
      1. I decided to sleep on the sofa so I wouldn't disturb my parents.
      2. By stages I came to know who was in the living room with me.

---

[9] *Mark Twain's Speeches* (New York: Harper & Row, Publishers, 1923), pp. 224-37.

3. My exit was sudden.
IV. A theatre date with "a peach" made a lasting impression on me.
    A. I slipped off my boots and couldn't get them on again.
    B. The trip home was miserable.
V. Once I rudely dismissed a "peddler of etchings" who called at our house.
    A. He turned out to be a friend of the family.
    B. I had to make amends.

Conclusion

I. I hope I taught you some inspiring lessons.
II. I know I enjoyed you more than I enjoyed that "peach" of fifty-three years ago.

POINTS TO KEEP IN MIND

1. Speaking to inspire and speaking to entertain are the two principal types of evocative speech. Both require:
    a) A high degree of speaker sensitivity.
    b) A high degree of audience involvement.
    c) A high degree of creative imagination.

2. Follow one basic method in developing inspirational speech—the implicative, comparison-contrast, chronological, or cumulative method. Others may be used helpfully in a subsidiary role.

3. The keys to entertaining speech are re-creation of the event, careful sequence, suspense, vivid details and language, dramatization, and good timing. Skill with humor contributes much to this type of speaking.

4. Use the topical outline on occasions when you speak to inspire or entertain.

EXERCISES

1. Select a great speech or sermon whose ideas stir you. Consult the Bible, Shakespeare's plays, or anthologies of speeches. Open your talk by reading portions of your selection. Then in your own words carry forward the ideas expressed.

2. Use this speech to stimulate interest in and appreciation for some person who is unknown or little known to your audience, but whose life in some way has affected theirs. He may be a founder of your college or university, a donor, a teacher who is only a memory to the alumni, an alumnus who has conferred distinction on alma mater.

3. Prepare a "This I do believe" type of speech. Begin with a concept such as democracy, education, happiness, courtesy, brotherliness, worship. Formulate a theme that crystalizes your credo. Develop the

speech by means of the most appropriate pattern of the four listed in this chapter.

4. Make a cutting of an entertaining speech or piece of writing by Mark Twain, Artemus Ward, Robert Benchley, Will Rogers, Stephen Leacock, James Thurber, E. B. White, or someone else whose works you enjoy and would like to share. Prepare an introduction of your own.

5. Work up an entertaining talk based on a personal experience or an imaginative commentary on human behavior. Before you give it, check over the keys to entertaining talk and the suggestions on humor given in this chapter. Use as many of them as you can.

twenty

Reading Aloud

Skill in reading aloud is of inestimable value to you as a speaker whenever you read from a manuscript, but this chapter also discusses oral reading as a form of communication in its own right. Listening to effective oral reading enables an audience to extract more of an author's meaning and feeling than they would get by reading the same work silently.

ORAL READING AND COMMUNICATION

The purpose of reading aloud, as it is of speaking, is to communicate with your listeners. This is true whether you read from a novel, a news story, a play, a market report, or a sonnet.

The oral reader has a dual obligation—to his audience *and* to his material. When you read silently, you are the only person who is "listening." You skim, and you slow down. If the meaning of a passage escapes you, you go back and read it again. You pick up the meaning of a new word or phrase from its context. As you read along, you adjust yourself to the writer's sentence structure and punctuation. But when you read aloud, your audience must depend entirely on you to convey the meaning. Hence, reading aloud is a more complex act than reading silently. As a reader, you must make the written word immediately intelligible, meaningful, and vital. It is through sensitive interpretation that you discharge your obligation to your material and to your audience.

All of this may strike you as obvious. But how many readers show *by their reading* any real competence to interpret the written word? The plain and painful fact is that good readers are rare. Absurd as it may seem, some people read lyric poetry in much the same way that they read the minutes of the last meeting of their club. Even remarkably fine speakers frequently lose their audience when they begin to read. They fence themselves off with wooden words. At the other extreme are the people who look on every opportunity to read as a chance to give a dramatic performance. They're out to make a show of it, and they go about it in the spirit of a prima donna. Listeners may be either amused or embarrassed by such histrionics, but they respond not at all to the writer's message.

Good reading, like good speaking, requires special preparation before you face your audience.

ANALYZING YOUR MATERIAL

Familiarize yourself with the intellectual content

Successive private readings of a selection may reveal new meanings. If it is your own composition, you may be surprised to discover as you read it aloud that it conveys meanings you hadn't intended. If the selection was written by someone else, first read it for the general sense. As you do so, look up unfamiliar words and allusions. And while you are at it, learn to pronounce the words you're not sure of.

In subsequent readings look for answers to these questions: What is the writer's purpose? What is the central idea or theme that holds the work together? What are the subsidiary ideas? Is the thought immediately apparent, or is it intricate and elusive? If you plan to read only a portion, know how it fits into the whole work. Answers may be easy to come by, or you may have to dig for them. When necessary, consult outside sources such as reviews, critical commentaries, and references books.

You will acquire a deeper understanding and appreciation of your selection if you know something about its background. By way of illustration, consider two quite different types of material. The first is *J.B.*, a play by Archibald MacLeish. If you are guided solely by the contemporary circus setting of the play, you will miss the profound and timeless problem with which the poet deals. When you compare this play with the Book of Job, from which MacLeish drew his inspiration, you will appreciate more fully man's search for an answer to the meaning of his afflictions. An awareness of this background will heighten your respect for a modern treatment of an ancient theme, and will enable you to bring to your reading greater breadth and depth of knowledge. In short, understanding establishes both the desire and the right to communicate the writer's message.

Thomas Jefferson's First Inaugural Address offers a second illustration. Take this paragraph:

During the throes and convulsions of the ancient world, during the agonizing spasms of infuriated man, seeking through blood and slaughter his long-lost liberty, it was not wonderful that the agitation of the billows should reach even this distant and peaceful shore; that this should be more felt and feared by some and less by others, and should divide opinion as to measures of safety. But every difference of opinion is not a difference of principle. We have called by different names brethren of the same principle. We are all Republicans, we are all Federalists. If there be any among us who would wish to dissolve this Union or to change its republican form, let them stand undisturbed as monuments of the safety with which error of opinion may be tolerated where reason is left free to combat it.

True, the general sense of Jefferson's remarks is not hard to figure out. His call for amity and his stand for civil liberty are familiar. But it is precisely because readers are too often content with such off-the-top-of-the-head reactions that their reading adds nothing to the listener's understanding or appreciation.

As a reader, you are somebody else's representative by your own choice. It would be a desecration to accept and read Jefferson's lines as if all he had done was to strike off shopworn platitudes, pious and empty generalizations wholly detached from the age in which they were written. Look at the passage again. It is filled with oblique references to past events and unsettling ideas. It carries intimations of the French Revolution and its impact on American politics, of bitter domestic struggles over the Alien and Sedition Laws, of the abusive political campaign of 1800, of Jefferson's persistent work in behalf of civil rights. Here also is a distillation of Jefferson's faith in the free mind. No one can expect to convey the inner meaning of the speech until he is steeped in the circumstances of its origin. And while we're on the point, note that the eighteenth century expression "it was not wonderful" should be understood as "it was not remarkable" or "it is to be expected that."

Discover the prevailing mood of the work

As you pursue your analysis, you will discover that some materials have little or no emotional content and that others pulsate with feeling. We want factual reports to be presented with lucidity, precision, and just enough highlighting to bring out the essentials. It is a mistake to inject emotion into materials that were free from emotion when they were written. But aside from strictly factual reports, in most prose compositions the writer's emotions are in some way involved. Often he makes a deliberate effort to involve your emotions too.

First of all, then, discover the *nature* and *intensity* of the writer's feelings. It would be hard to miss the fervor of Patrick Henry's peroration in his famous speech on the eve of the Revolutionary War:

> It is in vain, sir to extenuate the matter. Gentlemen may cry, Peace, Peace—but there is no peace. The war is actually begun! The next gale that sweeps from the north will bring to our ears the clash of resounding arms! Our brethren are already in the field! Why stand we here idle? What is it that gentlemen wish? What would they have? Is life so dear, or peace so sweet, as to be purchased at the price of chains and slavery? Forbid it, Almighty God! I know not what course others may take; but as for me, give me liberty or give me death!

Henry's appeal is directed to elemental emotions. His vivid words and jabbing sentences excite strong, sensory responses. Put the speech in its historical context and you will sense how inflammatory it was when it was delivered. This doesn't mean that you should read the passage as if it were a pyrotechnic display; neither should you read it as if you were reciting the multiplication table. Discover the authentic emotion and then suggest it to your listeners.

Now let's look at a passage from Lincoln's Second Inaugural Address:

> With malice toward none, with charity for all; with firmness in the right, as God gives us to see the right, let us strive on to finish the work

we are in; to bind up the nation's wounds; to care for him who shall have borne the battle, and for his widow, and his orphan—to do all which may achieve a just and lasting peace, among ourselves and with all nations.

Both Henry's and Lincoln's words have an emotional tone. But that is where the similarity ends. Henry was animated by and tried to arouse a combative spirit; Lincoln was moved by and sought to move others to compassion. Your appreciation of the mood of Lincoln's speech will be strengthened if you understand the moment in history at which he spoke. Here was a soul-tortured President presiding over the destiny of the Union during the only civil war that has ever afflicted it. The agony of Lincoln and his age is an essential fact in the mood of his speech.

Poetry vividly illustrates variety in kind and intensity of mood. A poem may express rapture, whimsey, melancholy; it may be pensive, contemplative, ecstatic, despairing, triumphant. You will develop and refine your perception by selecting poems for reading that exhibit these differences. A few selections will suggest what we mean. You will recognize at once the whimsey in these stanzas from Lewis Carroll's "Father William."

"You are old, Father William," the young man said,
   "And your hair has become very white;
And yet you incessantly stand on your head—
   Do you think, at your age, it is right?"

"In my youth," Father William replied to his son,
   "I feared it might injure the brain;
But, now that I'm perfectly sure I have none,
   Why, I do it again and again."

"You are old," said the youth, "as I mentioned before,
   And have grown most uncommonly fat;
Yet you turned a back-somersault in at the door—
   Pray, what is the reason of that?"

"In my youth," said the sage, as he shook his gray locks,
   "I kept all my limbs very supple
By the use of this ointment—one shilling the box—
   Allow me to sell you a couple?"

"You are old," said the youth, "and your jaws are too weak
   For anything tougher than suet;
Yet you finished the goose, with the bones and the beak—
   Pray, how did you manage to do it?"

"In my youth," said his father, "I took to the law
    And argued each case with my wife;
And the muscular strength which it gave to my jaw,
    Has lasted the rest of my life."

Move now to John Keats' poem "On the Grasshopper and the Cricket." Here is a contemplative comment on the ceaseless rhythm of nature's music.

The poetry of earth is never dead:
When all the birds are faint with the hot sun,
And hide in cooling trees, a voice will run
From hedge to hedge about the new-mown mead;
That is the Grasshopper's—he takes the lead
In summer luxury,—he has never done
With his delights; for when tired out with fun
He rests at ease beneath some pleasant weed.
The poetry of earth is ceasing never:
On a lone winter evening, when the frost
Has wrought a silence, from the stove there shrills
The Cricket's song, in warmth increasing ever,
And seems to one in drowsiness half lost,
The Grasshopper's among some grassy hills.

Now contrast the poems by Carroll and Keats with the last stanza of Matthew Arnold's "Dover Beach." Here you confront complex emotions—darkness and melancholy leavened by the affirmation of an enduring value.

Ah, love, let us be true
To one another! for the world, which seems
To lie before us like a land of dreams,
So various, so beautiful, so new,
Hath really neither joy, nor love, nor light,
Nor certitude, nor peace, nor help for pain;
And we are here as on a darkling plain
Swept with confused alarms of struggle and flight,
Where ignorant armies clash by night.

Finally, we perceive stark, unrelieved despair in these lines from Shakespeare's *Macbeth*.

Tomorrow, and tomorrow, and tomorrow,
Creeps in this petty pace from day to day
To the last syllable of recorded time,
And all our yesterdays have lighted fools
The way to dusty death. Out, out, brief candle!

Life's but a walking shadow, a poor player
That struts and frets his hour upon the stage
And then is heard no more; it is a tale
Told by an idiot, full of sound and fury,
Signifying nothing.

Sometimes the authentic mood of a poem is not easy to discover. It may be half-concealed and elusive. It may lurk in a word or a metaphor, in the music and rhythm of the language. Should you find that the essential feeling eludes you, either consult somebody who can help you or choose something else that is within the range of your understanding.

Know the structure of your selection

Meaning and mood will emerge more clearly if you analyze the design of a work. Lincoln's Gettysburg Address offers a classic example. On this occasion, Lincoln wanted to do two things: to honor the heroic sons, husbands, and fathers who had been killed, and to state the case for democracy. In order to blend these two purposes into one unifying theme, he developed his haunting metaphor of birth, death, and rebirth—in the life of man and in the life of a nation. Thus Lincoln not only suggested the historical parallels between the life of a man and a nation, but he projected his faith in eternal democracy by linking it with man's aspirations for eternal life.

We gain a sharper perception of a writer's or speaker's purpose and meaning by exploring the structural artistry of his work. Is the work composed of a chain of arguments, or is it discursively topical as in a familiar essay? Is it didactic exposition, or does it unfold through a succession of poetical metaphors? Does the work move on one plane, or does it build to a climax? Your interpretation of thought and mood may be greatly influenced by questions you ask about the structure of a work.

READ EXPERIMENTALLY BEFORE YOU
READ TO AN AUDIENCE

Having analyzed the thought, mood, and structure of a work, test the results of your study by reading the work aloud to yourself. Listen critically to your reading, and, if possible, make a tape recording or get the reactions of a friend. You may discover a great gulf between the way you want to read and the way it actually comes off.

First read through your selection without stopping, to catch the swing of the author's style and to locate trouble spots. A sentence that gives no trouble to the eye may prove sticky on the tongue: "Complex statistical statements excite us less than sensitively selected examples." Other things come to light—long, winding sentences that need to be punctuated by inflections; a patch of choppy phrases that needs to be smoothed out orally; a switch in the rhythm to which you must adapt.

Work on the specific problems you turn up. Slow down as you move through tongue-tangling sentences, and sharpen your enunciation. Pay attention to the way you group words. Stammering, illogical groupings break the thought and drive listeners to distraction. For example, "It has / been said / that / the Russians / have / given to science / some of / the aura that / they have denied / to religion." A more natural grouping would be, "It has been said / that the Russians have given to science / some of the aura that they have denied to religion." In addition to natural grouping, spot the sentences and passages that need to be highlighted, and experiment with several ways of giving them prominence. An increase in volume of voice is not the only way to gain emphasis. A change in rate or pitch, or a pause, may be a better way.

Reading smoothly, of course, is not enough. As you experiment, concentrate on communicating faithfully the facts, ideas, and images of your material. Factual material calls for clarity, accuracy, and objectivity. Be especially careful to avoid injecting personal attitudes into reportorial reading. "The governor suggested that the budget for the next fiscal year will require a slight and temporary increase in the sales tax" is a simple, straightforward statement. But if phrases such as "the governor" and "slight and temporary increases" are doctored with inflections, the meaning is colored by the reader's attitudes of admiration or derision.

Give ideas the stature they deserve. Suppose you were to read these lines from John Milton's *Areopagitica:* "Though all the winds of doctrine were let loose to play upon the earth, so Truth be in the field, we do ingloriously, by licensing and prohibiting, to misdoubt her strength. Let her and Falsehood grapple: Who ever knew Truth put to the worse in a free and open encounter?" Here is a ringing declaration of faith, not a mundane statement of fact. When sentiment and ideas are majestic, your reading should endow them with impressiveness. Conversely, avoid giving an idea an importance greater than it warrants. It would sound pretty silly if Joe were to announce his plans to walk to the corner grocery store as if he were embarking on an expedition into outer space.

The imagery of a work will be more vivid if you re-create sensory experiences that are similar to those indicated by the writer. You may not have had exactly the experience he describes, but you can approximate it by drawing on your memory and imagination. Let your mind's eye see "a crowd, a host, of golden daffodils . . . tossing their heads in sprightly dance," about which Wordsworth writes. Let yourself see, touch, and smell "the strong crust of friendly bread" about which Rupert Brooke writes. And "the cool kindliness of sheets," "live hair that is shining and free," "the musty reek that lingers about dead leaves." Consider the extreme distress that Coleridge describes in these lines:

> And every tongue, through utter drought,
> Was wither'd at the root;
> We could not speak, no more than if
> We had been choked with soot.

It's unlikely that you have ever had such a desperately parched feeling, but you do know what it's like to be thirsty. Recall the circumstance, and re-create accurately the specific sensations you felt at the time. Heightening your own empathic responses to a writer's imagery enables you to read with a vividness that is likely to stimulate listeners to re-create comparable sensory experiences of their own.

SOME PRACTICAL CONSIDERATIONS

Preparing copy

Even under ideal conditions it is hard to read small print set in lines tightly squeezed together. The problem is compounded when you read to an audience. Whenever the printed page is unsatisfactory, take the time to type up the material for the occasion. Typed copy, double spaced, is perferable to copy that you write out in longhand.

Establishing a context for your reading

When the material you are reading is just a small part of your whole speech, work it in through easy transitions. But when the reading is the main business at hand, work up a short extemporaneous introduction that identifies your selection and its author, stimulates interest in the selection, and establishes a congenial mood for your reading. You may or may not need to develop a conclusion of your own. Much depends on the material, your purpose in reading, and the circumstances.

Interpolating comments

If you are reading instructions or obscure technical material, stop and clarify the important points as you go along. Sometimes you may want to interrupt your reading momentarily to underscore your author's point in your own words. In short, feel free to interpolate your own comments whenever they will add significantly to your audience's interest, understanding, and appreciation. Refrain, however, from intruding excessively with comments of your own. You can ruin the fine edge of a poem, story, or a particularly well-written article with a disruptive commentary.

Handling your materials while reading

If you plan to read here and there in an article or book, always mark your places beforehand. You will be embarrassed and your audience will grow anxious if you have to fumble around while trying to find your place. These awkward moments dissipate any success you may have won up to that point.

The clumsy handling of a book, magazine, or manuscript may be enough to spoil an otherwise effective reading. The ideal is to manipulate these materials so that your listeners are hardly aware of them. If you are using a speaker's stand, you may want to place your materials there and leave them there. If you like more freedom and mobility, then hold your magazine or book in one hand. Hold it high enough so that you can read it easily, and a bit to one side so that you can see your audience readily. Avoid holding it up so high that it covers your face, or so low that your body looks like a question mark. Never let the book, magazine, or whatever you are using block your line of vision. If you are well prepared, you should be able to look directly at your audience most of the time.

POINTS TO KEEP IN MIND

1. The purpose of reading aloud is to communicate faithfully an author's meaning and feeling.

2. Prepare by familiarizing yourself with the intellectual content of your selection, its background, its mood, and its structure.

3. Before you read to an audience, practice reading your selection experimentally to test your preliminary analysis and to acquire skill.

4. Prepare and handle your text so that you can communicate easily when you read to your audience.

EXERCISES

1. Make a brief report on the content of an article or a book you have read recently. Read aloud selected passages that point up the writer's ideas in a way that will bring them home to your listeners.

2. Take a somewhat technical piece of writing that you understand and think you can explain to your audience. Skillfully weave in enough interpolations to make it clear.

3. Write out a speech or report of your own. Maintain your best oral style in your writing. Read it aloud to the class. Be as communicative as you can. See if you can make the audience forget you are reading from a manuscript.

4. Choose one of the sample speeches that appear at the end of this book for reading aloud to the class. Analyze it and practice reading it beforehand.

5. Poetry that deals in values people live by offers fine opportunities to combine reading and speaking. Robert Frost's "Mending Wall" is a good example. Prepare your own introduction to such a poem. Give your introduction extemporaneously and then read the poem.

6. Choose a play, speech, poem, or story that has been read aloud by someone else and has been recorded. Familiarize yourself with the work before you listen to it. Then listen several times to the recording. Evaluate the skill of the reader. Did your reactions to the way the work was read change after successive listening experiences? Could you suggest ways in which the reading might be improved?

twenty-one

Speaking in Public

We have been talking about the principles and methods of public speaking all through this book. But now we shall deal with some of the special forms and the conventional procedures and amenities associated with them. This information will help you apply what you already know about public speaking in situations that call for special adaptations—public deliberation, public policy making, and speeches for special occasions.

PUBLIC DELIBERATION

Dealing with public questions in a way that will induce learning and understanding is one of the most important functions of public speech. Inquiry, reporting, and advocacy serve this function. Here are some adaptations of these basic methods that are useful in public deliberation.

Panel discussion

This is an ingenious device for conducting group discussion in the hearing of an audience. We are all familiar with the unique values of give-and-take discussion in small, intimate, face-to-face groups. Panel discussion attempts to achieve these same values for larger groups.

The members of the panel, usually four to eight people, sit in a semicircle facing the audience, preferably around a table on a raised platform. The panel leader opens the discussion and acts as chairman. He tells the audience what the panel is going to discuss, introduces the members, and starts the discussion by asking a question or two.

The panel discusses the subject in conversation among themselves much as they would in private discussion, but they must never forget that they are talking for the benefit of the audience. They must speak clearly and loudly enough to be heard easily, and they must keep the discussion moving along at a brisk pace. The steps in reflective thinking explained in Chapter 16 provide a good general pattern for the discussion.

This kind of public conversation requires speakers who are both articulate and well informed. At its best, it is a lively interchange among knowledgeable people who hold different points of view and are prepared to explore their differences cooperatively.

The symposium

A symposium is usually made up of three to five persons who deliver short speeches on a problem in front of an audience. Its chief difference from the panel is that it uses public speeches rather than group discussion. And it differs from public debate in that it uses the methods of inquiry and reporting rather than the methods of advocacy. The purpose of a symposium is to instruct and to increase understanding, not to persuade.

A symposium opens up a problem and gives it a thorough airing. The best way to do this is to have each speaker explain his point of view on the problem as a whole. Another way—though usually less effective—is to assign a different phase of the problem to each speaker. The first speaker defines and lays out the problem, the second analyzes it, and the others suggest various solutions.

The leader of the symposium simply acts as chairman. He introduces the speakers, makes a few opening remarks, fills in between successive speeches, winds things up after the last speaker has finished, and takes charge of the question-and-answer period.

Debate

Debate is a familiar method of public deliberation in which speakers oppose each other on propositions of public interest. The debater uses the methods of advocacy. Admittedly partisan, he tries to win support for his position. Listeners benefit from the chance to hear different points of view advanced and defended—an experience that helps them to extend their own knowledge and thinking on the question being debated. In addition to these educational values, a good debate often provides stimulating entertainment.

Ordinarily, the opposing debaters speak from the same platform on the same occasion, and the debate is conducted according to procedures agreed upon in advance. Often, however, there are public debates in which the opposing speakers never meet each other face to face. In a sense, a national political campaign is a running debate that stretches out over several weeks or months. The candidates take sharp issue on public questions and pursue their interests in speech after speech, reply and counter-reply, before audiences all over the nation.

The essentials of a good debate are a carefully worded proposition or resolution, one or more speakers who support this proposition (the affirmative), one or more speakers who oppose it (the negative), and arrangements that permit opposing speakers to develop their cases and reply to each other. In a properly planned debate, the proposition is phrased so that the affirmative has the burden of proof (see page 237) and has the opportunity to open and close the debate. Here are some suggestions for arranging debates.

THE TWO-SPEAKER DEBATE

Affirmative constructive speech .... 10 minutes
Negative rejoinder (reply and constructive case) .... 14 minutes
Affirmative rebuttal .... 4 minutes

THE TEAM DEBATE

Constructive Speeches		*Rebuttal Speeches*	
First affirmative	10 minutes	First negative	5 minutes
First negative	10 minutes	First affirmative	5 minutes
Second affirmative ...	10 minutes	Second negative	5 minutes
Second negative	10 minutes	Second affirmative ...	5 minutes

THE CROSS-QUESTION DEBATE

The first affirmative presents the entire affirmative case .... 20 minutes
The first negative questions the first affirmative .... 10 minutes
The second negative presents the entire negative case ..... 20 minutes
The second affirmative questions the second negative ..... 10 minutes
The first negative presents the negative rebuttal .... 10 minutes
The second affirmative presents the affirmative rebuttal .... 10 minutes

In a good debate, no matter what arrangements are prescribed, the debaters hold close to the issues and make adaptations and replies to the arguments of their opponents throughout the debate. This requires a thorough knowledge of the ins and outs of the subject, analytical and tactical skills, and, above all, competence in extemporaneous public speaking.

The open forum

Every panel discussion, debate, and symposium requires an audience. Ideally, the members of the audience should be more than a group of passive onlookers. They should be brought in as active participants. The best way to let the listeners have their say is to arrange for an open forum after the regular program. This is a question-and-answer period conducted by the discussion leader or chairman.

One way to conduct on open forum is to have members of the audience write questions on slips of paper and send them up to the chairman. During a brief recess, the chairman can sift through the questions and arrange them in logical order. Written questions cut short the cranks and the frustrated orators who have their own little speeches all prepared.

But a better way is to invite questions from the floor. This makes for livelier, more spontaneous discussion. One question suggests another, and the audience has a chance to hear each question as it is presented. The chairman should keep the proceedings as informal as possible and should have the questions put directly to speakers on the platform. He should intervene only to clear up confusion or misunderstanding, or to decide which member of the audience has the floor when several speak at once.

Most audiences take a lively interest in the question-and-answer period. But if the leader suspects that an audience may be slow to respond, he may sum up the discussion in a way that spotlights vital and controversial issues. He may ask a few questions of his own that will suggest others to the audience. Or he may put the first question to one of the speakers. But he must never hint that he expects to have a hard time in getting questions from the audience. Once the forum is under way, the leader should be content to repeat questions that are inaudible, help clarify ambiguous questions, and keep each question and answer within reasonable time limits.

PUBLIC POLICY MAKING

Policy making goes beyond deliberation for educational purposes. Any policy-making body must express the will of the group in the form of specific decisions. It must come up with a firm conclusion on which other people can act. The policy-making groups with which you are most familiar are committees, boards, councils, and legislative bodies. Actually, any organized group or public assembly can adopt resolutions and take whatever actions its needs and interests may dictate. Many of these groups have their own procedural rules. Here are some tips on committee procedure and parliamentary debate that apply to most of the situations you are likely to face.

Committee procedure

Large legislative assemblies seldom talk through problems in full session, for too many participants make the discussion unwieldy. Instead, legislatures usually refer problems to committees for investigation and recommendation.

In the early stages of its work, at least, it is wise for a committee to proceed as a discussion group. If the discussion leads to a solution on which the members agree, their job is done; all they have to do is report their findings to the larger group. Very often this is exactly what takes place in a committee, especially where the members are accustomed to cooperative procedures and united in their desire to find the best answer to the problem.

If disagreement develops and persists, however, then the chairman of the committee should call for motions and conduct debate on these motions until a majority decision is reached (see below).

A committee uses formal debate only as a last resort after making every attempt to keep the discussion informal and cooperative. If the chairman calls for formal motions at the very outset, he runs the danger of crystallizing differences of opinion that might have been resolved in the opening discussion. An even greater danger is that the group may fail to analyze the problem carefully, because it has been hurried into a decision before developing the information and understanding it needs.

Parliamentary debate

Parliamentary debate is the most useful method of determining policy in any large assembly. Recommendations for consideration may come from committees or be initiated by any member of the assembly. In either case, these recommendations are presented as motions for debate and action. Often, agenda are worked out in advance to determine the order of business.

Most policy-determining groups use the standard rules of parliamentary procedure to govern debate. You are already familiar with some of these rules. They are used in class meetings, clubs, fraternities, and wherever business is conducted in public meetings. If you are hazy about these rules, it will be worth your while to get them firmly in mind. There are many excellent manuals on parliamentary law, but the brief résumé below will suffice for most occasions.

The *principal motion* is used to introduce a proposal when there is no other motion before the assembly. The maker of the motion states his proposal and may, if he chooses, explain it. The motion itself should be a clear, unambiguous proposal that the secretary can record in his minutes. If the motion is seconded, it is then thrown open to debate. During debate, *subsidiary motions* may be applied to the principal motion. For example, someone may move that the principal motion be amended; then the motion to amend becomes the subject of the debate. If this amendment is carried, then the principal motion as amended is before the house. Merely passing an amendment does not mean that the principal motion has been passed.

Each of the six *subsidiary motions* in the accompanying table takes precedence over those above it and yields to those below. Of the subsidiary motions, "the previous question" is puzzling to some people. Its purpose is to stop debate. In most assemblies, all you have to do is call for the question if you want to halt debate and get a vote on the resolution before the house. But if somebody objects to this method of stopping debate, you may then offer a formal motion to have the previous question brought to a vote. If your motion is seconded and carried by a two-thirds vote, the chairman must then put the question itself to a vote.

TABLE OF PARLIAMENTARY MOTIONS

Motions	Need a Second?	Amend-able?	Debat-able?	Vote Re-quired	May Inter-rupt a Speaker
I. Principal Motion					
1. Any main question or any independent matter of business before the meeting ..	yes	yes	yes	maj.	no
II. Subsidiary Motions					
2. To amend	yes	yes	yes	maj.	no
3. To postpone indefinitely ..	yes	no	yes	maj.	no
4. To refer to a committee ..	yes	yes	yes	maj.	no
5. To postpone to a certain time	yes	yes	yes	maj.	no
6. Previous question	yes	no	no	⅔	no
7. To lay on (or take from) the table	yes	no	no	maj.	no
III. Incidental Motions					
8. To suspend a rule	yes	no	no	⅔	no
9. To withdraw a motion	yes	no	no	maj.	no
10. Question of consideration ..	no	no	no	⅔	yes
11. A point of order	no	no	no	Chair[†]	yes
12. Appeal from decision of chair	yes	no	no	maj.	yes
IV. Privileged Motions					
13. To make a matter of business a "special order" for a given time	no	no	no	⅔	yes
14. Questions of rights and privileges	no	no	no	Chair[†]	yes
15. To adjourn (unqualified) ..	yes	no	no	maj.	no
16. To fix time for next meeting	yes	yes	no	maj.	no

Source: Quoted with some changes from Gregg's *Handbook of Parliamentary Law* (Boston: Ginn and Company, 1910) in J. M. O'Neill, ed., *Foundations of Speech* (Englewood Cliffs, N.J.: Prentice-Hall, Inc., 1941), p. 395.
[†] Requires only decision of Chair; no vote unless appealed.

Incidental motions arise out of other motions. Their purpose is to make it easier for these motions to be considered. The order in which they are listed in the table is not significant.

Privileged motions have to do with the general conduct of the meeting. They arise independently of other motions and take precedence over them. However, any incidental motion or subsidiary motion that is properly applied to the privileged motion itself takes precedence over the privileged motion to which it is applied.

For speed and convenience in using the table of motions, we have listed below the specific purpose or object of each motion in the table.

OBJECTS OF MOTIONS[1]

1. Main motion—to bring original business before the assembly.

2. To amend—to modify a question that is before the assembly.

3. To postpone indefinitely—(a) to dispose of a question for the session without voting on it directly; (b) used by the opponents of a question to determine their strength.

4. To refer to a committee—to secure the advantage of action by a smaller group, or of greater freedom in debate in dealing with a question.

5. To postpone to a certain time—to defer action on a question to some future time.

6. Previous question—to suppress debate and bring the assembly to a vote.

7. To lay on the table—(a) to postpone a subject so that it may be taken up at another time during the same session; (b) to stop debate and suppress a question for the session, provided a majority cannot be secured to take the question again from the table.

8. To suspend a rule—to make temporarily possible an action contrary to the standing rules or rules of order of an organization.

9. To withdraw a motion—to expedite business in case of a changed opinion by the maker of the motion.

10. Question of consideration—an objection to the consideration of a question to enable the assembly to avoid irrelevant, unprofitable, or contentious questions.

11. A point of order—to correct a breach of order or an error in procedure.

12. Appeal from decision of chair—(a) to invoke a rule that the chairman has ignored or misinterpreted; (b) to appeal to the assembly to overrule the chairman on any rule where an opinion or a judgment may be exercised.

13. Special order—to set a specific time to consider a certain matter of business when all other things will be set aside.

[1] From J. M. O'Neill, ed., *Foundations of Speech* (Englewood Cliffs, N.J.: Prentice-Hall, Inc., 1941).

14. Questions of rights and privileges—to secure to the assembly or any of its members some right with respect to safety, comfort, dignity, reputation, or freedom from disturbance.

15. To adjourn—to bring a meeting to a close.

16. To fix time for next meeting—to fix a time or place for reassembling.

Debate for the purpose of determining policy follows the methods of advocacy. Even though it follows the formal rules that we have outlined here, it is still debate. If you make a motion, you must state it clearly and assume the responsibility for defending it. Any motion is vulnerable unless you can present a convincing defense of it when the opposition raises objections. Opponents of the motion will defeat it if they can attack it successfully on one or more vital counts.

SPEECHES FOR SPECIAL OCCASIONS

Some speeches are designed primarily to recognize special occasions and to strengthen our ties with our fellow men. Often you are under something of an artistic obligation in handling these courtesies. Poise, graciousness, and appropriateness in style and manner are especially important on such occasions. The methods of evocation are appropriate to speeches for these occasions.

Speeches of introduction

When you introduce a speaker to an audience, your job is to establish good speaking relationships between him and his listeners. Think of yourself as a go-between, a situation-maker, not as a principal in the show.

Find out all you can beforehand about the person you are introducing. If possible, talk with him and with people who know him. Track down some reliable biographical sketches, but don't try to use everything you gather together. Don't make your introduction sound like a paragraph from *Who's Who*. If the audience doesn't know much about the speaker, choose information that will identify him, establish his qualifications to speak, and make him liked as a person. If you can, let the audience see for themselves what kind of a person he is by telling an anecdote that puts him in a favorable light. If he is already well known, keep your introduction short and concentrate on the warm sentiments the audience feels toward him.

Above all, be accurate. You may have heard introductions in which the speaker's name was mispronounced or completely garbled. Not every speaker can transform a blunder into a pleasantry, as Rabbi Stephen Wise did when he was introduced as Rabbi Mann. "These days," he retorted, "it's a wise man who knows his own name."

Avoid a long speech. Remember, the audience came to hear the main speaker, not you.

Speeches of welcome and farewell

You are a member of an organization or a community that is playing host to visitors, and you are selected to represent the host group. Make your greetings cordial and try to use a little originality. Most speeches on these occasions are dismally trite and are delivered in an inflated or perfunctory manner. Be direct, sincere, and brisk.

Make it clear that you really know whom you are welcoming, what they stand for, and what they have contributed. If the visitors represent a group dedicated to an ideal or to a program of public service, give your talk an inspirational note. Make your visitors feel at home. Show your hospitality by pointing out the services and facilities at their disposal, and the attractions and special events that will add to their pleasure. End by wishing your guests a pleasant and profitable stay.

Speeches of farewell are given at dinners or other ceremonies honoring someone who is leaving the group. When you make such a speech, feel free to reminisce about the past, express the esteem in which the departing person is held, and extend the group's good wishes.

What if you are the person who is departing? Here you have a chance to show publicly your affection and respect for the friends you are leaving, and to express appreciation for the pleasant associations you have had with them. If you have a personal philosophy that you want to share, this is a perfect occasion to put it into words. In short, show that you have responded warmly to your friends' sentiment.

Speeches of commemoration

Every society has certain anniversaries that it commemorates with special speeches. For example, we celebrate the Fourth of July, Memorial Day, United Nations Day, and the birthdays of distinguished men and women. Ordinarily, you will key a speech of commemoration to the immediate occasion, unless it is understood that you are free to use the occasion as a springboard to some related subject. If you are dedicating a park, talk about the work of the people who made it possible, about its values and uses for the community. If you are commemorating United Nations Day, build your talk around the history, purposes, work, and accomplishments of the organization. If you are offering a tribute, invite your listeners to look again at the life and career of the person whom you are praising.

But don't make your speech of commemoration a bloodless catalogue of facts. Go about it in an inspirational manner. Stir your listeners to contemplation and help them to look at the event, deed, or life as a symbol.

Speeches of presentation and acceptance

These talks reflect the prevailing mood of the occasion. They put into words what everyone is feeling. A football banquet at which varsity letters are awarded invites lightness and gaiety. When the senior class presents a gift to the college, dignity is the order of the day. Occasions of this sort are often charged with sentiment. But if you are making a speech of presentation, you must keep a nice balance between what you are feeling and what good taste permits. Suggest the appropriate sentiment, but don't parade it.

Bring out the reasons that have prompted the gift or award. For example, assume that you and your associates are honoring the school physician for long and faithful service. First, suggest the group's feelings toward him. Then supply the reasons for these feelings—reasons that grow out of his years of service to the group. You might climax your talk with a short citation, then present the gift or award.

A speech of acceptance should measure up to what is expected by those who are making the gift. A simple "thank you" is enough when numerous awards are handed out at one time, as at an honors convocation. If you are accepting an award in behalf of an organization, express your appreciation for the entire group and say why the award will be meaningful to all the other members. Single out the individuals who contributed most toward winning the award. If a presentation is being made to you personally, your acceptance should be a simple, sincere statement of gratitude. Speak of the gift as a symbol of mutual esteem and affection.

After-dinner speeches

Many after-dinner speeches are serious talks on serious subjects. Each day countless reports, political speeches, and other forms of serious speaking take place at mealtime. But most people associate the term *after-dinner speaking* with entertainment, and that is the sense in which we shall use it here.

Everything we said in Chapter 19 about speaking to entertain applies to after-dinner speeches. Look for a theme that lends itself to the light touch and that will make it easy for you to hold attention agreeably for a specified time. Your talk need not be predominantly humorous, but it should offer some chances for humor. Make it sprightly throughout. Concentrate on making what you have to say interesting in its own right, and let the humor show itself naturally from time to time.

POINTS TO KEEP IN MIND

1. *Panel discussions, symposiums,* and *debate,* followed by *open forums,* are useful methods for handling public deliberation.

2. Public policy making usually begins in exploratory *discussions in committees* and is concluded through *parliamentary debate* in larger legislative assemblies.

3. Courtesy speeches for special occasions include speeches of *introduction, welcome and farewell, commemoration, presentation and acceptance,* and *after-dinner speeches.*

EXERCISES

1. Organize the class in small groups. Some groups will plan panel discussions; others will plan symposiums. A group may choose to discuss a new book, a political question, the implications of a scientific discovery, a philosophical problem, and so forth. Devote one class period

to each panel or symposium. Reserve time for questions from the class and for criticism.

2. Plan a series of debates in which each type of debate is represented. Select propositions that can be debated without extraordinary preparation. Don't overlook the possibility of campus problems.

3. Have the class select several controversial problems, and let several students prepare speeches of advocacy on each of them. Elect a chairman for each period, and reserve half the period for an open forum following the speeches. Have a short critique on the prepared speeches and the open forum.

4. Devote two or more class periods to parliamentary debate. Organize the meeting and elect officers. Members of the class should come prepared to offer motions, experiment with the table of motions, and debate those that admit of debate. In the first period, appoint committees with responsibility for reporting at the next meeting. Committee reports offer opportunities for further parliamentary action.

5. Plan short talks that introduce people from many stations and walks of life. Evaluate the talks in terms of the propriety with which the people are introduced.

6. Prepare a tribute to some person. Choose someone from one of the following fields who is already well known to the class and whom you admire.

Politics	Science	Social work
Literature	Entertainment	Education
Art	Industry	Religion
Medicine	Agriculture	Communications
Engineering	Law	Sports

twenty-two

Microphone and Camera

We live in an age of electronics—of public-address systems, radio microphones, and television cameras. Doubtless, you will be called upon to use one of these devices at one time or another. So it is worth your while to learn how to get the best results from them. Good speech remains good speech whether or not you are speaking before a microphone or camera. *But there are important differences.* This chapter will tell you about the adaptations you need to make in your regular speech habits if you are to speak before the microphone and the camera with assurance and competence.

THE PUBLIC-ADDRESS SYSTEM

Amplification of your voice is often helpful, and when you are speaking in large auditoriums or out-of-doors it may be essential. On such occasions a public-address system in good working order with an experienced operator at the controls is often the only means of getting through to your audience.

But don't use a public-address system if you can make yourself heard easily without it. Without a microphone you are freer to move around the platform, and you avoid erecting a physical barrier between yourself and your audience. If you can speak without strain and be heard without strain, you will establish closer rapport with your audience without an amplifying system.

The principal advantage of a public-address system, apart from simple audibility, is that it enables you to talk to a large audience more intimately than you could without it. It lets you speak with exactly the same volume and inflections you would use in talking to a small group. In fact, you will get very poor results if you depart from the conversational level of speaking. Don't forget that you are using the system and begin to shout into the microphone as if you were trying to project your voice to the last man in the top balcony all by yourself. Nothing will put a listener's nerves on edge faster than a distorted voice that comes screeching out of a loudspeaker.

When you use a public-address system, then, let it work for you. Keep your lips about 18 inches from the microphone, and avoid moving your head abruptly. Talk as though you were addressing a group of 10 or 15 people in a small room. Keep your hands off the microphone and avoid coughing or laughing explosively into it.

Finally, public-address systems are notoriously capricious. Always make a point of personally checking in advance on the equipment to see that it is in good working order.

RADIO SPEAKING

Most radio speaking takes place in acoustically designed studios under the control of trained personnel. An engineer or producer will position the microphone and show you how to use it. On all technical matters, put yourself in the hands of the experts.

ADAPTING TO THE RADIO AUDIENCE

Radio audiences vary with locality, station, time, and program. But one factor remains constant: Most of the people listen by themselves or in small groups under informal circumstances. You can't talk to two or three people sitting in their living room or driving in their automobile as you would to a big audience assembled in an auditorium. The best radio speaking is man-to-man conversation. By and large, radio discussion programs have been successful because the participants speak as though they were talking directly with each listener in his own home. If you are confronted with a good-sized studio audience as well as a radio audience, to which audience should you accommodate your style, voice, and manner? To the audience that is more important to you or to your sponsors. Here we shall assume that you are interested in adapting to your radio audience.

A good way to learn the technique of effective radio speaking is to ask three or four people to sit in the studio with you. Then talk directly to them. Talk into the microphone, but concentrate on communicating your ideas *to the listeners who face you*. If you keep this technique in mind when you are actually on the air, your radio listeners will receive your message almost as if they were actually in your presence.

VOICE AND ACTION IN RADIO SPEAKING

Since radio listeners can't see you, you will have to pack your voice with meaning and feeling. You will have to depend on variety in force, pitch, time, and quality to convey fine shades of sense and attitude. What we have said in Chapter 14, on the use of your voice, applies directly to the radio speaker.

Many speakers sound stiff and wooden when they speak on the radio. The reason is that they become muscle-bound before a microphone. They forget that bodily action is part of normal speech. Whenever you suppress the movements of your arms, hands, body, head, and face, you cramp and impoverish your speech—and that goes for radio speech too. Most good radio speakers use just as much bodily action in the studio as they would if they were carrying on a spirited conversation with a friend or giving a public address. They find that bodily action reduces tension, makes their voice sound spontaneous and fresh, and adds variety. Don't pound the table or go streaking off out of the microphone's range. But remember that engineers in the control room are remarkably clever at adjusting their equipment to fairly active people.

NOTES, OUTLINES, AND SCRIPTS

When you can see and hear your listeners, you can sense how they are responding and adapt your speech to their shifting moods. Extemporaneous speaking is your best method on such occasions. But when you are sealed up in a studio, the only faces in sight may be those of the engineers—and they probably won't be paying much attention to what you say. In these circumstances, you may want to write out your talk and use a manuscript. It certainly helps you to stay within set time limits. Be sure to write the manuscript in your best oral style and to read it as if you are talking to a few people seated directly in front of you. Again, having two or three interested listeners in the studio helps you to come through to your radio audience with warmth and directness.

If you are preparing a radio roundtable discussion, get the participants together for a preliminary meeting and agree on a short discussion outline. Give each speaker a copy of the outline on which he can make notes. But when you go on the air, be sure that everyone speaks extemporaneously and uses the outline only as a working guide. A script kills the lively give and take that is the life blood of an effective discussion program.

TELEVISION SPEAKING

Television offers greater possibilities for speech than any other medium of mass communication that man has devised.

ADAPTING TO THE TELEVISION AUDIENCE

Most people who watch television are sitting comfortably at home —alone or in a small group. The total television audience is huge, but it is made up of individual viewers.

The best television speaker is the one who talks directly to his viewers rather than to the studio audience. If you want to get the most out of this medium, talk—don't shout or orate—with your listeners in a conversational manner. As with radio, your speaking should reveal the same warmth and vitality that you show in man-to-man communication at its best. Be as informal as the situation permits.

Television is ideally suited to panel discussions and interviews. The cameras can cover three or four people at fairly close range, and can give close-ups of individual speakers. The best setting for television discussion programs suggests a living room or a study or a conference room. Such a setting invites discussion and helps both speakers and viewers to forget about the cameras and the technical equipment.

CBS reporters Eric Sevareid and Bill Shadel stand outside the White House preparing to deliver a news broadcast. *(Wide World Photos)*

VOICE AND ACTION IN TELEVISION

You are seen as well as heard on television. And your audience gets a much closer look at you than it would in a public auditorium. The camera brings your eyes, mouth, facial muscles, and the movements of your head and shoulders into painfully close focus. If the picture on the television screen tells a story that is out of keeping with your words, your audience will dismiss the words as false, affected, or ridiculous. Television is hard on fakes. It is kind to honest and sincere people who speak with the confidence of their convictions. Your voice and actions must agree. Both must reveal in you a genuine desire to communicate.

NOTES AND SCRIPTS IN TELEVISION SPEAKING

Scripts and clumsy notes raise havoc. An ingenious gadget called the teleprompter has been devised to overcome just this difficulty. It enables you to read from enlarged type suspended before you, so that you look as though you were gazing directly into the camera. But in most cases this proves to be a poor substitute for directness. If often leads to a preoccupied, glassy stare or to furtive attempts to keep up with the moving script. Moreover, the teleprompter is one more mechanical device to be adjusted to.

It comes down to this: If you are a good extemporaneous speaker, you will have a tremendous advantage in television. If you must use brief notes or a short outline, don't try to disguise them. But avoid making them the center of your attention. Be so well prepared that you won't be at the mercy of your notes. Handle them unobtrusively and maintain direct contact with your audience.

PROPERTIES FOR TELEVISION SPEAKING

Television enables you to use visual aids that are out of the question on radio and often difficult to handle in public speech. It sends out a private copy of charts, pictures, diagrams, maps, and models to every member of your audience. But don't feel that you have to use visual aids because you are being televised. Use them only when they serve a real purpose.

POINTS TO KEEP IN MIND

Here are the key suggestions:

1. Speak before microphone and camera just as you do when you are talking effectively to another person or a small group in your home.

a) Maintain the best elements of conversational speech.

b) Use bodily action even if your audience can't see you.

2. Speak extemporaneously whenever possible. Reading from a manuscript may be a satisfactory substitute in a radio studio.

3. Stay within close range of a public-address microphone. Engineers will tell you what to do in a radio or television studio.

4. Television is ideally suited for visual aids—but don't drag them in unless they serve a real purpose.

EXERCISES

1. Choose several subjects suitable for panel discussions on radio or television programs. Assign four to eight students to each panel. Have one member of each group serve as chairman or moderator. Each panel will work as a group in preparing an outline for the program. When the panel "goes on the air," try to simulate actual studio conditions.

2. Have each student prepare a short talk suitable for a radio or TV program. Record the talk and play it back during a class period. Listen to each talk with these questions in mind: If I were dialing for a program, would this speaker and his speech invite my interest? Would his voice attract me? Is his language arresting? Are his ideas challenging? If time permits, have the students rework their talks in the light of the criticisms offered.

3. Devote a class period to a report, persuasive speech, or discussion on a radio or TV program. Immediately following the program or at the next class period, conduct a class discussion of what you heard. Did all the listeners derive essentially the same impressions as to what was said? Did the speech or discussion exemplify the standards and principles set forth in this book? To what audience was it directed? Did the speaker or speakers adapt to the medium of communication?

4. If facilities permit, present a short talk with the benefit of a public address system. After the talk, have the class make suggestions for improving your presentation. Repeat part of your talk in an effort to follow through on the suggestions.

Sample Speeches

The speeches that follow are examples of the four main types of speaking: inquiry, reporting, advocacy, and evocation. Read them critically. Evaluate how successfully each speaker puts into practice principles and methods offered throughout this book.

A SPEECH OF INQUIRY:
"MALAISE OF OUR TIMES"

GRAYSON KIRK

One evening last week I sat in my study confronted by an empty sheet of paper in my typewriter, and I wondered—as I always do at this season—just what I might most usefully say to you on this ceremonial occasion. From your standpoint the time allotted to me is mercifully short, but that, as any speaker knows, merely compounds the difficulty of his problem.

After a while, as I discarded mentally one after another of a list of possible topics, I began to speculate about your mood, your morale, your assessment of your years at Columbia, and what is more important, your attitude toward the years ahead. I wondered if you are filled today with the same restless anticipation and the same youthful optimism about the future that I felt when I sat in your place several decades ago and listened with half an ear to a long and dull Commencement speech.

I wondered, because I am told that this is not the case. I am told that you feel insecure, helplessly trapped by circumstances and events beyond your control, that life seems meaningless to you, and that your general outlook may be characterized by some current vernacular equivalent of *"Après nous, le déluge."* I recalled, for example, a conversation with a faculty colleague who reported a recent student interview. Apropos of some minor difference of opinion he had said, "You'll feel differently about this matter when you are thirty." And the student had replied, sourly, "Maybe so, if I live to be thirty."

If you do share this bleak feeling about the future, you are merely reflecting a general attitude of discontent and apprehension that appears to be widely prevalent in our society today. Since this social malaise does exist, perhaps it may be useful for us to look for a moment at some of its causes and manifestations. For all of us, the problem could become one of serious proportions.

From one point of view this uneasy state of public morale seems strangely irrational. No society in history has been so successful in providing material needs and even luxuries for such a large proportion of the population. Do you wish to travel? You can be at the ends of the earth in a matter of hours, and in the greatest ease. Are you eager to know what is happening elsewhere in the world? Your morning newspaper, or even the flick of an electronic switch, will make you fully aware, and even a spectator, of events in distant lands. Are you hungry for out-of-season or exotic foods? Your local supermarket has an array that was unavailable to the tables of royalty in past times. Are you worried about disease? A prescription filled at your corner drug-store will cope effectively with many an ill that may have taken your ancestors prematurely to their graves. Are you haunted by the fear of possible poverty and want? The whole mechanism of our society is organized to shield you from the hazards of indigence, much less the threat of starvation, that still hang over the vast majority of mankind. Thus viewed, your situation would seem to embody the fulfillment of the dreams of mankind over centuries of travail and hardship.

And yet it appears that happiness, confidence and optimism have eluded us. Our affluence seems not to have brought us contentment but uncertainty and apprehension. And we may ask ourselves, "Has the American dream failed us? Why do we have bitter fruit from the outstanding material success of our society? Why are we less optimistic about the future than our less privileged and struggling fathers were?

We are told by many persons that an answer to these questions is to be found in our uneasy feeling that our people today have less admirable ethical standards than those by which our fathers lived. We are constantly being made aware of what is said to be characteristic of modern life in America—of disintegrating family ties, of declining religious influences, of the prevalence of brutal and callous men whose sole criterion of conduct is the cynical question, "What's in it for me?" We are told that even in the universities student dishonesty has grown greater, and that it is limited, not by a sense of wrong-doing, but by the fear of being caught. We are alarmed by the growth of juvenile delinquency and by the social failure that has permitted it to develop. The law, it is said, is being obeyed only by those who are not clever enough to evade its limitations. Simple honesty and the Golden Rule are only for stupid people.

Are these really the guide-lines by which we live today, and are we worried because we are far from proud of them? I find it difficult to accept at face value such a jaundiced view of our contemporary life. As I shall say later, I do think we have cause for grave concern over some of the developments, but I have no hopeless feeling about them. Violence, reprehensible conduct and crime have existed in every society and in every generation. Because the news of the world is at our finger-tips, we may be more acutely aware of the evils of our time than our fathers were of theirs. Because history records more of human achievement than of human frailty, we may be less conscious of the sins of the past than of our own.

Nonetheless, though we may take some comfort from this exercise in historical perspective, it is cold comfort because it does not give us genuine reassurance about the state of our social health, and it gives even less reassurance that we are making progress toward that higher state of civilization for which men have labored and dreamed. We have yet to demonstrate to history that our own form of society is the best of all to enable men to live happily and harmoniously together. Our pride in our material progress must not blind us to the long hard road of social improvement ahead.

Others tell us that the malaise of our time is caused by the conviction that the individual has lost control over his own destiny. Society has become so complex in its organization and in its interrelationships that the ordinary citizen feels helpless and frustrated, a mere cog in a vast machine he but dimly comprehends. We have all read studies and analyses of the Organization Man, enmeshed in a huge impersonal group, unable to do more than follow the course others have set for him, unable to find self-fulfillment. We read George Orwell. We watch with anxiety the continued growth of completely totalitarian societies. We note the steady increase in social controls in our own society. And so we become pessimistic and apprehensive about our own prospects because we feel that the dignity and the independence of the individual are being engulfed by the sheer mechanism of modern society.

Such a feeling of frustration is particularly and understandably appropriate to younger people. As Bruno Bettelheim has said, "The buoyancy of youth is fed by the conviction of a full life to come, one in which all great things are theoretically attainable. But one cannot believe in the good life to come when the goal is suburbia. One cannot realize one's values by climbing the ladder of the business community, nor prove one's manhood on the greens of the country club. . . ." Has modern life, as he suggests, created a generation of youth "which has little belief in the romance of a better world, a generation whose dreams are not to be striven for but subjected to analysis"?

These are harsh words but they give us pause. They are romantic words because they disregard the plain fact that life in an urban, technological society does become steadily more complex, and does place greater restrictions upon the absolute freedom of the individual. This is the price we pay for the kind of society in which we live, the price for our membership in it, the payment for the benefits it confers upon us. Facing this situation, it is our obligation to redefine for our time the ancient paradox of all government, which is the principle of liberty through restraint.

We do not achieve this goal by a romantic rejection of society. Neither Rousseau nor the beatnik can be our guides. We cannot find an answer in futilitarian philosophies that deny the essential meaning of human existence, nor can a free people find an answer in the complete surrender of liberty to power. We must find our answer in a realistic appraisal of each new proposal for the extension of social control, and we can find it successfully only if our people have been educated to that level of comprehension that enables them to make such an evaluation responsibly and intelligently. Freedom of choice is the eternal essence of freedom. And each age must make its choices without being unduly hampered by the choices that other men have made at other times and under other conditions of life.

Perhaps our third—and greatest—source of worry today comes from the fear of physical destruction at the hands of a distant foe. We are fearful because we know the danger is genuine and because we feel helpless as individuals in the face of it. We shrink from an existence in which we may be destroyed by a single individual thousands of miles away who may encompass our fate merely by the impersonal act of pressing a button. And so we give way to our fears. We even demonstrate against measures designed to give us the best assurance that the button will not be pressed or that we may survive if it is. We picket the White House. We join protest organizations in the hope that by demonstrating our will to peace we can exorcize this fear from our lives. We have been so carefully protected against hardship in our individual lives, that we may not have formed the habit of courage in the face of new and unknown dangers.

We seem to forget that this threat of mass destruction is new only in its dimensions. The pioneer who tilled his little field with his rifle at his side lived in the constant presence of danger. He may not have had to worry about the fate of mankind, but the precarious safety of his family was worry enough for him. The feudal lord who watched from the battlements of his castle the horde of an approaching army was no stranger to fear. Most men, in most generations, have lived out their lives in the midst of danger, but they did not give way to it. They accepted it as a part of life. Shall it be said of us that we were less brave than our forebears?

It is customary to answer such a rhetorical question with a ringing denial. We proclaim that our people are as tough and as resilient as our forefathers were, that men will rise to meet adversity and peril as they always have done, that we will close our ranks and think only of the common good whenever a crisis comes.

Such talk is reassuring but it is not wholly convincing. History offers us too many uncomfortable examples of societies that became successful and affluent only to disappear under the onslaught of a tougher and more disciplined people that had a future to win and not a status to preserve. We sense from our reading of man's long record of successes and failures that sheer physical power will not in the long run suffice to protect a society that has grown soft at the core.

This, I think, is our greatest unspoken concern. We wonder if, spiritually, we are in the peak of condition to meet the challenge of a world that does not accept our values at their professed worth. We should be properly concerned about these manifestations to which I have alluded—the prevalence of disrespect for law, the ulcerous growth of juvenile delinquency, the cynical selfishness of great pressure groups, the failure to offer the prospect of a life of high adventure and significance to our youth. Unchecked, these social ills could direct our society down the Roman road.

I realize that this is a somber note for a Commencement Day, but I think we are all weary of the platitudes and clichés that normally adorn speeches on this occasion. I say this because I feel that you who are our newest graduates need to be aware of the dangers as well as of the promise of American life. You will have much to do with the leadership of our country in years ahead. Your influence will be greater than you now realize. It must be a good influence because all your sharpened intelligence and all your acquired skills will be meaningless unless you also have idealism, discipline and understanding.

Perhaps what I am really saying is that you must be worthy of the two-hundred year old heritage of this great university from which have come so many men of character and leadership. Sixty years ago, in his inaugural speech as President of this university, Nicholas Murray Butler spoke of the young Columbia men "who even now are lighting the lamps of their lives at the altar-fires of eternal truth." In these days we may say such things in a somewhat simpler fashion, but I hope the picture his words conveyed may be no less true of the class of 1962 than of the class of 1902.[1]

A SPEECH OF INQUIRY: "WHAT'S HAPPENING DOWNTOWN?"

One hundred million Americans live in metropolitan areas, and over half of them live in our twenty-three largest cities.

For these people "going downtown" is a trek to the heart of the city —a compact area of ten or twenty or more city blocks that contain the principal interests of the city. Downtown is the City Hall, the biggest department stores, the biggest office buildings, the biggest movie houses, the biggest medical centers, theaters, museums, libraries, hotels, restaurants, and an amazing array of shops and entertainment facilities of every kind and description.

Downtown is busy, bustling, crowded, exciting. It is the political, social, cultural, and economic center of the city. White-collar workers pour into the city in the morning and out at night. Shoppers dominate the midday flow, and pleasure-seekers the night hours. There is always somebody going downtown, or coming back—a lot of somebodies— literally millions of them!

To the casual observer, at least, downtown appears to be thriving. But let's take a closer look. The editors of *Fortune Magazine* took such a look and report their findings in a book entitled *The Exploding Metropolis*. This explosion appears to be leaving downtown with "falling retail sales, tax bases in jeopardy, stagnant real-estate values, impossible traffic and parking conditions, failing mass transit, and encirclement by slums." These are the words of one of the editors.

Does this picture sound exaggerated? Those of you who live in or near our big cities can probably answer the question for yourself. But an analysis of some of the basic forces at work in most metropolitan areas suggests pretty strongly that the core of the city is destined to lose some of its traditional strength unless action is taken to counteract these forces.

There is no question that millions of people are leaving the cities for the suburbs. The first to go vacate the old residences close to the core of the city for newer homes and greener lawns. The less fortunate move in behind them. Then the slums begin. And then the next layer moves out farther to escape the encroaching slums. This gives more room for slums. So on it goes—a powerful centrifugal force pulling people away from the heart of the city into a vast suburban sprawl. And the vacuum

---

[1] Given at Commencement Excercises, Columbia University, June 5, 1962. Text supplied by President Kirk and reprinted by permission.

their leaving creates is filled by some 17 million Americans living in dwellings now beyond rehabilitation—"decayed, dirty, rat infested, without decent heat or light or plumbing."

There is a second force at work which bears examination. Urban dwellers appear to be enamored with two things: a house in the suburbs and a car—perhaps even two cars. And anybody who invests three to five thousand dollars in a car wants to operate the car. Especially is this true if the alternative is an outmoded, rundown public transportation system. So the inevitable happens: Downtown becomes so congested with automobiles without adequate parking facilities that Mr. and Mrs. Suburbanite begin to look for some more convenient place to work, shop, and play, And anyone who has had any experience with recent suburban developments knows that they do not have to look far. Slick new shopping centers, dominated by acres of free parking are ready at hand. And many of them include office buildings for professional services, theaters, and even amusements for the kids.

Why go downtown? That is precisely the question most of our downtowns face. And there appear to be millions of people who are perfectly willing to let them worry along with their own problem. But before we settle for this attitude, let me raise a few questions: How much do the hearts of our cities mean to American life—to the culture and economy of the nation? And more particularly, what happens to the suburbs if the mother city loses its vitality? Are people abandoning the central city by choice or because circumstances force them to leave? In short, are the downtown areas of our cities worth rehabilitating and worth making more easily available to the people who want to use them? The keys to the problem appear to be imaginative planning and accessibility. Downtown must first be a place people want to go and, second, a place they can get to without paying too heavy a toll in time, energy, and patience.

Jane Jacobs raises this first question in her article *Downtown Is for People*. She asks, ". . . What makes a city center magnetic, what can inject the gaiety, the wonder, the cheerful hurly-burly that makes people want to come into the city and to linger there?" She continues, ". . . Downtown's values are its by-products. To create in it an atmosphere of urbanity and exuberance is not a frivolous aim."

Jane Jacobs' thesis is that we must exploit the unique compactness of downtown by making an enormous variety of goods and services available to people in the compass of a few blocks. Here is where all sorts of highly specialized enterprises can exist—enterprises with markets so selective, they need exposure to hundreds of thousands of people. She sums it up this way, "A metropolitan center comes across to people as a center largely by virtue of its enormous collection of small elements, where people can see them, at street level." And, I might add, where they can get to them on foot without risking life and limb in city traffic.

Whether this or some other picture of downtown sums up its magnetic potential, we cannot escape the problem of getting there to enjoy whatever it has to offer. Here is where the battle lines are really drawn: Should we rehabilitate, modernize, and add to our facilities for public transportation to the center of the city? This question raises a whole brood of related problems: Will people ride the subways, elevated lines, and buses even if they are improved? Who is going to pay for these improvements? The riders—or the public, through subsidies?

Or should we make it easier for people to get downtown by private car? Build bigger and better freeways for through traffic and bigger and better parking facilities in or near the downtown area? In fifteen of the nation's twenty-five largest cities, 60 per cent or more of all riders entering the downtown business district arrive by automobile. If this trend continues, how long will it take to reach car saturation? As Francis Bello asks in his article "The City and the Car," if we attempt to provide parking space for all the motorists who want to come, will there be anything left worth coming to?

One solution to this knotty problem that is receiving considerable attention is a proposal to keep cars out of the central city and turn it into "a pedestrian mall." The architect Victor Gruen has proposed such a plan for the redevelopment of downtown Fort Worth. This plan recommends perimeter parking facilities around a limited downtown area and express bus service that would deposit its customers at even more convenient points than their own cars.

I see that my time is up, and I know I have not given you any neat answer to the question that motivated these remarks. As a matter of fact I didn't intend to, nor am I at all certain that I know the answer. In all probability there is no *one* answer. I am convinced, however, that downtown faces problems. I have tried to suggest some of the causes contributing to these problems and to suggest directions that solutions might take. If enough people value the unique density and variety of opportunity that the central city can offer, I suspect that these values can be conserved and that we can find ways of getting to them. But most competent observers appear to agree on one thing: There is no time to waste!

A REPORT:
"HURRICANE EDNA"

EDWARD R. MURROW

This is the news:

Hurricane Edna is moving north-northeast faster and with higher winds at her center. The latest from the Weather Bureau is this: Edna's speed has increased from ten miles an hour to between seventeen and twenty-two miles an hour. When last reported, she was centered eighty miles slightly "east of south" of Cape Hatteras, North Carolina. The center is expected to pass the Cape at midnight. Previously the highest winds near the center were one hundred and fifteen miles per hour. Now they are one hundred and twenty-five miles per hour. The weathermen expect the hurricane to step up its forward speed in the next few hours. Tonight hurricane warnings—a central white light with two red lights on each side—are displayed from North Carolina to Maine. Here in New York, the weatherman has told us: "It could be one of the most serious hurricanes in the city's history." There is a slight possibility that it may go out to sea, but we have all been adequately warned. The phone companies here and in New England are ready with their "master disaster plan." Military and naval planes have been flown inland from all shore installations. Civil defense agencies, the Red Cross, are ready. Coastal residents of Connecticut have been urged to move inland before midnight. Sandbags have been piled around buildings in Providence, Rhode Island, hard hit by Hurricane Carol. On Martha's Vineyard, bulldozers are pushing up sand dikes to protect low inland areas. Ham radio networks have been set up to relay emergency messages. Three thousand National Guardsmen in New Hampshire have been ordered on a stand-by alert. Yesterday I flew into Hurricane Edna's eye, with the Air Force. I'd like to try to describe what I saw. . . .

We took off from Bermuda at 11:30 A.M. in a specially equipped B-29. The Air-Force boys were working for the taxpayers, going out to chart, measure, map and study the hurricane. We climbed to ten thousand, blue sky overhead, blue water without a single whitecap below, and headed West. For about an hour-and-a-half there was nothing to do except remember that flying is made up of many hours of boredom, interspersed with a few minutes of stark terror. Then there were a few whitecaps, but no clouds. Then the whitecaps grew in size—surface wind about thirty miles an hour; a few scattered cumulus clouds ahead. A big cloud seemed to summon its neighbors, and they built castles and lakes and cities on hillsides, all white against the blue of the sky. We bored through a few and skirted others. Then there was a big mountain of clouds ahead, and we went in. A few rain squalls, but little turbulence. The texture of the cloud changed, became a ghostly gray; we couldn't see the wing-tips of the aircraft. Twenty minutes later there was a little blue-gray light, but it seemed to come from all around us. Suddenly blue water again, no whitecaps, but the ocean was heaving as though a giant were shaking a rug. Into another cloud, out on the other side, and the ocean had changed its face.

Long irregular furrows, as if a drunken plowman had been plowing a field of blue velvet and turning up snow. We went down to seventy-five hundred—surface winds now estimated at sixty miles an hour; flew right along the top of a flat cloud, with the feeling that if the pilot let his wheels down he'd leave a track in it. The next time we saw water, the wind was cutting the top off the whitecaps, and there was a thin gauze of spray as far as we could see. Then into the cloud again, and that ghostly gray light that seemed to rub off on the faces of the crew members and to cause them all to look as if they were ill and hadn't slept.

Radar kept reaching out, looking for Edna's eye. It showed a high bank of clouds to the right and to the left. We were flying blind through that gray stuff in the valley between. Suddenly there was a hole in the cloud—maybe a quarter-mile across—and at the bottom there was seafoam. It was as if we were looking down a deep well, at a huge eggbeater churning up milk at the bottom. We flew on and began the real search for the eye of the hurricane. There were sudden changes in temperature—more rain. Radar reported, the engineer reported, the navigator wanted to know if anybody could see surface wind. The radarscope didn't show anything. We were bounced around a little. The skipper said: "There's a storm around here somewhere. Let's find it."

The navigator asked for a turn to the left, and in a couple of minutes the B-29 began to shudder. It was a twisting, tortured motion. The co-pilot said: "I think we're in it." The pilot said: "We're going up"— although every control was set to take us down. Something lifted us about three hundred feet. Then the pilot said: "We're going down"— although he was doing everything humanly possible to take us up. Edna was in control of the aircraft. We were on an even keel but were being staggered by short, sharp blows. We then hit something with a bang that was audible above the roar of the motors, and more than one man flinched. It was a solid sheet of water. Seconds later brilliant sunlight hit us like a hammer; a little rainbow spun off the starboard outboard prop. Someone shouted: "There she is," and we were in the eye. Calm air—flat, calm sea below; a great amphitheater, round as a dollar, with white clouds sloping up to twenty-five or thirty thousand feet. The water looked like a blue alpine lake with snow-clad mountains coming right down to the water's edge. A great bowl of sunshine. Someone, I think it was the right scanner, shouted: "So help me, there's a ship down there." And there was—right in the center of the eye. We guessed her to be a ten-thousand ton merchant ship, moving very slowly in that calm water, with only a thin feather of wake behind her. She appeared to be in no trouble, but trouble was inevitable sometime ahead, because she was surrounded by those cloud mountains and raging water.

The eye was twenty miles in diameter. We went down to fifteen hundred feet and flew back and forth across it, making shallow penetrations into the storm area. The temperature went up fourteen degrees. The altimeter said four thousand feet, but we were actually at fifteen hundred feet. The civilian weather officer aboard looked at Edna with a clinical eye and said: "She's a copybook hurricane—beautifully formed." We took her temperature, measured her speed, threw overboard scientific gear that might help to chart her future movements, while we continued to fly around in the calm at the bottom of that funnel of white clouds.

The eye of a hurricane is an excellent place to reflect upon the puniness of man and his works. If an adequate definition of humility is ever written, it's likely to be done in the eye of a hurricane.

The engineer reported some trouble with the number three engine. We climbed to ten thousand feet and bored into the wall of the white cloud that surrounded the eye. It was not as rough going out as it was coming in because the navigator had picked his exit well.

Going back to Bermuda, we talked of hurricanes. One of the pilots said: "We certainly were disappointed in Carol; we just didn't think she would do what she did." He had flown through Carol so often that he regarded her as a friend who had committed a major misdemeanor.

These young men who fly the Air Weather Service are doing all that can be humanly done to provide information upon which adequate warning can be based. After all, the only thing you can do about a hurricane is to watch it and get ready for it.

After flying yesterday for only nine hours with these young men of the Air Force, on a routine mission, I think they deserve combat pay.[2]

A REPORT:
"TODAY'S TENSIONS"

MARJORIE CARPENTER

Time was when speeches about women centered around the question: Is woman's place in the home? We now know that her place is wherever she decides to place herself. There is some historical authority for the topic stated by Rozanne Brooks: "Woman's place is in the Wrong." Ever since Adam she has been blamed for the sins of mankind; and she is forever feeling guilty about her rightful duties. It is not my intention in the title I have chosen for my remarks to do more than suggest that we can boil down all of the findings about women as they have appeared in numerous periodicals over the past years to the observation that women have discovered that they are more than females. This throws them into the midst of the tensions of all human beings.

[2] Given over C.B.S. Network, September 10, 1954. Published by permission.

Laurens van der Post comments: "With more and more women of our own day there is an urge to creativeness which lies underneath and deeper, above and beyond the begetting of children. These women have a contract with life itself which is not discharged with the mere procreation of their species. Men recognize and try to honor this contract in themselves as a matter of course; they do not so readily honor it in a woman." Let us consider, then, what the special assets and liabilities of a woman are when she realizes that she is a human being suffering from the same fears and loss of direction that men feel in today's world.

Perhaps all of us need to reconsider the bad connotation we have given certain words. We all suffer from "tensions." At their door we lay the responsibility for divorce, bad health, and war. Actually the word implies a stretching to the point of tautness. The arrow cannot fly with any force unless the bowstring is held taut. Trouble comes if the archer does not know where the target is and has not the skill to hit it. Also, we speak with horror of conflict. In reality the meeting of two opposing forces, the contact of negative and positive, of male and female is essential to the creative process. Perhaps we need to concern ourselves with conditions which will create the best possible new idea and welcome the conflict which produces creativity. So, too, we feel abused at living through a time of crisis. The Chinese people use two characters to express the idea of crisis: one the symbol for danger, and one the sign which means opportunity. Again, we act as though insecurity were the cause of most neurosis; we give it as the basic reason for crime and delinquency. Actually, static security is death; and insecurity is the growing point of learning, the frontier of progress.

If we cannot object then to "tensions" and "crises" as such, surely we can complain about the tremendous changes which overwhelm us and confuse us. Here, the title of your seminar is encouraging. You consider that there is a challenge in our changing world. In the United States we are especially conditioned to change; we are restless without it. A Canadian colleague of mine asked me once if I knew the difference between an Englishman, a Canadian, and an American. He then proceeded to make the distinction: The Englishman says, "As it was in the beginning, is now and ever shall be, world without end, Amen." The Canadian says, "As it was in the beginning, is now, and if any of you gentlemen think there ought to be a change, we shall appoint a committee to investigate it." The American says, "As it was in the beginning, is now, and by God, there has got to be a change!" Change is inevitable; change is everywhere today and such rapid change that one cannot keep up. Scientific discoveries bring constant technological change. Barbara Ward comments on the dangers for our society if everything changes but its institutions. "No one can stay sane if no one is to innovate except technologists."

It is at this point that women may be accused of being a part of the problem. They do resist change—unless it is one which fashion decrees, or one which simplifies housework. Traditionally women are the consolidators. They want to keep the members of the family safe and secure in a pattern of living which has become familiar—provided, of course, that they have been comfortable. Consider, for example, the attitude of many women in the South about civil rights. They will fight for the rights of children and husband; but extend the idea to minority groups, and they become resistant because this might endanger the advantages they have enjoyed.

Consider, also, the changes in the labor market. Here women are directly concerned. We can read from Leaflet #18 of the Labor Department (What's New About Women Workers, 1963) about the great increase in the number of women workers:

> In April, 1962, about 24 million women were workers. This was 4½ million above the figure reached in April, 1945. In 1940, the average age of women workers was 32 years. Since then it has advanced about nine years. 36% of all women of working age are in the labor force.

Women use their earning power to help husbands through school, and later they add to the family income; but they do not recognize in adequate numbers that women are needed in professions. They do not take advantage of all the possibilities now open to women and really live up to their highest potential. Is it laziness, line of least resistance or a fear of being considered "not feminine"?

Even though women resist change unless it serves their immediate interests, and although they are lazy about learning difficult facts—especially in science and mathematics—they have some very real assets in these days of crisis and change. I overheard one wise educator, Dr. Max McLain, put it this way: "Women have the kind of instinct which is invaluable. They know when to lean on their friends in time of disaster, when to withdraw and think things out, and when to fight. Most tragedies occur when an individual reacts in one of these ways at the wrong time." Some men—not enough—have developed this instinct. Winkler claims that civilization would be better off if men worked to claim this sort of sensitivity, and women worked to know more facts and take a more objective view. We need both approaches from both sexes.

A similar observation is made by Cleanth Brooks in his recent book, *The Hidden God*. He is analysing with much insight the women characters in the novels of our recent authors. In discussing Faulkner's *Sanctuary*, he comments that the men characters "have to lose their innocence about evil, confront a hard choice, and through a process of initiation discover reality." "Women are always in possession of this knowledge naturally and instinctively." Again in considering Dilsey in *The Sound and the Fury,* he says that "she affirms the ideal of wholeness in a disintegrated family . . . she knows a concrete world of values." Lena, he comments, "represents the principle on which the human community is founded. She is the carrier of life."

Woman as the consolidator, then, has social significance. In the past, we have assumed in our American culture that she would keep alive a sense of values—both religious and aesthetic. Mass communications have contributed to a dulling of her aesthetic judgment; they appeal to what is cheap and tawdry in emotions; and in presenting stereotypes, they have blunted genuine emotion. Scientific gadgets have assisted in speeding up work; but they have increased an emphasis on material comforts and the sort of mechanization which speeds "dehumanization." The speed of today's living reduces many women to days spent in trivia; and it becomes difficult to break the bonds of what is expected in choosing a deodorant, or hair rinse. She must be glamorous to her husband. This is set up as normal. One woman commented: "I am just a normal woman with husband and children." Deep is the fear of being thought different, "not feminine."

Marriage is the only goal of many women. Statistics about the population explosion give abundant proof that as a female, woman has reached her highest potential. Most critics are very sure that she has not reached her highest potential as a woman. In a contracting world there is need for an expansion of her powers. The very essence of the feminine—the power to love, the instinct to understand what does not appear on the surface, the ability to face tension and crises with both instinct and knowledge, and make them serve creative purposes—these need to be used in units larger than the small family unit. In fact, women will rise to the occasion when they realize that this small family unit is not secure unless all of their powers are thrown into the conflicts, tensions, and crises of the day. Rapid changes must be evaluated and embraced as a challenge. They can work *for* today's woman unless she allows herself to be tied to trivia and guided by glamour, unless she is paralyzed by a fear of not being "feminine."

In closing, let me read a poem with apologies to James Oppenheim. This is a parody or paraphrase of his poem, "The Slave."

> They set woman free, giving her a vote and job.
>   She is just as frustrated as ever
>   She is still chained to triviality
>   She is still manacled to mental indolence
>   She is still bound by fear of not being feminine
>   By ignorance of what is potentially hers.

Her slavery was not to the home
But in herself.

They can only set free women free
And there is no need of that
Free women set themselves and all men free.[3]

A SPEECH OF ADVOCACY:
"THE CASE OF THE SPLENDID SPLINTER"

CLAUDE COLEMAN

Today our society suffers from a plethora of splendid splinters—fractional adults who never become men and women in any real sense of the word. I had better define my term, perhaps. Ask who someone is and the reply invariably comes back, "Why, he is a plumber," or a "surgeon," or an "economist," or a "geographer," or a "dean," or a "policeman"—not a man at all but only a splinter.

It hardly matters what special field a young man chooses to prepare himself for nowadays. Any department in any college in the land will prescribe as many courses for him as it can persuade its deans to approve. Every professor within the department believes he has something absolutely essential to the splinter's welfare. In the graduate school, the splinter must dedicate his entire existence to the business of becoming a sharper and more highly polished splinter.

Do I mean that our society has educated its best minds in the wrong directions and with a false sense of values? Yes, that is exactly what I mean. Along with a false estimate of itself. Socrates tells how in search of someone wiser than himself he went among the artisans, and found them not only vain about their one talent but, because of their one skill, inclined to believe they knew a great deal about other matters, too.

The situation still prevails. The skillful surgeon sounds off in the barbershop about the political situation and reveals a greater ignorance than the barber's. The professor of English gains the hearty applause of his colleagues by making scornful remarks about the college of education. The professor of Romance languages joins the John Birch Society. The professor of physics labels all courses in humanities and social studies "trash" and declares that anyone interested in these fields can learn enough about them by reading magazines. The professor of sociology solemnly declares that knowledge is the prerogative of departments and can only be taught within the appropriate departments, and there is not

[3] Given at a seminar for women, St. Louis, Missouri, November 9, 1963. Reprinted by permission from *Vital Speeches of the Day*, January 1, 1964, pp. 184-86.

a twinkle of humor in his eye. And the professor of mathematics solemnly agrees with him.

These are the splendid splinters. The examples I have given are those within my own experience and knowledge. Here are some of the best minds of the nation, no doubt doing excellent work within narrow limits, whose total contribution leads to confusion and unhappiness. Most scholars work long hours turning out scholarly articles for other blind scholars to read in their own fields. They are finely trained scholars, but they are not men. They are fractions of men.

What a man is so greatly surmounts what he says that what he says scarcely matters. He must first be a man, for his failure to be a man will shine clearly through the most opaque rhetoric. An economist who has no understanding of history or anthropology or psychology is no economist at all. It is, to quote Thoreau, "as if the main object were to talk fast and not to talk sensibly."

Our foolish society has confounded itself with its tools of communication. No one has much of anything to say, but every tongue clacks away. Our splendid splinters have constructed vocabularies so involved and complex that they can talk only to other splinters from the same woods as themselves. Did you ever hear two physicians talk to each other about a sick patient? Or two economists discussing a sick economy?

Sometimes one gets the strong impression that our intellectuals have removed themselves from the world of affairs as effectively as the monastic scholars did in the Middle Ages.

Our entire society is made up of specialists. Governors govern. Doctors doctor. Plumbers plumb. Auditors audit. Engineers engineer. And so on and so on. Here we go round the mulberry bush.

Professors of English strive vainly to teach students to write. College students should have learned writing competence in the seventh grade, but they still make ghastly errors—in spelling, sentence structure, agreement of tenses, paragraphing and organization. Why, they ask, should they learn to write? They can hire writers. Look at Senator Barry Goldwater, whose ghost-written "Conscience of a Conservative" has sold 700,000 copies. "I am going to be an engineer," they say, "and I am willing to put any amount of time into my studies in engineering. Writing is for the birds—or for would-be writers."

For the same reason the public no longer reads much of anything but comic books, newspapers and thrillers. Why should anyone read "The Iliad" or "The Odyssey" when he plans to be a doctor or a lawyer or an engineer? Why should anyone ever read a book of poems? Why should anyone ever run a mile just for the sake of running? Why climb a mountain or swim a channel? Or take a long walk by oneself? Or a bicycle trip across the continent?

Well, if there's money in it, we understand. Otherwise the chap is an oddball. The national yell is "Get a job." The national theme is "Specialize, specialize, specialize." Get a job. Make money. Work, study, go to college, get a job. Marry a wife and see that she gets a job. Have children and see that they have jobs.

All this rings false in my ears. It is a foolish kind of economy. These job-getting, money-making specialists are not only dullards; they are building up an economy that may collapse through the neglect of more substantial values. There may be jobs for 175,000,000 Americans one day and no jobs at all the next day, if we have not the character and the intelligence to avoid a global war.

Further than this, I find myself a little bit in sympathy with the beatniks. If our economy reduces us to a dull, meaningless round of working at jobs, going home to nothing, and coming back the next day to work at the same old job, we hardly have lives worth living.

The kind of culture I visualize will give us greater stability in the society of nations and greater day-to-day enjoyment. If we do not have both greater individual happiness and greater international security, then the beatnik pattern of behavior becomes good sense.

Commonly nowadays we hear the remark, "It is a world I never made." This pernicious thought appears to excuse the individual from the mistakes of his society, but we cannot shrug off our responsibility. It would indeed be pleasant to retire to some ivory tower and live out our lives serenely, but our universities cannot provide such a retreat and they must not.

There are people who accept responsibility by proclaiming themselves 100 per cent American. They try to solve all problems by the simple process of approval of everything within the United States and disapproval of everything without. Their organizations feed on ignorance and specialization. In a well-educated society these groups could not be born.

To quote Thoreau once again: "A man must first be a man and a subject afterwards." We cannot make up for our deficiencies as men by being subjects.

I expect the masses of people to be faulty in reasoning, irresponsible and personally unhappy for a long, long time. College graduates in America, however, now number several millions. Within this group we must build a strong and deep reservoir of intelligence, good taste and character.

We must not permit our college students to be led into narrow specialization without a broad substructure of understanding. We need more psychology, more literature, more history and anthropology, more philosophy, more of all the fine arts and humanities. If we abdicate to the technologists and the engineers, they may indeed take us to the moon or even to Mars, but why transport this crazy society beyond earth?

I should be much for the study of all sciences, especially biology, for

I believe a man needs to understand his relation to the stream of life and to the physical forces that underlie it. But I do not want to abandon the noble dreams men have had.

A healthy, happy, peaceful stable society can be developed on earth. We cannot build such a society out of splinters. We can build it only out of strong, healthy, happy, responsible men—and women.

Women are quite as important as men. Every day I encounter attractive, dedicated mothers who have given up everything else to a career in motherhood. I like casual mothers much better, mothers who love and work for their children but do not remove themselves from public issues, mothers who insist upon pursuing the arts or sciences even as men, mothers who even before they are mothers are women.

Not *ladies*—just responsible, happy, informed and interested women who are only casually concerned about finding the right liquid detergent, the right tissue, the right stuff to put up their hair with, but are deeply interested in building a society in which their children can be happy.

We have a complicated society in which we must have plumbers, auditors, surgeons, editors, teachers, lawyers, chemists, physicists, engineers, and on and on. If these technologists are only technologists and nothing else, however, they become the most obnoxious and crashing bores. Nine-tenths of the faculty at any university are bores, simply because they become complete nincompoops outside their specialties. Most of them take their coffee breaks with their own colleagues in order to avoid the viruses of other disciplines. They are not happy until their undergraduate majors become as narrow as they are themselves.

We must have colleagues, of course. But they should return to their original business of educating men and women. Our society needs specialists—but it is desperate for men and women. The splendid splinter must be replaced by the splendid man.[4]

A SPEECH OF ADVOCACY:
"THE INTELLECTUAL AND THE POLITICIAN"

JOHN F. KENNEDY

It is a pleasure to join with my fellow alumni in this pilgrimage to the second home of our youth.

---

[4] Given at the National Student Association Congress, Madison, Wisconsin, August 8, 1961. Reprinted by permission from *The New York Times Magazine*, September 24, 1961, pp. 35-39. © 1961 by The New York Times Company. The title used here is the one under which the speech was first given by Professor Coleman. The title used by *The New York Times Magazine* is "Needed: Whole Men, Not Fractions."

Prince Bismarck once remarked that one third of the students of German universities broke down from overwork; another third broke down from dissipation; and the other third ruled Germany. As I look about this campus today, I would hesitate to predict which third attends reunions (although I have some suspicion), but I am confident I am looking at "rulers" of America in the sense that all active informed citizens rule.

I can think of nothing more reassuring for all of us than to come again to this institution whose whole purpose is dedicated to the advancement of knowledge and the dissemination of truth.

I belong to a profession where the emphasis is somewhat different. Our political parties, our politicians are interested, of necessity, in winning popular support—a majority, and only indirectly truth is the object of our controversy. From this polemic of contending factions, the general public is expected to make a discriminating judgment. As the problems have become more complex, as our role as a chief defender of Western civilization has become enlarged, the responsibility of the electorate as a court of last resort has become almost too great. The people desperately seek objectivity and a university such as this fulfills that function.

And the political profession needs to have its temperature lowered in the cooling waters of the scholastic pool. We need both the technical judgment and the disinterested viewpoint of the scholar, to prevent us from becoming imprisoned by our own slogans.

Therefore, it is regrettable that the gap between the intellectual and politician seems to be growing. Instead of synthesis, clash and discord now characterizes the relations between the two groups much of the time. Authors, scholars, and intellectuals can praise every aspect of American society but the political. My desk is flooded with books, articles, and pamphlets criticizing Congress. But, rarely if ever, have I seen any intellectual bestow praise on either the political profession or any political body for its accomplishments, its ability, or its integrity—much less for its intelligence. To many universities and scholars, we reap nothing but censors, investigators and perpetrators of what has been called "the swinish cult of anti-intellectualism."

James Russell Lowell's satiric attack more than one hundred years ago on Caleb Cushing, a celebrated attorney general and member of Congress, sets the tone:

> Gineral C is a dreffle smart man,
> He's ben on all sides that give places or pelf,
> But consistency still wuz a part of his plan—
> He's ben true to *one* party, that is himself.

But in fairness, the way of the intellectual is not altogether serene;

in fact, so great has become popular suspicion that a recent survey of American intellectuals by a national magazine elicited from one of our foremost literary figures the guarded response, "I ain't no intellectual."

Both sides in this battle, it seems to me, are motivated by largely unfounded feelings of distrust. The politician, whose authority rests upon the mandate of the popular will, is resentful of the scholar who can, with dexterity, slip from position to position without dragging the anchor of public opinion. It was this skill that caused Lord Melbourne to say of the youthful historian Macaulay that he wished he was as sure of anything as Macaulay was of everything. The intellectual, on the other hand, finds it difficult to accept the difference between the laboratory and the legislature. In the former, the goal is truth, pure and simple, without regard to changing currents of public opinion; in the latter, compromises and majorities and procedural customs and rights affect the ultimate decision as to what is right or just or good. And even when they realize this difference, most intellectuals consider their chief function that of the critic—and politicians are sensitive to critics (possibly because we have so many of them). "Many intellectuals," Sidney Hook has said, "would rather 'die' than agree with the majority, even on the rare occasions when the majority is right."

It seems to me that the time has come for intellectuals and politicians alike to put aside those horrible weapons of modern internecine warfare, the barbed thrust, the acid pen, and—most sinister of all—the rhetorical blast. Let us not emphasize all on which we differ but all we have in common. Let us consider not what we fear separately but what we share together.

First, I would ask both groups to recall that the American politician of today and the American intellectual of today are descended from a common ancestry. Our nation's first great politicians were also among the nation's first great writers and scholars. The founders of the American Constitution were also the founders of American scholarship. The works of Jefferson, Madison, Hamilton, Franklin, Paine, and John Adams —to name but a few—influenced the literature of the world as well as its geography. Books were their tools, not their enemies. Locke, Milton, Sydney, Montesquieu, Coke, and Bolingbroke were among those widely read in political circles and frequently quoted in political pamphlets. Our political leaders traded in the free commerce of ideas with lasting results both here and abroad.

In these golden years, our political leaders moved from one field to another with amazing versatility and vitality. Jefferson and Franklin still throw long shadows over many fields of learning. A contemporary described Jefferson, "A gentleman of thirty-two, who could calculate an eclipse, survey an estate, tie an artery, plan an edifice, try a cause, break a horse, dance a minuet, and play the violin."

Daniel Webster could throw thunderbolts at Hayne on the Senate floor and then stroll a few steps down the corridor and dominate the Supreme Court as the foremost lawyer of his time. John Quincy Adams, after being summarily dismissed from the Senate for a notable display of independence, could become Boylston Professor of Rhetoric and Oratory at Harvard and then become a great Secretary of State. (Those were the happy days when Harvard professors had no difficulty getting Senate confirmation.)

The versatility also existed on the frontier. An obituary of Missouri's first senator, Thomas Hart Benton, the man whose tavern brawl with Jackson in Tennessee caused him to flee the state, said:

With a readiness that was often surprising, he could quote from a Roman law or a Greek philosopher, from Virgil's *Georgics,* the *Arabian Nights,* Herodotus, or Sancho Panza, from the Sacred Carpets, the German reformers or Adam Smith; from *Fénelon* or *Hudibras,* from the financial reports of Necca or the doings of the Council of Trent, from the debates on the adoption of the Constitution or intrigues of the Kitchen Cabinet or from some forgotten speech of a deceased member of Congress.

This link between the American scholarship and the American politician remained for more than a century. Just one hundred years ago today in the presidential campaign of 1856, the Republicans sent three brilliant orators around the campaign circuit: William Cullen Bryant, Henry Wadsworth Longfellow, and Ralph Waldo Emerson. Those were the carefree days when the "egg-heads" were all Republicans.

I would hope that both groups, recalling their common heritage, might once again forge a link between the intellectual and political professions. I know that scholars may prefer the mysteries of pure scholarship or the delights of abstract discourse. But, "Would you have counted him a friend of ancient Greece," as George William Curtis asked a century ago during the Kansas-Nebraska controversy, "who quietly discussed of patriotism on that Greek summer day through whose hopeless and immortal hours Leonidas and his three hundred stood at Thermopylae for liberty? Was John Milton to conjugate Greek verbs in his library or talk of the ancient Shunamites when the liberty of Englishmen was imperiled?" No, the duty of the scholar—particularly in a republic such as ours—is to contribute his objective views and his sense of liberty to the affairs of his state and nation.

Secondly, I would remind both groups that the American politician and the American intellectual operate within a common framework—a framework we call liberty. Freedom of expression is not divisible into political expression and intellectual expression. The lock on the door of the Legislature, the Parliament, or the Assembly Hall—by order of the King, the Commissar, or the Fuehrer—has historically been followed or preceded by a lock on the door of the university, the library or the printer's. And if the first blow for freedom in any subjugated land is struck by a political leader, the second is struck by a book, a newspaper, or a pamphlet.

Unfortunately, in more recent times, politicians and intellectuals have quarreled bitterly—too bitterly in some cases—over how each group has met the modern challenge to freedom both at home and abroad. Politicians have questioned the discernment with which intellectuals have reacted to the siren call of the extreme left; and intellectuals have tended to accuse politicians of not always being aware, especially here at home, of the toxic effects of freedom restrained.

While differences in judgment where freedom is endangered are perhaps inevitable, there should, nevertheless, be more basic agreement on fundamentals. In this field we should be natural allies, working more closely together for the common cause, against the common enemy.

Third and finally, I would stress the great potential gain for both groups resulting from increased political cooperation.

The American intellectual and scholar today must decide, as Goethe put it, whether he is to be an anvil—or a hammer. Today, for many, the stage of the anvil, at least in its formal phases, is complete. The question he faces is whether he is to be a hammer—whether he is to give to the world in which he was reared and educated the broadest possible benefits of his learning. As one who is familiar with the political world, I can testify that we need it.

For example: The password for all legislation, promoted by either party, is progress. But how do we tell what is progress and what is retreat? Those of us who may be too close to the issue, or too politically or emotionally involved in it, look for the objective word of the scholar. Indeed, the operation of our political life is such that we may not even be debating the real issues.

In foreign affairs, for example, the parties dispute over which is best fitted to implement the long-accepted policies of collective security and Soviet containment. But perhaps these policies are no longer adequate, perhaps these goals are no longer meaningful—the debate goes on nevertheless, for neither party is in a position to undertake the reappraisal necessary, particularly if the solutions presented are more complex to, and less popular with, the electorate.

Or take our agricultural program, for another example. Republicans and Democrats debate long over whether flexible or rigid price supports should be in effect. But this may not be the real issue at all—and in fact I am convinced that it is not, that neither program offers any long-range solution to our many real farm problems. The scholars and the universities might reexamine this whole area and come up with some real answers—the political parties and their conventions rarely will.

Other examples could be given indefinitely—where do we draw the line between free trade and protection, when does taxation become prohibitive, what is the most effective use we can make of our present nuclear potential? The intellectuals who can draw upon their rational disinterested approach and their fund of learning to help reshape our political life can make a tremendous contribution to their society while gaining new respect for their own group.

I do not say that our political and public life should be turned over to experts who ignore public opinion. Nor would I adopt from the Belgian Constitution of 1893 the provision giving three votes instead of one to college graduates; or give Harvard a seat in the Congress as William and Mary was once represented in the Virginia House of Burgesses.

But, I would urge that our political parties and our universities recognize the need for greater cooperation and understanding between politicians and intellectuals. We do not need scholars or politicians like Lord John Russell, of whom Queen Victoria remarked, he would be a better man if he knew a third subject—but he was interested in nothing but the Constitution of 1688 and himself. What we need are men who can ride easily over broad fields of knowledge and recognize the mutual dependence of our two worlds.

"Don't teach my boy poetry," an English mother recently wrote the Provost of Harrow. "Don't teach my boy poetry; he is going to stand for Parliament." Well, perhaps she was right—but if more politicians knew poetry, and more poets knew politics, I am convinced the world would be a little better place to live on this Commencement Day of 1956.[5]

A SPEECH OF EVOCATION: "SHE WOULD RATHER LIGHT CANDLES"

ADLAI E. STEVENSON

I stand here for the second time in little more than a year sad in heart and in spirit.[*] The United States, the United Nations, the world, has lost one of its great citizens. Mrs. Eleanor Roosevelt is dead; a cherished friend of all mankind is gone.

Yesterday I said I had lost more than a friend; I had lost an inspira-

[5] Given at Commencement Exercises, Harvard University, June 14, 1956. Reprinted by permission.
[*] On September 18, 1961, Dag Hammarskjöld, Secretary General of the United Nations Organization, was killed in an airplane crash in Central Africa. Mr. Stevenson eulogized Mr. Hammarskjöld in a statement to the General Assembly on September 20, 1961.

tion. She would rather light candles than curse the darkness, and her glow had warmed the world.

My country mourns her, and I know that all in this Assembly mourn with us. But even as we do, the sadness we share is enlivened by the faith in her fellowman and his future which filled the heart of this strong and gentle woman.

She imparted this faith, not only to those who shared the privilege of knowing her and of working by her side, but to countless men, women and children in every part of the world who loved her even as she loved them. For she embodied the vision and the will to achieve a world in which all men can walk in peace and dignity. And to this goal, a better life, she dedicated her tireless energy, the strange strength of her extraordinary personality.

I do not think it amiss to suggest that the United Nations is, in no small way, a memorial to her and to her aspirations. To it she gave the last fifteen years of her restless life. She breathed life into this organization. The United Nations has meaning and hope, for millions, thanks to her labors, her love, no less than to her ideals—ideals that made her, only weeks after Franklin Roosevelt's death, put aside all thoughts of peace and quiet after the tumult of their lives, to serve as one of this nation's delegates to the first regular session of the General Assembly. Her duty then, as always, was to the living, to the world, to peace.

Some of you in this hall were present at that first historic Assembly in London seventeen years ago. More of you were witnesses to her work in subsequent Assemblies in the years that followed. The members of the Third Committee—the Committee on Social, Humanitarian and Cultural Questions—and the Commission on Human Rights, which she served so long as chairman—you in particular will remember the warmth, the intelligence and infectious buoyancy which she brought to her tasks. You know, better than any of us, the unceasing crusade that helped give the world, after years of painstaking, patient travail, one of the noblest documents of mankind: The Declaration of Human Rights.

This is not the time to recount the infinite services of this glorious, gracious lady; the list is as inexhaustible as her energies! But devotion to the world of the Charter, to the principles of the United Nations, to a world without war, to the brotherhood of man, underscored them all. And, happily for us all, she could communicate her devotion, her enthusiasm to others. She saw clearly; she spoke simply. The power of her words came from the depth of her conviction.

"We must be willing," she said, "to learn the lesson that cooperation may imply compromise, but if it brings a world advance it is a gain for each individual nation. There will be those who doubt their ability to rise to those new heights, but the alternative is not possible to contemplate.

"We must build faith in the hearts of those who doubt, we must rekindle faith in ourselves when it grows dim, and find some kind of divine courage within us to keep on till on Earth we have Peace and Good Will among Men."

While she lived, Mrs. Roosevelt rekindled that faith in ourselves. Now that she is gone, the legacy of her lifetime will do no less. Albert Schweitzer wrote: "No ray of sunlight is ever lost, but the green which it wakes . . . needs time to sprout, and it is not always granted to the sower to live to see the harvest. All work that is worth anything is done in faith."

Mr. President, I trust you will forgive me for having taken the time of this Assembly with these very personal thoughts. The issues we debate in this hall are many and grave. But I do not think we are divided in our grief at the passing of the great and gallant human being who was called the First Lady of the World.[6]

A SPEECH OF EVOCATION: "A NEW DEAL FOR DAD"

ADLAI E. STEVENSON

I have come here today not so much to accept an award as to strike a much needed blow for fatherhood in America.

There was a time when father amounted to something in the United States. He was held with some esteem in the community; he had some authority in his own household; his views were sometimes taken seriously by his children; and even his wife paid heed to him from time to time.

In recent years, however, especially since World War II, father has come upon sorry times. He is the butt of the comic strips; he is the boob of the radio and TV serials; and the favorite stooge of all our professional comedians.

In short, life with father seems to have degenerated into a continuous sequence of disrespect or tolerance at best. It appears that the poor fellow is unable to hang a picture or hit a nail without some mishap; no radio or clock will ever work again after he fixes it; he can't boil water or even barbecue a steak, at least not without burning it.

Every time the so-called head of the household attempts to assert himself or express his opinions, the whole family is convulsed with indulgent if not scornful laughter.

Personally, I think all this has gone far enough, and father certainly

---

[6] Given to the General Assembly of the United Nations Organization, November 9, 1962. Text taken from Adlai E. Stevenson, *Looking Outward*, ed. Robert L. Schiffer and Selma Schiffer (New York: Harper & Row, Publishers, 1963), pp. 113-15. Reprinted by permission.

needs his Day! So all of us fathers should be grateful to you for contriving this brief hour of recognition. I am honored that you have chosen me, a father and a grandfather.

I do not think we would want father restored to his nineteenth-century role of absolute monarch, but, even though we don't want him to be the autocrat of the breakfast table, I think we might consider giving him at least a polite seat at the table.

After forty or fifty years of life, after hard experience in the world of affairs, after education both in college and in the school of hard knocks, and after sweating away at earning a living for the whole family, it is conceivable that father could have learned a thing or two, and the rest of the family could listen to him with profit once in a while for the honor of raising a plaintive voice on behalf of so many. We might even have some better-behaved children if they did listen to him now and then. But of course I except my own children. I have to—or I might not survive Father's Day!

In all candor, I cannot say that I know for sure just how seriously my own children listen to me, but, God bless them, they at least pretend they do.

So all things considered, I have this suggestion to offer: Instead of a Father's Day, maybe we should try a Father's Year for a change. In any case, whatever we call it, let's have a New Deal for Dad!

Now it has been said that paternity is a career imposed on you one fine morning without any inquiry as to your fitness for it. That is why there are so many fathers who have children but so few children who have fathers.

Is there truth or cynicism in this remark? A bit of both, I imagine, but far too much of the former for my taste.

It is an all too visible truth that fatherhood is no longer the sacred duty it was once held to be. There are, today, far too many absentee fathers, fathers in name only. Paradoxically, and this is an insight into the nature of contemporary society, they are, in many cases, men whose ability, sense of responsibility and moral integrity outside the home are of the first order.

Apologists for these errant progenitors (in most instances, offenders themselves) have called up a multitude of rationalizations in their defense —two world wars in less than half a century, the pressures of modern urban life, business before pleasure, country before self and other tired old saws.

What nonsense. There is absolutely no excuse for a parent to abdicate his most important duty—the proper raising of his children. No father should be allowed to get away with the cowardly logic which concludes that his only job in the family is to pay for the bacon.

His role is much more grandiose than that. If it is to be properly fulfilled, he should be, in his realm, a man of many faces—an artist, a philosopher, a statesman and, above all, a prolific dispenser of good sense and justice.

But it is vitally important, especially in the early years, that his children see in father a working model of the social order in which, not so many years hence, they will be expected to play a dynamic part.

How can we, the parents, hope to secure a just and rational society if we neglect the development of those very instruments, our children, most necessary for its implementation? What good does it do to conceive grand moral, social or political plans for a better world if the children who will have to live them out fail to see their importance?

I know there are utopians who believe that human progress is inevitable, a divine trajectory irreversible in its upward motion. Let me just point out to them that in the last few thousand years we have blazed what I consider to be a trail of questionable glory—from Abraham and Isaac to Dennis the Menace.

I fear that no logic, no optimism can controvert the irrefutable equation that a father brings to his son what his son brings to the world. For sure, leaders in the Soviet Union believe this. In Russia, children are barely out of diapers before the full attention of the stage is focused squarely upon them. They are prodded, led and coaxed through the intricate social, moral and political byways of the system into which they were born. By the time they reach maturity their values are crystallized and they know their duties as responsible Soviet citizens.

In a democracy—in America—the state does not presume to be the father of the man. That responsibility is left to our schools, our churches and, most of all, to our parents.

On the contrary, to our way of thinking, it is the individual who is destined to become the father of the state. And to succeed in his parenthood, he must himself be well trained.

In a very real sense, a father's relations with his children should be a microcosmic reflection of their relations with the society in which they live. Through his actions a father must teach his children the intrinsic meaning of the democratic concept—freedom with restraint and the nature of integrity.

Several years ago, at a "Father-and-Son Team of the Year" ceremony held by the National Father's Day Committee, the father was the first to speak and said:

I claim no credit for my son being what he is . . . people make their own intellectual and moral characters. If he was helped in making his by me . . . it was he who decided to accept the help. The decision in such matters is finally with ourselves. To say that responsibility begins at home should mean, I think, that it begins—and ends, too—in the individual. Sooner or later he must help himself. There are no alibis.

The son then spoke of his father:

He has been able to move me, to laughter and to tears, for as long as I can remember, both in public and in private—and that's of the greatest importance. For my father has been to me both a public and a private man.

But my experience has reminded me of something that he taught me—not consciously, I'm sure, but as an example. For the extraordinary thing about my father is that his public face and his private face have been the same. He has been the same man to the world as he has been to his family. And that is harder than it sounds.

It is the very definition of integrity, I suppose.

In modern society everyone faces in some degree the problem of making his public face the same as his private face.

How far any individual succeeds in this effort—which is indeed harder than it sounds—may be taken as a rough measure of "public ethics" for our time and place. Thus in an era of growing artificiality of tinsel and packaging and makeup, and "falsies" of mind and body, the highest compliment that can be paid to a public man is paradoxically that he is made of the same stuff all the way through, inside and out. The more public responsibility he carries, the more important it is to have a private face that can without embarrassment be displayed in public.

I hope no one asks my sons how I've performed in that respect.[7]

[7] Remarks to the National Father's Day Committee, New York City, May 25, 1961. Text taken from Adlai E. Stevenson, *Looking Outward*, ed. Robert L. Schiffer and Selma Schiffer (New York: Harper & Row, Publishers, 1963), pp. 273-76. Reprinted by permission.

Index